Designing Cities with Children and Young People

D0420796

Designing Cities with Children and Young People focuses on promoting better outcomes in the built environment for children and young people in cities across the world. This book presents the experience of practitioners and researchers who actively advocate for and participate with children and youth in planning and designing urban environments. It aims to cultivate champions for children and young people among urban development professionals, to ensure that their rights and needs are fully acknowledged and accommodated.

With international and interdisciplinary contributors, this book sets out to build bridges and provide resources for policy makers, social planners, design practitioners and students. The content moves from how we conceptualize children in the built environment, what we have discovered through research, how we frame the task and legislate for it, and how we design for and with children. *Designing Cities with Children and Young People* ultimately aims to bring about change to planning and design policies and practice for the benefit of children and young people in cities everywhere.

Kate Bishop PhD is a Senior Lecturer in the Faculty of Built Environment at the University of New South Wales. Her background in environment-behaviour research underpins her teaching, research and her particular area of interest: children, youth and environments. She specializes in the design of environments for children with special needs, pediatric facilities and participatory methodologies with children and young people.

Linda Corkery is an Associate Professor of Landscape Architecture in the Faculty of Built Environment at the University of New South Wales. Her research and teaching focuses on the social dimensions of urban landscapes, including public parklands and open space, urban landscape planning and design, and collaborative design processes. Linda is a Fellow of the Australian Institute of Landscape Architects and a member of the Environmental Design Research Association.

WITHDRAWN

LIVERPOOL JMU LIBRARY

3 1111 01513 3356

"Whether your interest is in researching children's needs or turning such research into practice, you will here meet a panel of proven experts drawn from three continents. If you wish to mount successful advocacy for the rights of the child as citizen, you will meet here pathfinders who know from their experiences the practical and political challenges you will inevitably face."

Christopher Spencer, Emeritus Professor of
Environmental Psychology, University of Sheffield, UK

Designing Cities with Children and Young People

Beyond Playgrounds and Skate Parks

Edited by Kate Bishop and Linda Corkery

Routledge
Taylor & Francis Group

NEW YORK AND LONDON

First published 2017
by Routledge
711 Third Avenue, New York, NY 10017

and by Routledge
2 Park Square, Milton Park, Abingdon, Oxon, OX14 4RN

Routledge is an imprint of the Taylor & Francis Group, an informa business

© 2017 Taylor & Francis

The right of Kate Bishop and Linda Corkery to be identified as the authors of the editorial material, and of the authors for their individual chapters, has been asserted in accordance with sections 77 and 78 of the Copyright, Designs and Patents Act 1988.

All rights reserved. No part of this book may be reprinted or reproduced or utilised in any form or by any electronic, mechanical, or other means, now known or hereafter invented, including photocopying and recording, or in any information storage or retrieval system, without permission in writing from the publishers.

Trademark notice: Product or corporate names may be trademarks or registered trademarks, and are used only for identification and explanation without intent to infringe.

Library of Congress Cataloging in Publication Data
Names: Bishop, Kate (Lecturer on the built environment), editor. | Corkery, Linda, 1951- editor.
Title: Designing cities with children and young people : beyond playgrounds and skate parks / edited by Kate Bishop and Linda Corkery.
Description: New York, NY : Routledge, 2017. | Includes index.
Identifiers: LCCN 2016033799| ISBN 9781138890817 (hardback) | ISBN 9781138890824 (pbk.)
Subjects: LCSH: City children. | City planning. | Architecture and children. | Play environments.
Classification: LCC HT206 .D47 2017 | DDC 307.1/216—dc23
LC record available at https://lccn.loc.gov/2016033799

ISBN: 978-1-138-89081-7 (hbk)
ISBN: 978-1-138-89082-4 (pbk)
ISBN: 978-1-315-71004-4 (ebk)

Typeset in Frutiger
by Keystroke, Neville Lodge, Tettenhall, Wolverhampton

MIX
Paper from
responsible sources
FSC® C014174
FSC
www.fsc.org

Printed and bound in the United States of America by Sheridan

Table of contents

List of contributors

Penelope Carroll is a Researcher at the SHORE & Whariki Research Centre, Massey University. Her current research with children includes exploring their perceptions of city living, their well-being and sense of place; facilitating child-led research; and helping ensure the voice of children and young people is heard in policy forums.

Louise Chawla is Professor Emerita in the Environmental Design Program at the University of Colorado, Boulder. With a doctorate in Environmental Psychology and a master's degree in Education and Child Development, her research areas are children and nature, children in cities and the development of committed action for the environment.

Victoria Derr is an Assistant Professor in Sustainability Education in the Environmental Studies Program at California State University, Monterey Bay. For more than 20 years, Victoria has engaged communities in participatory research, design and planning for natural and built communities. Her published research includes topics of participatory planning with children and youth; environmental education; sense of place; and sustainable, resilient and socially just communities. Victoria was the Co-Coordinator of Growing Up Boulder as a Senior Instructor at the University of Colorado, Boulder. She holds a master's and PhD from Yale University.

Katina Dimoulias is a Sessional Lecturer and Senior Researcher in the School of Education, Western Sydney University. She received a PhD in Environment and Behavior Studies at the University of Sydney. Her doctoral research was concerned with the influence of physical, social and organizational characteristics on young people's participation in youth centers. She is also a consultant and has been involved in the development of several purpose-built youth facilities.

Patsy Eubanks Owens is a Professor of Landscape Architecture in the Department of Human Ecology at University of California, Davis. She holds a MLA from the University of California, Berkeley and a BLA from the University of Georgia. Her research focuses on the relationships between people and place, including the role of the physical environment in the development, health and well-being of youth, and methods for youth and adult engagement in design and policy development.

Debra Flanders Cushing is a Lecturer of Landscape Architecture at Queensland University of Technology in Brisbane, Australia. Debra was the Co-Coordinator for Growing Up Boulder during its first three years and has studied youth councils and youth masters plans across the United States. She currently focuses her research on design pedagogy, innovative intergenerational park design to address childhood obesity, and youth participation in design.

Karen Malone is Professor of Sustainability (Education) and Deputy Director of the Centre for Educational Research (CER), Western Sydney University. She was Chief Investigator on a number of international research projects, including UNESCO's Growing up in Cities, UK Policy Institutes Children's Independent Mobility project and numerous current UNICEF Child Friendly Cities projects. Her current publications include a sole-authored book, *Sustainability and Childhoods*, and the co-edited collection *Reimagining Sustainability in Precarious Times*.

Fredrika Mårtensson is Associate Professor in Environmental Psychology at the Swedish University of Agricultural Sciences (SLU). In the multidisciplinary field of children's outdoor environments she is investigating the role of the physical environment for children's play and independent mobility in daycare settings, schools and neighborhoods. She pays special attention to the processes of restoration, play and learning associated with going outdoors and staying in natural environments.

Angela Million is Professor of Urban Design and Urban Development at the Berlin Institute of Technology and Adjunct Professor at Michigan State University. She studied urban design and planning in Germany, Spain and the US. She holds a Dipl.-Ing. from BTU Cottbus and a PhD from TU Dortmund. Her research focuses on participatory urban design, building and planning culture (Baukultur), with a special interest in cities as educational settings, children and youth.

Mara Mintzer is Co-Coordinator of Growing Up Boulder, a child and youth friendly city initiative based out of the Program in Environmental Design at the University of Colorado, Boulder. Her career has focused on designing and implementing programs for low-income children and families across the United States.

Maria Nordström holds a PhD in psychology and is Senior Researcher at the Swedish University of Agricultural Sciences, where she does research on children's environments from a developmental psychology perspective. She has recently been involved with planners in urban developments, studying building developments and conducting child impact assessments (CIAs). She is a member of the steering group for the European Network of Child Friendly Cities.

Fiona Robbé is a Landscape Architect who has specialized in the design of outdoor children's environments. Her work encompasses public playgrounds in parks, as well as play areas in schools, childcare centers, zoos, churches, museums and anywhere children play outside. Fiona's commitment to the design of quality play spaces includes caring advocacy for the right of children to participate in the design of outdoor environments.

Cathy Sherry is a member of the Faculty of Law, University of New South Wales, Australia. She researches property law, with a focus on strata and community title. Dr. Sherry has a particular interest in the social, economic and political implications of private communities. She provides advice to government and the private sector and is a General Editor of the international property journal *Property Law Review*.

Willem van Vliet, Professor Emeritus, is interested in planning and design as tools for including the voices of underrepresented population groups in the creation of livable and sustainable communities. From 2004 to 2014, he served as director of the Children, Youth and Environments Center at the University of Colorado.

Karen Witten is a Professor of Public Health at the SHORE & Whariki Research Centre, Massey University. She is investigating how the design and infrastructure of urban neighborhoods influence the well-being of residents, and led *Kids in the City*, a study of children's use and experience of diverse Auckland neighborhoods.

Helen Woolley is a Chartered Landscape Architect and Reader in Landscape and Society in the Department of Landscape at the University of Sheffield, England. Her research has focused on green and open spaces and people, especially children, and their outdoor environments. Helen often works with non-academic partners including government departments, non-governmental organizations, charities, practitioners, communities and commercial organizations. She is currently building on research undertaken in the post-disaster area of Japan.

Foreword

The NSW Commission for Children and Young People (now the Advocate for Children and Young People) has been at the forefront of addressing issues surrounding children, young people and the built environment for more than a decade. In 2012 the Commission, in collaboration with Dr. Kate Bishop and Associate Professor Linda Corkery, ran a four-part seminar series on children, young people and the built environment called 'Beyond playgrounds and skate parks: Advocating for children and young people in the built environment'.

This series was one of a number of commitments made by the NSW Government in response to parliamentary inquiries into children, young people and the built environment conducted by the NSW Joint Parliamentary Committee on Children and Young People in 2006 and 2010. As the Chair of the original inquiry noted, the Committee hoped that its findings would not only enhance the built environment for children and young people in New South Wales but also help inform the wider debate within Australia and internationally on child and youth friendly environments.

The seminars, out of which this book has grown, were intended to continue this debate in the context of ever-evolving built environments and knowledge about the needs and interests of children and young people. The seminars were also intended to inspire champions in the built environment professions and amongst policy makers; build bridges between them to ensure the right of children and young people to healthy environments in which to live and develop; and enable young people to have their voices heard in civic processes.

As with the seminar series, the book aims to discuss areas of major challenge to the creation of supportive built environments in children's lives. This important new book takes our knowledge in new and exciting directions again, and will inform and inspire a broader audience to make great places for children and young people.

On behalf of the former NSW Commission for Children and Young People, I would like to thank Kate Bishop and Linda Corkery for their work in devising the original seminar series and for their contribution to the Commission's work in this area over many years. I would also like to thank all of the outstanding speakers who contributed to the success of the seminars, a number of whom are represented in this book.

Gregor Macfie
Former Director of Policy and Research
NSW Commission for Children and Young People

Acknowledgments

The editors would like to thank the NSW Commission for Children and Young People (now the Advocate for Children and Young People) for inviting us to collaborate with them on the original seminar series in 2012 that led to this book, and for their continued cooperation and support throughout the journey of assembling it. We would also like to thank all the original speakers and participants in that series for providing us with a rich background of ideas from which to draw for this book.

We would like to express our gratitude to the former NSW Commissioner for Children and Young People, Gillian Calvert, for her input to our discussion of the origins of the Parliamentary Inquiries.

We would like to thank the Faculty of Built Environment, UNSW Australia, for their book support subsidy which allowed us to add the talents of Rachel Cogger to our team. A big thank you to Rachel for her ever-willing assistance and support.

Finally to all our contributors—of chapters, case studies and photographs—thank you for your time and commitment to this project. We hope we have done you proud.

Introduction

Kate Bishop and Linda Corkery

The challenges of designing and planning the twenty-first-century city are shared by nations all around the world. Increasing urbanization and densification in global cities raise the social, economic and environmental pressures on the people that live in them now, and this is set to only increase for future populations. Children and young people, from birth to 18 years of age, represent a vulnerable and marginalized segment of the urban population, susceptible to having their needs and considerations overlooked by the prevailing adult agendas and priorities. What might cities look like in 50 years if the children and young people of today were active participants in imagining the built environments of *their* future?

In compiling this book, we want to draw attention to some of the gaps and limitations in the way society considers children and young people as fellow citizens. We believe these breaches undermine our capacities as urban design and planning professionals to deliver optimal environmental opportunities for this age group. The sorts of *problems* and *solutions* cross many professional boundaries, so we present an interdisciplinary discussion to address the spatial, environmental and social challenges that children face in cities today.

In *Designing Cities with Children and Young People*, we seek to build bridges and understanding between the different professions of the community involved in the creation of the built environment, and to provide a resource for policy makers, urban planners and design professionals. The co-editors have a long-standing interest in children, youth and environments, with more than 60 years of combined experience in designing children's environments and in researching children's environmental experiences. And as the subtitle of the book—*Beyond Playgrounds and Skate Parks*—emphasizes, we want to highlight the fact that there are many other settings that play significant roles in the everyday lives of children and young people.

The genesis for this book lies in a series of seminars held in Sydney, Australia, in 2012, which were co-facilitated by us with the New South Wales (NSW) Commission for Children and Young People (the Commission). The seminars were part of a significant effort by agencies of the NSW State Government to highlight the built environment as a major factor impacting children's health and well-being. In 2005, the NSW Joint Parliamentary Committee for Children and Young People launched the first Parliamentary Inquiry into children, youth and the built environment. The idea for this inquiry grew out of a conversation between the Chair of the Committee and the then NSW Commissioner for Children and Young People,[1] when they recognized the need to address and respond to some of the challenges that children were facing in their communities. In recent correspondence with the former Commissioner, she reflected: "[We] were just responding to what kids were saying, i.e. the need for free play areas; the need for public facilities like netball courts; not being able to easily move around; being harassed by police or council statutes when moving around; housing; the continued desire to position children as citizens not as 'victims'" (G Calvert 2015, pers. comm.).

The Parliamentary Inquiry received 57 submissions and generated a series of recommendations which were acted upon by the Commission. In 2009, a follow-up inquiry was convened to assess progress made on the recommendations in the intervening years. The follow-up inquiry produced a new round of recommendations aimed at bringing about change in children's and young people's experience of the built environment. One outcome was the seminar series that had a very similar title to this book: 'Beyond playgrounds and skate parks: Advocating for children and young people in the built environment'.

The life cycle of this political focus on children, young people and built environments by the NSW State Government and associated organizations now spans 10 years and still represents a remarkable political feat which is unique around the world, as discussed in Chapter 4 and Chapter 12. It also illustrates what many who campaign for children's issues know: that making progress on children's issues largely depends on the support of champions in high places who are prepared to assign them real resources and political time (Chawla 2002a).

The 2012 seminar series sought to cultivate champions for children and young people among those diverse professions that commission, create and construct the built environment. It consisted of five half-day events in which the processes that create the built environment were discussed and illustrated. The series particularly sought to address points of breakdown that can occur in these processes, which can have major impacts on the quality of the environments available to children in cities and their potential value in children's lives. The seminars also challenged participants to formulate strategies for achieving better outcomes, including the essential role of children's participation, and to commit to implementing them.

Many of the aims and ambitions for the seminar series are the same ones we have identified for this book. We have briefed our contributors to focus on *processes* rather than focusing on built *products*. Throughout the chapters, we also want to draw out examples of points of breakdown, while featuring how children's and young people's participation can contribute to achieving successful outcomes. Rather than concentrating on Australian initiatives—of which there are many—we have expanded the scope to include international perspectives from four major regions of the world: USA, the UK, Sweden and Germany, alongside Australia and New Zealand.

The decision to focus on process rather than product stems from our cumulative experience in this field. We can learn a lot from studying photos, drawings and case studies of the many remarkable, beautifully constructed projects which enrich the public domain and provide valued places in children's lives. However, the success of each of these projects frequently results from a unique set of circumstances and people. While we celebrate these stand-alone places and projects, we recognize that we are aiming for consistent success in everyday design and planning for children and young people. We want to see good built environments become an everyday reality for children and young people, and this will result from the quality of the processes that commission, create and construct them. We want to highlight client initiatives and innovative processes and examine the barriers that arise: what works, what does not. Above all, we are advocating for more inclusive urban design and planning—that is, processes that invite and take account of children's and young people's participation. With more of this, we believe we can get to a point where the processes that produce the built environment are so sound that a good outcome *for everyone* is more likely to be achieved.

By 'process', we mean all levels of process, including *thinking* about children and young people, establishing who they are, and what they need in a specific contemporary context; *planning* with them and for them to meet their social and environmental needs; and *collaborating* in design, and sometimes construction, in both general public and child-centered settings. As built environment professionals understand, there are many potential points of breakdown in the journey from project conception to project implementation that can compromise the final result for children and young people. For example, there may be a fear of or disinterest in participatory processes, or the view that it takes too much time, thus preventing these stakeholders from taking part in any aspect of the project. Other problems may include poor communication between professionals, a lack of shared understanding, a lack of the specific and relevant knowledge about children and childhood that would ensure good decision-making on their behalf. A number of the chapter authors tackle these and other issues.

Defining terms

There are a number of terms we felt important that everyone understand, and that we have tried to use consistently throughout the book. To begin with, unless otherwise stated by the chapter author, we use the term *children* to refer to people aged newborn to 12 years, and *young people* to refer to adolescents aged 13–18 years. The chapters focus on how these age groups experience public space.

By *public space* we mean all types of formal and informal public space that young people perceive to be freely accessible, even if it is privately owned. This includes, but is not limited to, streets, parks, malls, plazas, vacant spaces and parking lots. We have taken a broader scope in reaction to the traditional view that children's environmental needs are served by schools, childcare facilities, parks and recreational settings. We think this represents a limited view of children's and young people's environmental needs in cities. Also, we want to draw attention to the fact that public space—as we have broadly defined it—is often overlooked as an important aspect of children's and young people's everyday experience of the city.

Public space is also consistently shared with adults and it can be a contested and politically charged arena where community values are on display in relation to many issues, including the community's response to young people. As Christensen and O'Brien (2003) note, children and adults are involved in a constant process of spatial negotiation in cities which often results in a mismatch between what adults want and what children and young people want in relation to public space. Studying shared public spaces allows a greater opportunity to explore the dynamics of adult-child relations in planning and design processes than when the attention is on child-only environments. Focusing on children alone will not help to bring about changes in adult-led processes such as planning and design (Mannion 2007). As Cockburn (2005, p. 115) states, "in order to bring this forward, attention must be paid to issues of engagement, co-construction and partnership".

Although some of the references used throughout the book are more than 10 years old, the points they make remain salient today, which is another reason for this book: change and improvements in this area are happening at a glacial pace. Why is this? The chapters that discuss political and social contexts surrounding children's participation in the design and planning of cities reveal some unique and some commonly held attitudes that influence children's environmental outcomes. For example, there is a decreasing proportion of children in some urban populations brought about by falling birthrates in some countries. In research findings and media reporting, there is evidence of resentment from people who do not have children. A typical economic argument is: why should people without children have to pay subsidies, through their taxes, for childcare and education of other people's children (Mannion 2007)? This, coupled with the aging populations in many countries, threatens children's social acknowledgment. It is not unrealistic to suggest that the interests of children and young people will face an increasingly difficult task to remain on political, social and environmental agendas. Interpreting the 'specialness' of children and childhood across all social domains will require increasing diligence from adults in positions of power as there are fewer children to make the case for themselves.

While our contributors come from countries that have been working in the area of child-sensitive design and planning for some time, we believe the issues discussed in this book are relevant to cities and people around the world. Interesting questions for us are: in those countries that have adopted the child friendly/participation agenda of the United Nations Convention on the Rights of the Child (UNCRC, 1989), how embedded in planning and design processes *are* these agendas? If they are not embedded, why not? What inhibits their progress? More than a simple spot check, this book aims to reflect the practice and progress of organizations and individuals who have embraced these philosophies and approaches, and have been practicing them for years. We want to bring to light how these practices have evolved and what has been learned along the way and to see how they have advanced, 25 years on.

In research carried out over the past two decades, there is growing acknowledgment that children's interactions and relationships with the built environment are changing. The conclusions point to two sets of drivers: changes in social attitudes about children and childhood, and changes in environmental opportunity and experience. These two realities, coupled with children's continued lack of opportunity to participate in community development processes, mean that children are literally losing ground in all urban contexts in the developed world.

Research from the health sector confirms that children are leading more sedentary lives than any generation before them. Childhood is increasingly spent indoors in private spaces, which fundamentally changes children's relationship with their neighbors and their neighborhoods. From research on child and youth across several disciplines, it is clear that these changes in environmental experience are partly the result of increasingly risk-averse western societies, which is reflected in risk-averse approaches to parenting. Broader social attitudes also reveal that communities frequently have a polarized view of their young people as either 'angels' or 'devils', and this also greatly impacts the way they are regarded, and included in the community and in community development projects—or not.

Since the introduction of the UNCRC in 1989, much has been heard in relation to acknowledging children's voices and children's rights to be part of community decision-making processes. The UNCRC has been used for many years as the framework to define how to go about meeting children's needs in urban environments (Bartlett et al. 1999; Chawla 2002b; Malone 2001). As Malone (2001) discussed, these global movements provide the framework for local authorities to develop policies that are respectful of what it means to meet the needs of children alongside adults.

Those who advocate for a new conceptualization of children and young people emerged in force, post 1989, from the so-called *new sociology of childhood*. This group of researchers sought to redress the balance and social view of children from biological becomings to social citizens and beings with rights as children (Corsaro 2005; Mayall 2002; Prout & James 1990; Qvortrup et al. 1994). This is known as the rights-based approach. Since then this conceptual approach has underpinned much of the reported participatory research with children and young people. The rationale for this research is that involving children is the right action to take as it responds to children's rights as citizens to participate in processes that affect their lives (Knowles-Yánez 2005).

In 2005, Knowles-Yánez synthesized components from various approaches to children's participation, which she argued provides a holistic and applied approach to children's participation in land use planning (p. 12). This model provides a useful framework for the discussions that occur throughout this book from the perspectives of research, planning and design practice, education and policy. From the *scholarly/research approach*, she took the need to respect the capabilities of children as a fundamental starting point. From *practice*, she took the many creative methods and approaches that could be used. From the *educational approach*, she took the need to integrate these processes with other developmental programs. And from the *rights-based approach*, she took the use of participation as the basis for instilling citizenship and an understanding of the tools of democracy. Many of the chapters in this book also discuss these elements as core elements of their discussions of participation in contemporary contexts. Throughout the chapters, readers will see that many of these starting points operate either as conceptual frameworks or methodologies for practice, education or research.

Child-centered research is essential for understanding children's lived experience. It provides perspectives that adults do not have and cannot do without if they are trying to meet children's needs—of any kind. However, to alter adult-led processes, there must also be a focus not only on hearing children's voices but also on positioning them within adult discourse, values and operations. It has long been argued that children's participation must be 'institutionalized', that is, it should become 'business as usual' in all aspects of civic life (Barlett et al. 1999; Chawla 2001, 2002a, 2002b). However, that still remains a rare thing.

One of the persistent themes to emerge from research in this area is the difficulty in managing knowledge transfer between different professions or the different sectors of research, policy and practice. Researchers also identify a kind of 'deafness' to children's voices as a recurring theme—a lack of receptivity to children's input. These themes are also part of the struggle with spatial provision for children and young people in our cities and communities. For example, are they going to get a skate park or a play-ground or not? In research, these themes are often framed as either a reflection of, or an expression of, child-adult power relations in any community.

Children's participation is often championed as an indicator of positive child–adult relations: an acknowledgment of children's capacities; an expression of their rights; an opportunity for citizenship training; an empowering experience for children. Likewise, for adults the claims are that the adult world will be better off if it understands and meets the needs of its children; and that adults will be enlightened by the process and the outcomes of children's involvement. However, in reality, the proponents of participation are rarely in a position to evaluate the enduring outcomes of experiencing participatory processes or projects in either the children's or the adults' lives. There is very little research evidence that looks at how the experience of one of these processes or projects continues to benefit either the expectations and interests of the children involved, or the professional practices or policies of the adults involved.

In their discussion of children's participation in policy decision-making more than a decade ago, Tisdall and Davis (2004) made the point that participatory processes are often only used on a single or one-off project basis. This inhibits the potential effectiveness of the outcomes to change embedded processes and well-structured prevailing networks because children's presence is transient, as is the group of people championing them. They argued that in the case of 'policy communities', these usually have a tight membership and ideology and established systems of players and negotiation whereas 'issue networks' have more members and less established power networks and systems. "Thus policy communities are more likely to influence policy than are issue networks" (p. 133). This kind of challenge has not changed and still faces all those who engage in participatory processes in research, policy and practice.

Although participatory processes can be very successful in one-off projects, bringing about cultural change in organizations or institutions of power in our societies remains difficult, despite the countless models for success in evidence. Chapters 2 and 15 of this book discuss different aspects of a long-running project, called Growing Up Boulder, that breaks through this set of barriers. This project, now running since 2010, has achieved an enduring and unique status, well entrenched in the local community-building processes. The project provides a substantial model of best practice for other communities to follow.

The discussion around children's participation also intersects with other major global movements and agendas such as social inclusion and social sustainability. Participation has long been considered a process that is fundamental to social inclusion (Davis & Edwards 2004). As stated by Hill et al. (2004, p. 78), "multidimensional participation must be part of the processes and part of the answer for social inclusion as a dynamic concept emphasizing society's barriers rather than individuals' failings". The first chapter of this book reframes the international Child Friendly Cities (CFC) movement as part of a model for sustainable planning and development. Children's participation in the design and planning of cities has always been a fundamental component of the CFC because this movement grew out of the UNCRC, which established children's participation as a basic human right.

The four sections of the book represent what we consider to be crucial processes and key considerations which influence environmental outcomes for children. As with the seminar series, our intent is for the book to promote better designed and more inclusive built environments for children and young people in cities. And to address this we have presented an interdisciplinary, cross-sectoral and multi-national discussion which spans the whole process associated with developing the built environment. It consists of four parts:

1 Global and regional initiatives with local value
2 Researching with children and young people
3 Instruments with impact: legislation and policy
4 Perspectives on participatory practices with children and young people

At the beginning of each of the four sections we offer a brief synopsis of the discussions that follow. At the end of the book we provide a set of case studies which showcase long-running and successful participatory projects in addition to those discussed in the chapters.

The collective resources of this book provide a contemporary discussion and reflection on persistent challenges and key processes within the design and planning of urban environments for children and youth. They also offer effective approaches for future practice from experienced points of view which we hope all readers will find beneficial.

Note

1   Gillian Calvert was the first Commissioner of the NSW Commission for Children and Young People, and held that position for 10 years from 1999 to 2009.

References

Bartlett, S, de la Barra, X, Hart, R, Missair, A & Satterthwaite, D 1999, *Cities for children*, Earthscan, London.

Chawla, L 2001, 'Evaluating children's participation: seeking areas of consensus', *Participatory Learning and Action Notes*, vol. 49, pp. 9–13.

Chawla, L 2002a, 'Insight, creativity and thoughts on the environment: integrating youth into human settlement development', *Environment and Urbanization*, vol. 14, no. 2, pp. 11–21.

Chawla, L (ed.) 2002b, *Growing up in an urbanising world*, Earthscan, London.

Christensen, P & O'Brien, M (eds) 2003, *Children in the city: home, neighborhood and community*, Routledge Falmer, London.

Cockburn, T 2005, 'Children's participation in social policy: inclusion, chimera or authenticity?', *Social Policy and Society*, vol. 4, pp. 109–119.

Corsaro, WA 2005, *The sociology of childhood* (2nd ed.), Pine Forge Press, Thousand Oaks, California.

Davis, J & Edwards, R 2004, 'Setting the agenda: social inclusion, children and young people', *Children & Society*, vol. 18, pp. 97–105.

Hill, M, Davis, J, Prout, A & Tisdall, K 2004, 'Moving the participation agenda forward', *Children and Society*, vol. 18, no. 2, pp. 77–96.

Knowles-Yánez, K 2005, 'Children's participation in planning processes', *Journal of Planning Literature*, vol. 20, no. 1. DOI: 10.1177/0885412205277032.

Malone, K 2001, 'Children, youth and sustainable cities (special edition editorial)', *Local Environment: The International Journal of Justice and Sustainability*, vol. 6, no. 1, pp. 5–12.

Mannion, G 2007, 'Going spatial, going relational: why "listen to children" and children's participation needs reframing', *Discourse: Studies in the Cultural Politics of Education*, vol. 28, no. 3, pp. 405–420.

Mayall, B 2002, *Towards a sociology of childhood: thinking from children's lives*, Open University Press, Buckingham, England.

Prout, A & James, A (eds) 1990, *Constructing and reconstructing childhood*, Falmer Press, London.

Qvortrup, J, Bardy, M, Sgritta, G & Wintersberger, H 1994, *Childhood matters: social theory, practice and politics*, Avebury, Aldershot, England.

Tisdall, EKM & Davis, J 2004, 'Making a difference? bringing children and young people's views into policy-making', *Children & Society*, vol. 18, pp. 131–142.

PART 1

GLOBAL AND REGIONAL INITIATIVES WITH LOCAL VALUE

The four chapters in this section have been written by professionals and academics in four different regions of the world, yet they clearly share a common set of conceptual reference points. The conceptual conversations presented in each of these chapters effectively reduce the geographical distances to zero. With the exception of Corkery's chapter, which includes a discussion on the nature of children's and young people's participation, the other three chapters write to an audience that is familiar with common concerns, universal considerations and techniques for activating children's rights and, in particular, participation.

All the authors situate their discussions of children's lived experiences and involvement in design in the envelope of sustainability—both social and environmental, even if only briefly—as this reflects the contemporary discourse that underpins urban design and planning. Karen Malone, academic and researcher in education and sustainability, has a long association with United Nations initiatives and the Child Friendly Cities (CFC) in particular. She introduces these international conventions and programs, reflecting on their efficacy and integration into shifting environmental and social priorities, expressing optimism that children's participation and capacities will be embedded in the UN's recently issued Sustainable Development Goals.

Louise Chawla and Willem van Vliet have been at the forefront of children, youth and environment research and advocacy for many years. Their work champions the participation of children and young people in urban environments around the world. Chawla also has a long association with project implementation and program evaluation for the United Nations. With colleague, and fellow champion of participatory research, design and planning, Victoria Derr, they highlight the implicit compatibility and essential relationship between children's participation—central to the CFC approach—and the creation of resilient, sustainable cities—the primary aim of the Rockefeller Foundation's Resilient Cities program.

Environmental psychologists Fredrika Mårtensson and Maria Nordström offer a Swedish perspective with their expertise in the importance of children having access to their local environments. They challenge the notion that a city can consider itself sustainable if it does not include children's participation in planning and design processes. Linda Corkery, a landscape architect and planner, also reflects on the relationship between children's participation and healthy, livable and sustainable cities, and provides a view from Australia where CFC principles have been successfully built into local government policies and implemented at the scale of suburban development.

(Source: Fiona Robbé)

These first chapters set the conceptual scene for the book with their shared outlook on the challenges faced by modern urban design and planning, and their insistence on the involvement of children and young people as a meaningful way forward. They also highlight the universal challenges—social, economic and environmental—faced by all nations dealing with increased urbanization and urban densification. They spell out the need to involve end users in planning and design for better social outcomes and more enduring built environments. At the same time, they reflect the specific nature of the social and governance contexts, planning policies and processes, and varying concepts of public space and public use in various locales.

Comparing the similarities and differences that arise in these discussions helps make the case for this book and underscore its timeliness. Twenty-five years on from the UNCRC, we still struggle with many of the basic challenges associated with involving children in urban planning and design. Twenty-five years on, these challenges are well understood and experienced around the world. However, we still have to advocate for children's capacities, and search for indications that children's rights and capacities are becoming embedded in civic processes. These chapters reveal that we have made limited progress, but there are some hopeful signs.

CHAPTER 1

Child Friendly Cities

A model of planning for sustainable development

Karen Malone

Introduction: impacts of rapid urbanization for children and sustainable development

Globally, for the first time in human history, more people live in urban areas than rural areas, and it is believed more than 200,000 new inhabitants move into cities each day. Currently, over half of the world's population resides in cities and by 2050 this will rise to 7 out of 10 people. Recent figures state total urban populations are growing by nearly 60 million people, with global urban population being expected to grow roughly 1.5 percent per year between 2015 and 2050 (WHO 2010). That is, by the middle of the twenty-first century, the world's urban population will almost double. An estimated 3.4 billion people in 2009 living in cities will become 6.4 billion by 2050 (UNICEF 2012; WHO 2010). The ongoing consequence of this rapid urbanization for children and young people will be a significant issue that city planners and designers, in developed and developing nations, will need to address (UNICEF 2012).

Sustainable development is often perceived to be mainly associated with the non-human environment. However, taking a broader focus on the issue leads to considering how communities, locally and globally, can meet the needs of humans and non-humans, to achieve development that can both be sustainable, and be sustained. This means continuing to address issues of poverty eradication, human rights and equity, while also realizing the need for more sustainable patterns of consumption and production, calming climatic forces (UNICEF 2012, 2013) and attending to our relations with the more-than-human world. Urban growth and sustainable development may not seem like compatible partners, but if human populations do continue to grow at the rates predicted, then cities might be the only way the planet will support a sustainable future. That is, high-density urban environments will be the most cost-effective and sustainable way to accommodate and provide infrastructure to the billions of new human inhabitants and provide places for non-human beings to also co-exist (UNICEF 2012). The introduction by the United Nations of the post-2015 Sustainable Development Goals (UNDP 2015) is the stepping off point for new conversations on how the global and local communities in developed and developing nations can plan and respond to the rise in rapid urbanization, while still maintaining equitable rights of the most vulnerable within our communities and the ecological sustainability of the planet.

This chapter will argue that the participation of children and their communities should be central to the implementation of the new United Nations Sustainable Development Goals (SDGs) (see also Malone 2015). Specifically, it will argue that through their participation in the planning and implementation of urban projects and policy at the local level, such as those exemplified in the Child Friendly Cities initiative (CFC) and Growing Up In Cities (GUIC) project, children and young people can begin to play a significant role in addressing the challenges of urbanization and sustainability, preparing them for ongoing participation as active citizens.

Children's rights, planning and sustainable development

> Most of the environmental policies which would improve the lives of children in our cities would benefit adults, too. In particular, everything that would make the city a more tolerable place for the old, would make it more enjoyable for the young.
>
> —Colin Ward, *The Child in the City* (1978, p. 203).

Studies of human-environment relationships reveal unequivocally that humans learn through engagement with their environments (Kellert 2012; Lynch 1977). Stephen Kellert (2012, p. ix), environmental philosopher and advocate of the biophilia hypothesis, argues:

> Humanity is the product of its evolved relationship to nature, countless yesterdays of ongoing interaction and experience of the natural world. Our senses, our emotions, our intellect, and even our culture developed in close association with, and in adaption response to, the non-human world.

Sipe, Buchanan and Dodson (2006) noted that, historically, the aim of urban planning was to separate children from the social and physical decay of working-class city environments and the isolation of rural country environments by supporting greenfield suburban development and encouraging families to relocate. It was asserted that suburban spaces offer greater opportunities for mobility for children, who can meet other children, visit friends locally, travel to school on their own, access community and commercial services, and that all these activities contribute to their environmental competence, their capacity to contribute to the social capital of their community, and their own personal health and well-being through active lifestyles and quality of life (Hillman et al. 1990; Kytta 2004; Malone 2006; van Vliet 1985). However, this potential for suburban spaces to be healthy spaces for children is reliant on the quality of urban planning and the potential for children to access what is available in those neighborhoods.

Sustainable Development Goals

The principles of sustainable development clearly demand that the simultaneous achievement of the goals of sustainability should meet the needs of the present generation without compromising the needs of future generations. The goals of sustainability insist national governments maintain the integrity of their global partnerships and local policies and plans through processes that are participatory and equitable (UNDP 2015). The United Nations Convention on the Rights of the Child (UNCRC, 1989) identifies a child's well-being and quality of life as the ultimate indicators of a healthy environment, good governance and sustainable development

(UNICEF 1996, 1997). The principles of the UNCRC reinforce these goals of sustainability when they challenge governments to uphold the child's right to live in a safe, clean and healthy environment with their human and non-human companions. As one of the most vulnerable groups in our community, there is a lot at stake for children in these goals. The detrimental impacts of unchecked urbanization, where principles of sustainability are not considered, affect children profoundly and limit their potential for a future life. In policies and documents emerging from the United Nations since the late 1980s, there has been a convergence, and in many instances a symbiotic relationship, between the principles of sustainable development and children's rights (Malone 2006). In particular, two projects launched in the late 1990s, and in which I have been involved as a key researcher, have made a significant impact in government and academic circles by creating a climate for exploring ways to engage with communities in designing and implementing sustainable planning policies focused on children's rights: UNICEF's Child Friendly Cities Initiative and UNESCO's Growing Up In Cities project.

UNICEF Child Friendly Cities

The Child Friendly Cities Initiative fully emerged in 1996 after the presentation of the *Children's Rights and Habitat Report* by UNICEF representatives at the United Nations Conference on Human Settlements in Istanbul. At this same time, the goals of sustainable development and children's rights were being expressed through Local Agenda 21—the action plan for local governments, communities and stakeholders to promote and implement sustainable development. Building on the global launch of CFC in the late 1990s, the CFC was recognized as a central UNICEF program for supporting *A World Fit for Children*, the document emerging from the United Nations General Assembly Special Session on Children in May 2002. Child Friendly Cities also featured widely in other documents emerging from UNICEF around this time, including the *Partnerships to Create Child Friendly Cities* (2001) and *Poverty and Exclusion among Urban Children* (2002b). Over time many countries have devised accreditation or child friendliness indexes and recognition programs for cities wanting recognition as achieving child friendly status.

There is no single definition of what a child friendly city is or ought to be. In fact, the documents on the program go to great lengths to reiterate cities may never achieve child friendly status due to a city's ongoing transformation in response to an ever-changing local and global landscape. For some cities, especially in high-income nations, the emphasis of child friendly and sustainable programs tends to be on environmental issues such as improving recreational spaces and green spaces, reducing young people's alienation and controlling traffic to make streets safe for young citizens. In low-income nations, the focus is predominantly on issues requiring immediate attention, such as providing access to basic services to alleviate the impacts of poverty and environmental degradation.

The CFC has continued to build momentum since its introduction in 1996. At present over 62 countries and thousands of cities are involved to some degree in a Child Friendly Cities program. With a focus on policy development and planning designed with families and communities the examples of cities addressing children's needs have been viewed by UNICEF as instrumental in the steps needed to address the intensification of urbanization.

Developing child friendly indicators

To support child friendly initiatives, there was an emphasis on designing national indicators and strengthening data collection and monitoring of children, using community-based assessment tools. As a UNICEF report on the Asia-Pacific region stated, "often, national averages conceal the adverse health conditions dispropor- tionately experienced by the poor, and a lack of reliable statistical data disaggregated by geography and socio-economic groups makes analysis of the Asia-Pacific region difficult" (2008, p. 55). In response, a UNICEF CFC research advisory board devised and piloted a set of indicators and self-assessment tools, to support cities to monitor progress over time and make their accreditation programs more rigorous (UNICEF 2008). These assessment tools have been designed for use by parents, community service professionals and children. The primary intention was for local communities (including children), with the support of municipal councils and other stakeholders, to be able to collect data that would inform priorities for a children's plan of action to be implemented at the city level.

The main aim of using the assessment tools was to support ongoing monitoring of action plans and targets over time to be able to show evidence of changes in children's living conditions. Using these assessment tools revealed that despite the diversity of cities investigated, children around the world valued similar qualities in urban environ- ments and that these principles or indicators of child friendliness aligned very closely with the core principles of ecological and social sustainability (Malone 2001, 2012; UNICEF 1997).

Figure 1.1 Children working with adults to support CFC projects at Dapto, NSW, Australia (Source: Karen Malone)

UNESCO Growing Up In Cities project

The early 1990s saw an increase in visibility of children and children's rights in urban planning agendas and, in particular, intergovernmental discussions about how to address the needs of children in the rapidly urbanizing world. It was through both global projects—Child Friendly Cities (CFC) and Growing Up In Cities (GUIC)—that the true agenda for children's rights of participation in urban planning was articulated and became part of the UN and scholarly intellectual agenda of urban planning. It was also from these and many subsequent projects that the 'tools' for engaging children in authentic participatory planning with city officials began to gain currency in academic and non-academic circles. Models of good practice began to circulate and be shared in the developed and developing worlds.

At the same time that the CFC initiative was gaining momentum, interest was developing in a revisitation of the international UNESCO Growing Up In Cities project, previously initiated in the 1970s by Kevin Lynch (1977), an urban designer and planner. In 1995, Louise Chawla championed a newly conceptualized study (Chawla 2002), using a model of participatory action research involving children and young people in collaboration with adults. The new GUIC project evaluated the quality of low- and mixed-income urban environments such as the historical port neighborhood of Boca-Baraccas in Buenos Aires, Argentina; a low-income public housing site in the western suburbs of Melbourne, Australia; a peri-urban slum in Bangalore, India; the Nordic city of Trondheim in Norway; an immigrant Hispanic neighborhood in Oakland, California; the working-class district of Powisle, Warsaw, Poland; a squatter camp in the city of Johannesburg, South Africa; and the English city of Northampton, United Kingdom. The research included five new sites and three of the original sites. It had three main goals: "to collect information about young people's contemporary urban experience; to develop models of participatory urban planning with children and youth; and to compare the projects' present and past results" (Chawla 2002, p. 29). This iteration of the project involved children and adolescents aged 10–15 years old, and has been described extensively in two landmark publications (Chawla 2002; Driskell 2001).

In these projects, child participants were invited to engage in a variety of activities, including interviews, drawings of their area, small group discussions, child-led walks (walking interviews) and child-taken photographs and commentaries (photovoice). Project facilitators at the sites also documented each location's history, geography, economy and demographics; observed the roles that young people play in local public life; and talked with parents, community leaders and urban officials about their views of how the city functions for its children. Wherever possible, the information derived from these research activities with children and youth was then used as the basis for implementing actions to improve urban environments for young people and to design more child-sensitive urban policies and plans.

An important outcome of the project was a set of child-based indicators of environmental quality. Across all the locations, children expressed a concern for equitable distribution of resources, services and facilities as well as the need for communities to improve the quality of the social, cultural and natural environments by conserving and living within their means rather than increasing material consumption (Chawla 2002). The final product of the project was a core set of research tools (the toolkit). The toolkit combined quantitative methods, such as surveys and questionnaires, with

Figure 1.2 Children taking adults on guided tour in La Paz, Bolivia (Source: Karen Malone)

a range of qualitative methods, including cognitive mapping, drawings, photography, spatial observations and mapping, interviews, storytelling and time schedules. Having a range of methods provided for flexibility in the field where children as co-researchers could identify which data collection methods provided the best fit between their own interests and skills and the context of the study and the study site.

The following short case study provides an example of the application of GUIC and CFC planning activities within a community in Sydney, Australia. This case study was unique because of the extensive application of the toolkit with kindergarteners (5- to 6-year-olds) and children in middle childhood (9- to 10-year-olds). Unlike many research projects that hope to influence urban planning outcomes, this case is also unique because, from its inception, it was embedded in progressing urban development that was happening in real time in the children's lives.

Dapto Dreaming, a child friendly and sustainable planning project

The Dapto Dreaming project provided an opportunity for primary school-aged children to have input into the design of a new residential development by Stockland, a nationally known urban developer in Australia. This study ran from April to July 2011 using the global Child Friendly Cities framework. It replicated a number of studies, particularly in Australia, that have been conducted by the author, who has implemented a similar research design drawing on the child friendliness toolkit and with the inclusion of the internationally tested Children's Independent Mobility (CIM) instrument (Malone 2011; Rudner & Malone 2011). The CIM instrument was developed by Hillman in the early 70s and has been replicated throughout the world (Hillman et al. 1990). Writing on the value of replicating the CIM instrument in a variety of communities and cities globally, Malone (2011) stated: "How CIM has changed over time and how it is enacted in diverse global locations is a significant question at a time when we continue to battle concerns over children's declining health and quality of life" (p. 162). The methods and tools of the child friendliness toolkit had grown out of the author's involvement in the UNESCO Growing Up In Cities participatory research project (Chawla 2002; Driskell 2001).

The project was located in a community on the southern outskirts of Sydney's urban sprawl in the suburb of Horsley. This area boasts a number of large and small playgrounds and parks, with almost every child having a playground or park within walking distance of their home. Dapto Public School is a large school with a population of around 700 children enrolled from kindergarten to sixth grade. In their research brief, Stockland stated they were committed to the adoption of child friendly principles and to creating a nurturing, supportive and stimulating environment for children in the Brooks Reach development and surrounding communities (Stockland 2010).

Using the toolkit methods, the place-based participatory research and educational workshops supported the children to collect data about their experiences of their neighborhood, and then to evaluate the child friendly qualities of the existing physical neighborhood. The team conducted two research workshops with 150 children; 30 from the kindergarten and 120 fifth-grade children.

Kindergarten children

One group of kindergarten children was engaged in two sessions—the first, exploring how they experienced the local neighborhood; the second, focused on their dreams of what a child friendly community in Dapto would look like. All kindergarten classes were invited to complete the drawing activities, but no other grades took up this offer. Children had the opportunity to share their opinions and explain their drawings to the researchers. Adult researchers, using a storytelling strategy, conducted individual interviews with each child and completed the survey of child friendliness (CFC survey) of a neighborhood on their behalf.

Fifth-grade children

The older children were engaged in three sessions. The first session explored their mobility around the neighborhood using the CIM survey that has been conducted in a number of locations around the world (Hillman et al. 1990). The second session explored how children felt and experienced the local area. This included filling in the CFC survey and drawing their neighborhood. Each child was also given a disposable camera for a weekend to take photos of their local neighborhood. To ensure the process was open-ended and did not limit their data collection, the children were not given any specific instructions of what to photograph. The third session focused on their dreams of what a child friendly community in Dapto would look like and ideas of child friendliness that could be applied in the new urban design.

On completion of the in-class workshops, a smaller group of 12 children worked with the adult research team to collate and analyze the children's data, and develop a children's report. This group also generated a list of child friendliness indicators from the data to be used as the foundation of the design recommendations to the developers. Table 1.1 provides an overview of the final list of child friendliness indicators, the icons that represented each one and the comments from the children as to why these indicators were important.

Table 1.1 Final list of child friendly neighborhood themes/indicators with representative icons derived from children's drawings and the children's rationale.

Child icon	Indicator/theme	Comments from children why these indicators are important
	A place supporting play and has playgrounds	To let children have fun – Jason; So children don't just sit on the lounge and get unfit, so they could be running around – Kimberley; So people can develop their climbing skills and have fun – Logan; To have safe playgrounds – Paul
	A place that keeps and protects nature	Saves old trees, keeps our heritage and your families future – Aaron; Keep scar trees and indigenous things – Jack; To keep animals and plants from extinction and let animals have freedom and feel safe – Jason
	A place where we create communities	Have street parties, where people can get together, be nice to neighbours, share ideas – Aaron; So other people meet people and make more friends – Georgia; Groups or parties to get to know your neighborhood, create a good atmosphere, socialise and make new friends – communal gardens – LA; So we can share our ideas and make friends – Olivia
	A place that allows you to be active	It can be fun and children will be healthy and a good weight – Georgia; Let kids run free – Jack; It can be fun and you can run and play – Kimberley; So we can be healthy and fit – Olivia; Exercise keeps everyone fit and healthy and living a long life – Tiegan; It can be fun – Logan
	A place that promotes learning	People don't throw rubbish, play safe and learn to look after the environment – Jason; Important to teach children about the environment – Aaron; To teach kids to respect the environment, like at our school we have a green team – LA
	A place that is safe and clean	No pollution keeps us, animals and plants safe so there should be no litter – Connor; So no animals or people step on needles or pins and other sharp objects – Georgia; Keep us healthy and nature healthy – LA; Prevents animals, plants and ourselves from injury – Tiegan
	A place that values children	Because the future is in our hands – Paul; Valuing children is important because we can pass on our education to future generations – Tiegan
	A place that has pathways	Have pathways so you don't have to be worried about being hurt or run over by cars and motorbikes – Connor; Keep safe and so you don't step on nature – Jack; Keep safe so you're not walking on the road – Paul; So you don't tramp on plants – Logan

Once the indicators were identified, children in small groups designed the children's report *Dapto Dreaming*, which was produced *for* children and *by* the children. Children wrote in the introduction:

> Our Dapto Dreaming report is about the things we like about our neighbourhood and the things we think could be changed to make it even better. It's about making sure adults listen and value us and include our dreams in their designs for our place. The report is organised around the eight things children told us help make this neighbourhood child friendly (Malone 2010, p. 1).

A play space and pathway design were developed by the children and presented to the developers. Three months later, the developers presented the playground design with all the children's ideas to children, parents and staff of the school at a school assembly. Almost a year after their involvement, a number of children who had participated in the project were taken to the new Brooks Reach site to perform a 'turning of the soil' ceremony to initiate the playground development (Figure 1.3).

After the playground was completed and opened in late 2012, Stockland Developers and the research team were awarded the prestigious 2013 Planning Institute of Australia project of the year Presidential Award and their Child and Youth Planning Award for the entire Dapto Dreaming project. This was the first time ever for a university-school-developer collaboration to win such recognition.

Figure 1.3 Children and Stockland staff turning the soil at the new playground site (Source: Karen Malone)

Sustainable Development Goals and planning for the future

Toward the end of 2015, the implementation of the Millennium Development Goals (MDGs) concluded, and the global United Nations Sustainable Development Goals (SDGs) for the next 15 years were released. The UN report describing the SDGs states:

> Young people will be the torch bearers of the next sustainable development agenda through 2030. We must ensure that this transition, while protecting the planet, leaves no one behind. We have a shared responsibility to embark on a path to inclusive and shared prosperity in a peaceful and resilient world where human rights and the rule of law are upheld (United Nations 2014, Article 3).

Seventeen sustainable development goals were agreed on globally. These will frame the ongoing work of all UN organizations, in particular UNICEF and UNESCO. These goals are listed in Table 1.2.

Table 1.2 United Nations 17 Sustainable Development Goals (United Nations 2014).

Goal 1	End poverty in all its forms everywhere
Goal 2	End hunger, achieve food security and improved nutrition and promote sustainable agriculture
Goal 3	Ensure healthy lives and promote well-being for all at all ages
Goal 4	Ensure inclusive and equitable quality education and promote lifelong learning opportunities for all
Goal 5	Achieve gender equality and empower all women and girls
Goal 6	Ensure availability and sustainable management of water and sanitation for all
Goal 7	Ensure access to affordable, reliable, sustainable and modern energy for all
Goal 8	Promote sustained, inclusive and sustainable economic growth, full and productive employment and decent work for all
Goal 9	Build resilient infrastructure, promote inclusive and sustainable industrialization and foster innovation
Goal 10	Reduce inequality within and among countries
Goal 11	Make cities and human settlements inclusive, safe, resilient and sustainable
Goal 12	Ensure sustainable consumption and production patterns
Goal 13	Take urgent action to combat climate change and its impacts
Goal 14	Conserve and sustainably use the oceans, seas and marine resources for sustainable development
Goal 15	Protect, restore and promote sustainable use of terrestrial ecosystems, sustainably manage forests, combat desertification, and halt and reverse land degradation and halt biodiversity loss
Goal 16	Promote peaceful and inclusive societies for sustainable development, provide access to justice for all and build effective, accountable and inclusive institutions at all levels
Goal 17	Strengthen the means of implementation and revitalize the global partnership for sustainable development

Source: Report of the Open Working Group of the General Assembly on Sustainable Development Goals (A/68/970).

To deliver these goals, six essential elements have been designed to "help frame and reinforce the universal, integrated and transformative nature of a sustainable development agenda" (United Nations 2014, Article 66). These six elements include people, dignity, prosperity, justice, partnerships and the planet. They provide a useful, holistic and systemic approach for considering how local city planning that is focused on responsible 'sustainable development' and the rights and participation of children and young people can be achieved. Child Friendly Cities, as an example of a global initiative which is realized at a local level, is a useful model for operationalizing these goals, children's rights and sustainable development.

Conclusion

According to the most recently released UNICEF (2013) report on SDGs, investing in children yields high and long-lasting results for children, their families and their societies. The report refers to the need to address unfinished business and fulfill the promises made to cities, that is, to continue to tackle the challenges of rapid urbanization and to ensure the poorest and most disadvantaged children are not being left behind (UNICEF 2013). To ensure this happens, data collected by cities on their progress towards the SDGs will need to be clearly disaggregated so that good planning can be designed and implemented and equitable progress achieved at all levels (Malone 2015). Children and young people should be part of this planning and monitoring process and be given opportunities to be effective advocates, problem-solvers and agents for positive sustainable change. As stated in the UNICEF report, the wellbeing of children and their participation in planning of cities could serve as the main indicator of the progress of a city to meet the challenges of sustainable development.

> Children's needs and rights are thus interdependent with sustainable development. To achieve the greatest impact on the lives of children, the forthcoming Sustainable Development Goals (SDG) framework should include goals and targets that purposefully consider children's rights and needs within each of the dimensions of economic development, social development and environmental sustainability, while building on their synergies and adequately addressing the fair and inclusive application of the rule of law (UNICEF 2013, p. 6).

If this bold statement is true, that at the center of the SDG framework must be children and child's rights, then CFC and other planning projects based on these initiatives should be viewed as critical and strategic in encouraging local governments to engage with children and young people in sustainable planning, design and development. Internationally, CFC has created a network of thousands of cities which have been addressing the very planetary challenges a rapidly urbanizing world is likely to present. I offer a challenge to city planners around the world to consider how they can support the goals of sustainable development by promoting their own child friendly projects, and be best practice models for other cities, nationally and globally. Just as many planners and researchers worked closely with children, communities and national governments on the reporting and monitoring of CFC, they now can play a significant role as leaders in the development and implementation of the SDGs for the benefit of children and young people.

LIVERPOOL JOHN MOORES UNIVERSITY
LEARNING SERVICES

Bibliography

Chawla, L (ed.) 2002, *Growing up in an urbanising world*, Earthscan/UNESCO London.

Driskell, D 2001, *Creating better cities with children and youth*, Earthscan/UNESCO, London.

Hillman, M, Adams, J & Whitelegg J 1990, *One false move . . . a study of children's independent mobility*, PSI, London.

Kellert, S 2012, *Birthright: people and nature in the modern world*, Yale University Press, New Haven, Connecticut.

Kytta, M 2004, 'The extent of children's independent mobility and the number of actualized affordances as criteria for child friendly environments', *Journal of Environmental Psychology*, vol. 24, no. 2, pp. 179–198.

Lynch, K 1977, *Growing up in cities*, UNESCO, MIT Press, Cambridge, Massachusetts.

Malone, K 2001, 'Children, youth and sustainable cities (special edition editorial)', *Local Environment: The International Journal of Justice and Sustainability*, vol. 6, no. 1, pp. 5–12.

Malone, K 2006, 'United Nations: key player in a global movement for Child Friendly Cities' in *Creating child-friendly cities: reinstating kids in the city*, eds B Gleeson & N Sipe, Taylor and Francis, London, pp. 13–32.

Malone, K 2010, 'Dapto Dreaming children's friendly guide', unpublished report, University of Western Sydney, Sydney.

Malone, K 2011, 'Changing global childhoods: the impact on children's independent mobility', *Global Studies of Childhood*, vol. 1, no. 3, pp. 161–166.

Malone, K 2012, '"The future lies in our hands": children as researchers and environmental change agents in designing a child friendly neighborhood', *Local Environment: The International Journal of Justice and Sustainability*, vol. 18, no. 3, pp. 372–395.

Malone, K 2015, 'Children's rights and the crisis of rapid urbanization: exploring the United Nations post 2015 Sustainable Development Agenda and the potential role for UNICEF's Child Friendly Cities Initiative', *International Journal of Children's Rights*, vol. 23, pp. 1–20.

Rudner, J & Malone, K 2011, 'Childhood in the Suburbs and the Australian Dream: how has it impacted children's independent mobility?', *Global Studies of Childhood*, vol. 1, no. 3, pp. 207–225.

Save the Children 2012, *Born equal: how reducing inequality could give our children a better future*, Save the Children UK, London.

Sipe, N, Buchanan, N & Dodson, J 2006, 'Children in the urban environment: a review of research' in *Creating Child Friendly Cities*, eds B Gleeson & N Sipe, Routledge, Abingdon, pp. 86–102.

Stockland 2010, *Brooks Reach: child-friendly communities research and community engagement project brief*, Stockland, Sydney.

UNDP 2013, *Human Development Report 2013: the rise of the south: human progress in a diverse world*, UNDP, New York.

UNDP 2015, *Delivering the post 2015 development agenda: opportunities at the national and local levels*, United Nations Publications, New York.

UN-HABITAT 2003, *The challenge of slums—global report on human settlement*, UN-HABITAT, Earthscan, London.

UNICEF 1992, *Convention on the rights of the child*, United Nations Publications, New York.

UNICEF 1996, *Towards child friendly cities*, UNICEF, New York.

UNICEF 1997, *Children's rights and habitat: working towards child friendly cities*, UNICEF, New York.

UNICEF 2001, *Partnerships to create child friendly cities: programming for child rights with local authorities*, UNICEF/IULA, New York.

UNICEF 2002a, *A world fit for children*, UNICEF, New York.

UNICEF 2002b, *Poverty and exclusion among urban children*, UNICEF Innocenti Centre, Florence.

UNICEF 2004, *Building child friendly cities: a framework for action*, UNICEF Innocenti Research Centre, Florence.

UNICEF 2008, *The state of Asia-Pacific's children 2008*, UNICEF, New York.

UNICEF 2012, *State of the world's children 2012: children in an urban world*, UNICEF, New York.

UNICEF 2013, *A post-2015 world fit for children: sustainable development starts and ends with safe, healthy and well-educated children*, UNICEF, New York.

United Nations 1992, *Agenda 21: the Rio declaration and statement of forest principles*, United Nations Publications, New York.

United Nations 2012, *The future we want*, United Nations Publications, New York.

United Nations 2013, *A new global partnership: eradicate poverty and transform economies through sustainable development*, United Nations Publications, New York.

United Nations 2014, *The road to dignity by 2030: ending poverty, transforming all lives and protecting the planet*. Advance unedited copy tabled December 2014, United Nations, New York.

van Vliet, W 1985, 'The role of housing type, household density, and neighborhood density in peer interaction and social adjustment' in *Habitats for children: the impacts of density*, eds JF Wohlwill & W van Vliet, Lawrence Erlbaum Associates, New Jersey pp. 165–200.

Ward, C 1978, *The child in the city*, Pantheon, London.

WHO 2010, *Hidden cities: unmasking and overcoming health inequities in urban settings*, UN-HABITAT/WHO, New York.

Worldwatch Institute 2007, *State of the world 2007: our urban future*, Norton & Company, London.

CHAPTER 2

Children as natural change agents

Child Friendly Cities as Resilient Cities

Victoria Derr, Louise Chawla and Willem van Vliet

Introduction

Discourse about resilient cities includes processes of societal change and adaptation (Pearson & Pearson 2014) as well as knowledge transfer and exchange between organizations of civil society and citizens (Wamsler 2014). This discourse replaces the dominant view of cities as 'engines of growth' (Freeman et al. 1992) with one that sees cities as 'agents of change' (Van Vliet 2002). Evaluations of child friendly cities document that even at young ages, children can act as 'agents of change' and meaningfully participate in civic processes (Chawla & Van Vliet in press; Derr & Kovács 2015). Yet references to children are virtually nonexistent in the literature about resilient cities. Pearson and Pearson (2014, p. 247) describe resilient cities as those where "everyone has a role, an idea, an insight and the ability to participate in delivering cities where our children will *want to live*, rather than those where they will *have to work*". Yet within their framework, there are no clear mechanisms for including children in the planning process. Integration of children into processes where people help shape their cities and the structures that govern them is, thus, a logical and important progression. Children and adolescents are important stakeholders in our urban future, entitled to have their voices heard on all matters that affect them (United Nations 1989). They are also a tremendous resource for positive change. This chapter considers how principles of the UN Convention on the Rights of the Child that underlie Child Friendly Cities can contribute to thinking about resilience, and simultaneously, how Child Friendly Cities can learn from resilience planning in its consideration of nature and green infrastructure within the city. It examines these relationships through the evolution of one child friendly city project, Growing Up Boulder (GUB), and its recent inclusion of children in resilience planning.

In 2015, Boulder became the first city within the Rockefeller Resilient Cities network to engage children and adolescents in its planning efforts. Boulder was well placed to include children in resilience planning because of six years of prior child friendly cities work through its Growing Up Boulder program, which integrates children and youth into urban planning and design. As described in Chapter 15 by Mintzer and Flanders Cushing, GUB brings together the rights focus of the United Nations Convention on the Rights of the Child, as represented by the Child Friendly Cities Initiative, with the participatory approaches of Growing Up In Cities (Chawla 2002). Over time, this partnership has helped expand the culture of participation to many departments within the city, from community planning and sustainability, to parks and recreation, transportation, arts and culture, open space and mountain parks, and, most recently, the city's resilience program via the Rockefeller Foundation. The structure of GUB, as a partnership between the city, school district, university and many youth-serving organizations, has allowed participants to build relationships. Over time and many projects, people have come to know each other and build trust. This bonding and bridging social capital, which are essential components of GUB's success, are also essential for urban resilience. In this way, initiatives that promote participatory planning through a child friendly cities framework contribute to resiliency and have the potential to create the "capacity to respond to, create . . . and thrive in change" (Magis 2010, p. 404).

Multiple facets of resilience

When Holling (1973) introduced the idea of resilience in the 1970s, he changed people's thinking about ecosystems, from systems that are static and stable to those that are changing and flexible. Holling's thinking included three factors that are central to ecosystems: 1) the potential for change; 2) connectedness and flexibility; and 3) adaptive capacity, or resilience. This idea of adaptive cycles and states has gained momentum within the ecological literature and more recently in the fields of planning and urban design. Recent publications consider resilience in the context of governance (Pearson & Pearson 2014), community well-being (Astbury 2013) and social sustainability (Magis 2010). Resilience thinking in social-ecological systems accepts that change is an inherent part of the system. Magis (2010) suggests that resilience not only contributes to survival, sustenance and renewal, but also can be transformative. Circumstances arise that push an individual or community to a point where the old norms and adaptations are no longer sufficient and an entirely new system is needed. These transformations are considered healthy and provide opportunities for renewal. Critical factors for resilience include community agency and capacity; natural, financial and social capital; opportunities for self-organization; diversity and different forms of knowledge; opportunities to learn about and steward ecosystem functions; and landscape design that makes ecosystem processes visible and understandable (Astbury 2013; Berkes & Seixas 2005; Magis 2010).

In individuals, psychological resilience is evident when people become competent, confident and caring individuals despite major adversities such as poverty, war, natural disasters and family losses (Masten 2014). Like ecosystems, community systems that promote psychological resilience are constituted by interdependencies. Fifty years of research to understand protective factors that support resilience have yielded a 'short list' that has remained largely consistent across different populations, cultures and types of adversity (Luthar 2006; Masten 2014). Some protective factors are internal to a person: social competence; intelligence and problem-solving skills; self-control and disciplined planning to achieve goals; the motivation to succeed; a sense of self-efficacy; a belief that life has meaning. These internal strengths, however, develop from early childhood in relation to protective factors in the environment: effective parenting and caregiving; supportive relationships with other capable adults; close friendships and, later, adult life partners; effective schools; and effective neighborhoods that demonstrate collective efficacy. Resilience reflects an interactive process that occurs when children exhibit personal strengths by reaching out to find care and support, and people and places around them provide the resources that they need.

Resilience can follow a number of pathways, including *resistance* when people continue to function well during a crisis; *recovery* when they return to capable functioning after a period of decline; and *transformation* when they experience personal growth through positive adaptations to challenges. Similar pathways can be seen in community responses to disaster (Masten & Obradovic 2008). These individual and community levels are connected. The recovery of individuals and families is embedded in community contexts, and reliant on whether communities rally to provide their members with critical resources. Whether communities respond effectively to adversity, however, depends on the strengths of the individuals and social groups that constitute them. Community resilience is defined as networked adaptive capacities that are facilitated by economic resources, information and communication, social capital and community competence in the sense of collective know-how and effectiveness (Norris et al. 2008). Collective efficacy happens when groups function well because they are composed of people who bring individual strengths, and people feel encouraged to mobilize their strengths because they value the capacities of their group (Bandura 1997).

Intersections between Child Friendly Cities and Resilient Cities frameworks

Although the UN Convention on the Rights of the Child does not mention resilience directly, the government obligations that it specifies to secure children's rights are intended to protect children from harm, ensure their healthy development and full participation in society, respect their dignity and capabilities, and provide resources such as high-quality health care and education (United Nations 1989). Protective factors for resilience are implicit in these conditions.

UNICEF conceived of Child Friendly Cities as a way to advance children's rights in city decision-making and governance. These rights-based principles provide a framework for resilient cities to acknowledge the importance of children's wellness, the full development of children's talents and capabilities, and children's inclusion in civic processes: topics on which resilience planning has been largely silent. Because ideas about resilient cities emerged from the study of ecosystems, they address the general omission of the natural environment in the Convention on the Rights of the Child. Bringing children's rights and urban resilience together can enlarge the conceptualization of wellness and agents of change in resilient cities, and highlight the importance of well-functioning ecosystems for children's realization of their rights in child friendly cities. Concerns for multilevel, multisectoral governance and social equity, which thinking about resilience and child friendliness already share, provide opportunities for this expanded vision (see Figure 2.1).

It is noteworthy that the natural world is only mentioned once in the UN Convention on the Rights of the Child, when Article 29 includes "the development of respect for the natural world" as one of the goals of education. Neither the Convention nor current guidelines for *Building Child Friendly Cities* (UNICEF 2004) articulate the right of children to informally play in nature (Derr & Rigolon 2016). This is a serious omission, as research shows that childhood play in nature is the most frequent experience associated with lifelong respect and care for nature (Chawla & Derr 2012). Recent initiatives in GUB demonstrate that when children are included in urban planning and design, they spontaneously weave nature into their work (Figure 2.2). Children's own definitions of child friendly cities integrate all ages into city life, through welcoming public spaces and public processes that take their ideas seriously, and extend consideration of

Figure 2.1
Intersections
between Child
Friendly and
Resilient Cities
frameworks,
highlighting the
strengths and
contributions from
each framework

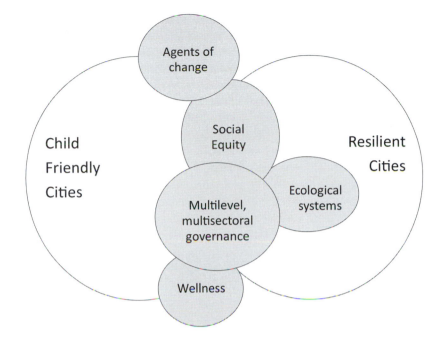

Figure 2.2 Mural
by Boulder Journey
School children,
"we want the grass
to tickle our toes"
(Source: Boulder
Journey School)

the rights of others to the rights of nature to exist within a city (Derr & Kovács 2015). Nature also emerges as an important element when children discuss resilient cities.

The values of nature that children express extend beyond the concept of ecosystem goods and services that is featured in the resilient cities literature. They are consistent with recent evidence that has been amassing about benefits of everyday access to nature for the health and well-being of all ages (Chawla 2015; Hartig et al. 2014). This research shows that people function better physically, cognitively and socially when they have trees, other vegetation and biodiversity around their homes, school and workplaces, and in nearby parks. For children, in particular, it indicates the importance of greening playgrounds, schoolyards and childcare centers. For both Child Friendly Cities and Resilient Cities, this research deepens the link between wellness and ecological systems.

Participatory processes produce agents of change and foster social capital

Growing Up Boulder's six years of engagement laid the groundwork for children's inclusion in resilience planning. In our review of GUB projects, we find several central tenets of Child Friendly Cities that support resilience within cities. These include participation as a process that supports children as agents of change; promotion of social equity; integrated, multilevel, multisectoral approaches to governance; attention to wellness; and a strong value that children place on access to nature. Brief descriptions of selected GUB projects show how these principles evolved.

Early on, adolescents involved with Growing Up Boulder worked in action groups to support public art, teen friendly businesses, and safe and affordable nightlife (Derr et al. 2013). Teenage mothers were concerned about Boulder's housing policy, which prohibited anyone under the age of 18 from applying for public housing. Some teen mothers were concerned that they would become homeless (Derr et al. 2013). Young people worked with GUB staff and discussed their concerns with adults, including business leaders and city councilors. In turn, adults identified existing services and possible policy changes (Derr et al. 2013). While no action group was specifically focused on resilience, when youth identified aspects of the city they liked and did not like, they helped to identify core components of child friendliness, such as access to basic services, as well as urban resilience, through their desire for supportive services and bridging capital. Through this process they developed their own capacity to be agents of change within their cities.

GUB's first park planning project—the 'Burke Park' project—emerged when shifts in land use led to an opportunity to collaborate in a participatory design process for a city park and the adjacent primary schoolyard. Historically, a ranch stock pond had become a lake amenity for a city park in a growing neighborhood. Lake levels were maintained by pumping treated municipal water into the lake. When the city proposed halting the unsustainable practice of pumping water, long-time residents, especially those living at a nearby neighborhood retirement center, staged a 100-person protest. Meanwhile, the school had expanded its buildings and needed to construct a new playground. The city saw this as an opportunity to bring together the school, the community and the Growing Up Boulder initiative to rethink the park and playground through an intergenerational planning process. Many partners identified the *process* as the most significant aspect of the Burke Park project. It facilitated community dialogue through a four-week elective class at the school, several community meetings and a university design-build course (Rigolon et al. 2015).

The value of the social capital generated within the community during the Burke Park planning process became significant during a major flood in 2013. In what has been called a "1,000-year rain event" (Brennan & Aquilar 2013), the retirement community was inundated with water. Many neighborhood residents came out to help. The outreach coordinator of the retirement center directly attributed this willingness to help to the connections made in the community meetings for the park project (Rigolon et al. 2015). This is an example of how participatory planning can create opportunities for groups to understand and care for each other, with ramifications that can go far beyond project timelines and outcomes, and extend into ideas of resiliency. In the case of more vulnerable populations, such as children or senior citizens, bridging capital seems particularly important in resilience to natural disasters. Intergenerational participatory processes, such as this one, can create both social capital and community cohesion, via the park and its resources that facilitate resilience.

Ecological systems considered and integrated

GUB's 'Great Neighborhoods' project involved children and adolescents in exploring options for dense, affordable, child friendly housing in anticipation of the city's Comprehensive Housing Strategy. The housing area chosen for study was heavily impacted by the 2013 flood, with some child participants being evacuated during the time of the project. While flood response was not the primary focus of the project, it played a role in shaping students' interest in ways to make neighborhoods and housing more resilient. Local experts presented mechanisms for flood mitigation during the project, and students designed hills and berms for flood protection and play. This project particularly facilitated the nurturing of different forms of knowledge and consideration of ecosystem services, with nature integrated at multiple scales.

In both the Burke Park and Great Neighborhoods projects, students expressed a desire to experience, learn about and care for nature (see Figure 2.3). This was reflected in the students' desire to restore the wetland, remove invasive fish species and increase plant diversity (Rigolon et al. 2015). It was similarly reflected in the desire of students in the Great Neighborhoods project to create hills and berms that could be used for flood mitigation as well as for play (see Figure 2.4). These desires are natural extensions in young people's thinking, from imagining possibilities for access to nature to intentions to actively care for it. This idea of stewardship is a fundamental concept of resiliency. In this sense, GUB's child friendly cities work helps foster both young people's *desire* to become active stewards and *capacity* to steward, which the Rockefeller Foundation includes in its basic definition of resiliency. In this realm, Child Friendly Cities could learn from Resilient Cities by increasing stewardship opportunities, thereby teaching children project-specific skills. Resilience planning could also learn from children: green infrastructure can play a role not only in supporting ecosystem services, but also in providing community opportunities for access to nature for play and restoration.

Figure 2.3 Students were entranced by cattails during the Burke Park project (Source: Lynn M. Lickteig)

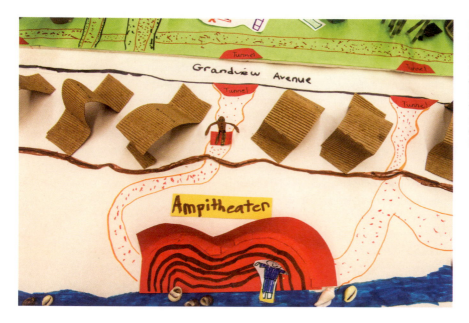

Figure 2.4 Children created a 'Great Neighborhoods' model which integrated nature throughout the site, including hills for flood protection, rooftop gardens and orchards (Source: Lynn M. Lickteig)

Promotion of social equity

In 2013, Boulder became a Resilient City under the Rockefeller Foundation's program. Selected cities partner with the Foundation and receive financial support to plan for resilience. The Foundation's resilience framework considers health and well-being, economy and society, leadership and strategy, as well as infrastructure and environment (Rockefeller Foundation 2014). While Boulder's implementation of the framework is broad, the initial emphases responded to the fire and flood that significantly impacted the city in 2010 and 2013, respectively. On its website, the Rockefeller Foundation considers Boulder and San Francisco as "cities [which] understand that investing in residents' capacity to steward their community's resilience is an essential step in building urban resilience" (Rockefeller Foundation 2014). However, website examples focus on disaster response and rebuilding and not on the transformative processes described initially by Holling (1973) or in recent definitions of community resilience (Magis 2010; Norris et al. 2008). When GUB began to work with the city's Chief Resilience Officer in the spring of 2015, broader conceptions of resilience began to emerge.

At that time, the city was gathering community perceptions of resilience. GUB decided to explore children's and adolescents' perceptions of resilience in an open-ended context, by focusing on Boulder's most underrepresented population. The goal was that these perceptions would help the city develop an understanding of local issues that impact resilience during their Preliminary Resilience Assessment phase, which was designed to identify priority areas for resilience planning. GUB partnered with the city's Youth Services Initiative (YSI), an after-school program that serves children and adolescents who live in Boulder's public housing sites. Most of the children who participate in the program are Latino, primarily of Mexican heritage. To qualify for public housing, families must earn an income close to federal poverty levels.

Using a variety of art-based methods over several weeks (see Figure 2.5), children and adolescents developed their ideas about resilience and shared them through

Figure 2.5 YSI
students planning
their resilience
mural (Source: Emily
Tarantini)

Figure 2.6
A resilience box
created by a YSI
youth. On the side
of the box she
wrote: "Nature
makes me feel
relaxed and free
from the world"
(Source: Emily
Tarantini)

informal presentations to Boulder's Chief Resilience Officer, Rockefeller Foundation
staff and the city's parks and recreation staff. Both age groups expressed feeling most
resilient among family and friends, as well as in nature. Adolescents identified that the
beauty of nature, interactions with animals and the seasons, and physical activity in
nature, such as hiking or riding horses, contributed to feelings of resilience (see Figure
2.6). While the literature addressing the role of nature in fostering resilience is relatively
new, children and adolescents have often expressed a desire for nature in child friendly
cities research (Chawla 2002) and other studies (Chawla 2014). It is in this realm that
Child Friendly Cities could learn from Resilient Cities in considering a diversity of ways

to integrate and make visible natural processes within the city (Astbury 2013). Similarly, social equity intersects with environmental justice: in many cities, children from families with lower incomes have less access to nature (Rigolon & Flohr 2014), yet in GUB's processes, they repeatedly express their desire for access to nature in their city.

In reflecting on resilience planning as a specific component of child friendly cities research, it appears that resilience as a construct provides a broader venue for identifying issues within a community. When GUB approached resilience using the wide-ranging definition from the Rockefeller Foundation, young people expressed concerns over economic issues (such as rising prices for housing and rent) and chronic negative influences of global and systemic issues (such as poverty, racism, violence and climate change). These issues do not affect all parts of cities equally. Therefore, it is important to ask "whose city" and "whose resilience"? As Vale (2014) observed, uneven resilience threatens the ability of cities as a whole to function economically, socially and politically, and resilience can be a useful concept and practice to the extent that it helps improve the life prospects of disadvantaged groups. A special issue of *Urban Studies* examines the role of governance in connecting these issues of social justice and progressive change to ecological realities (Beilin & Wilkinson 2015). The possibility of intentional resilience (Porter & Davoudi 2012, p. 305) creates opportunities for creating a moral compass to guide resilience-enhancing actions.

Integrated, multilevel, multisectoral approaches to governance

Following its Preliminary Resilience Assessment, Boulder identified priority areas for resilience planning. One of these is to improve governance so that resilience is integrated throughout planning processes rather than seen as a separate endeavor (G Guibert, Chief Resilience Officer, City of Boulder 2015, pers. comm., May 18). In particular, city leadership has underscored that residents within Boulder do not feel much ownership over decision-making. Exactly how resilience planning will unfold in the city remains to be seen, but city leaders are clear that it will not happen through city planning initiatives alone. It will rely on a citizenry that engages in issues and helps lead efforts.

UN-Habitat has compiled a worldwide database of best practices for alleviating poverty and promoting equity in diverse sectors including governance, environmental quality, housing and infrastructure, among others (e.g., UN-Habitat n.d.). Its evaluation of partnership practices showed that the most effective approaches integrate thematically interrelated sectors, coordinate different levels of government and involve complementary roles for stakeholders in the public sector, the private sector and civil society (Van Vliet 2009). As the City of Boulder's resilience planning moves forward, GUB can contribute to these processes through its history of support networks that build competence and capacity.

The experimental approach to GUB's work has resulted in much intergenerational learning and the formation of social capital. Resilience planning could learn from GUB's approach to child friendly cities, which develops participants' capacity to participate, deepens participants' knowledge through collaborative research and dialogue, and integrates participant ideas into tangible outcomes across city departments. As GUB's work has grown and partnerships with additional city departments have expanded, the value of a multisectoral approach is increasingly realized. Children naturally bridge sectors when they conceptualize a city. GUB can act as a bridge between departments, by integrating children's ideas from a single project into sectors from transportation to parks or housing.

Wellness and protective factors

As described earlier, protective factors can be internal as well as external to an individual. When teachers identified benefits that their students derived from participation in GUB's participatory processes, their observations included many protective factors. As one teacher stated:

> Today's students thrive when they are engaged in meaningful school work that provides rigor and connection with the community in which they live. Growing Up Boulder provides that critical bridge between the City of Boulder and the voices of her youth . . . Students come to know that their voices matter, they realize that civic engagement is an important lifelong action, and their emotional intelligence matures while working within diverse cooperative groups (Cathy Hill, GUB partner teacher, 2015, pers. comm., July 30).

Children develop such protective factors as social competence, problem-solving skills, a sense of self-efficacy and a belief that life has meaning. By interacting with adults in decision-making capacities, they also come to understand resilience as an interactive process in which people care and support each other, while also striving to make their shared communities better. These protective factors contribute to individual resilience while the participatory processes also contribute to community resilience.

The way forward

At the time of this writing, initial steps have been taken to connect GUB and the Boulder Department of Parks and Recreation to a statewide initiative for green space enhancement and ecological restoration, with broad implications for social and ecological resilience. The Department of Parks and Recreation hosted a series of events to promote nature play by creating spaces designated for children's free play in natural areas around the city. They held a public charrette to engage city residents of all ages, beginning with the ideas for child friendly green spaces and nature-based activities that GUB children and teens have already expressed. GUB will further advance these efforts by working with the city to map existing natural assets, overlay these with public housing and park amenities, and identify opportunities for intergenerational planning and community-based design and construction in city parks. To connect this initiative to the state vision of 'rewilding' ecosystems, the design and creation of nature play areas will need to include planning to enhance habitats for biodiversity, with the goal of connecting neighborhood habitats to regional ecosystems. How these initiatives can contribute to social and ecological resilience will need to be explored, but by bridging multiple city agencies, the school district and community-based organizations that work with children and adolescents, GUB has built a foundation for these next steps.

GUB has also begun a collaborative research process with partners at the National Autonomous University of Mexico to explore children's perceptions of resilience at varying scales within the cities of Boulder and Mexico City. Mexico City is part of the Rockefeller Foundation's 100 Resilient Cities network, yet it was the pairing of two universities involved in child friendly cities research that provided a framework to expand children's participation in resilience planning to Mexico's process. In this case, the social capital common both to resilience and participatory processes provided the catalyst for children's inclusion in another city's resilience planning.

Conclusion

When children's rights and urban resilience are considered together, they expand our conceptualization of wellness, promote social justice and well-functioning ecosystems, support children as agents of change and highlight the importance of multilevel, multisectoral structures of governance. Integration of child friendly principles into larger urban processes can thus encourage the transformative processes that cities seek to create through resilience planning.

References

Astbury, J 2013, 'Interactive urban landscapes for well-being and sustainability' in *Landscape, well-being and environment*, eds R Coles & Z Millman, Routledge, Abingdon, UK, pp. 72–86.

Bandura, A 1997, *Self-efficacy*, W.H. Freeman, New York.

Beilin, R & Wilkinson, C 2015, 'Governing for urban resilience: introduction to a special issue', *Urban Studies*, vol. 52, no. 7, pp. 1205–1217.

Berkes, F & Seixas, CS 2005, 'Building resilience in lagoon social-ecological systems: a local-level perspective', *Ecosystems*, vol. 8, pp. 967–974.

Brennan, C & Aquilar, J 2013, 'Eight days, 1,000-year rain, 100-year flood: the story of Boulder County's flood of 2013', *The Daily Camera*, Available from: www.dailycamera.com/news/boulder-flood/ci_24148258/boulder-county-colorado-flood-2013-survival-100-rain-100-year-flood.

Chawla, L (ed.) 2002, *Growing up in an urbanising world*, UNESCO/Earthscan Publications, New York.

Chawla, L 2014, 'Children's engagement with the natural world as a ground for healing' in *Greening in the red zone: disaster, resilience and community greening*, eds ME Krasny & K Tidball, Springer, Dordrecht, pp. 111–124.

Chawla, L 2015, 'Benefits of nature contact for children', *Journal of Planning Literature*, vol.30, no. 4, pp. 433–452.

Chawla, L & Derr, V 2012, 'The development of conservation behaviors in childhood and youth' in *The Oxford handbook of environmental and conservation psychology*, ed. S Clayton, Oxford University Press, New York, pp. 527–555.

Chawla, L & Van Vliet, W (in press), 'Children's rights to child-friendly cities' in *Handbook of children's rights: global and multidisciplinary perspectives*, eds M Ruck, M Peterson-Baldali & M Freeman, Taylor and Francis, New York.

Derr, V & Kovács, I 2015, 'How participatory processes impact children and contribute to planning: a case study of neighborhood design from Boulder, Colorado, USA', *Journal of Urbanism: International Research on Placemaking and Urban Sustainability*. Available from: www.tandfonline.com/doi/full/10.1080/17549175.2015.1111925.

Derr, V & Rigolon, A 2016, 'Participatory schoolyard design for health and wellbeing; Policies that support play in urban green spaces', in *Risk, protection, provision and policy*, eds C Freeman and P Tranter, vol 12 of *Geographies of Children and Young People*, pp. 125–148.

Derr, V, Chawla, L, Mintzer, M, Flanders Cushing, D & Van Vliet, W 2013, 'A city for all citizens: Growing Up Boulder's approach to engaging children and youth from marginalized populations', *Buildings*, special issue on Designing Spaces for City Living, vol. 3, pp. 482–505. DOI:10.3390/buildings3030482.

Freeman, C, Glaeser, EL, Kallal, HD, Scheinkman, JA & Sheifer, A 1992, 'Growth in cities', *Journal of Political Economy*, vol. 100, no. 6, pp. 1126–1152.

Hartig, T, Mitchell, R, de Vries, S & Frumkin, H 2014, 'Nature and health', *Annual Review of Public Health*, vol. 35, pp. 207–228.

Holling, CS 1973, 'Resilience and stability of ecological systems', *Annual Review of Ecological Systems*, vol. 4, pp. 1–23.

Luthar, SS 2006, 'Resilience in development: a synthesis of research across five decades' in *Developmental psychopathology, volume 3: risk, disorder, and adaptation* (2nd ed.), eds D Ciccetti & D Cohen, Wiley, Hoboken, NJ, pp. 739–795.

Magis, K 2010, 'Community resilience: an indicator of social sustainability', *Society and Natural Resources*, vol. 23, pp. 401–416.

Masten, A 2014, *Ordinary magic*, Guildford Press, New York.

Masten, A & Obradovic, J 2008, 'Disaster preparation and recovery: lessons from research on resilience in human development', *Ecology and Society*, vol. 13, no. 1, p. 9. Available from: www.ecologyandsociety.org/vol13/iss1/art9/.

Norris, F, Stevens, S, Pfefferbaum, B, Wyche, K & Pfefferbaum, R 2008, 'Community resilience as a metaphor, theory, set of capacities, and strategy for disaster readiness', *American Journal of Community Psychology*, vol. 41, pp. 127–150.

Pearson, LJ & Pearson, C 2014, 'Adaptation and transformation for resilient and sustainable cities' in *Resilient sustainable cities*, eds LJ Pearson, PW Newton & P Roberts, Routledge, New York, pp. 242–248.

Porter, L & Davoudi, S 2012, 'Applying the resilience perspective to planning: critical thoughts from theory and practice', *Planning Theory & Practice*, vol. 13, no. 2, pp. 299–333.

Rigolon, A & Flohr, TL 2014, 'Access to parks for youth as an environmental justice issue: access inequalities and possible solutions', *Buildings*, vol. 4, no. 2, pp. 69–94. DOI: 10.3390/buildings4020069.

Rigolon, A, Derr, V & Chawla, L 2015, 'Green grounds for play and learning: an intergenerational model for joint design and use of school and park systems' in *Handbook on green infrastructure: planning, design and implementation*, eds D Sinnett, S Burgess & S Smith, Edward Edgar Publishing Limited, Cheltenham, UK, pp. 281–300.

Rockefeller Foundation 2014, *Rockefeller Foundation's 100 Resilient Cities*. Available from www.100resilientcities.org/#/-_/ .

UN-Habitat n.d., *Best practice database: award winners*. Available from: http://mirror.unhabitat.org/bp/bp.list.aspx?bpTag=Best%20Practice.

UNICEF 2004, *Building Child Friendly Cities*, UNICEF Innocenti Research Centre, Florence.

United Nations 1989, *United Nations convention on the rights of the child*, United Nations Publications, New York.

Vale, LJ 2014, 'The politics of resilient cities: whose resilience and whose city?', *Building Research and Information*, vol. 42, no. 2, pp. 191–201.

Van Vliet, W 2002, 'Cities in a globalizing world: from engines of growth to "agents of change"', *Environment and Urbanization*, vol. 14, no. 1, pp. 31–40.

Van Vliet, W 2009, 'Broad-based partnerships as a strategy for urban livability: an examination of best practices', *Human Settlements Global Dialogue Series #2*, UN-Habitat, Nairobi.

Wamsler, C 2014, *Cities, disaster, risk and adaptation*, Routledge, New York.

CHAPTER 3

Nordic child friendly urban planning reconsidered

Fredrika Mårtensson and Maria Nordström

Introduction

In the Nordic countries children have high levels of independent mobility due to the merits of earlier planning regimes. Children's needs for outdoor places have been safeguarded by regulation, but today each community decides its own policies on the quality of their outdoor environments. What will the consequences be for children when the communities where they live choose differently? In this chapter, the strategies for child friendly urban planning in two Swedish cities will be described and discussed. We want to highlight the adoption of an inclusive strategy in which children's perspectives inspire urban planning. The history of child friendly planning and the UN Convention on the Rights of the Child provide a backdrop to this discussion.

The publication of *Growing up in an Urbanising World* by Louise Chawla (2002) made us aware of the fact that most children will grow up in urban environments, and this includes the Nordic countries. Like many regions in the world, the Nordic countries are changing in fundamental ways in response to increased urbanization. Sweden is a sparsely populated country and the population continues to diminish in the countryside as people move into the big cities. The region where the capital Stockholm, with 890,000 inhabitants, is situated gains 35,000 people every year. Malmö, Sweden's third-largest city, with 350,000 inhabitants, is also growing but more slowly. In this chapter we will share our reflections on the relationship between city development and children from a Nordic perspective, by describing planning related to children in these two cities. In Malmö we find planning initiatives inclusive of and sometimes even inspired by children, while in Stockholm, children's perspectives more easily get turned into an obstacle and a problematic issue. When looking at the planning history of Stockholm, however, we see that once it was as child friendly as Malmö is today.

Researchers on children's environments have been asking if there is a place for children in the city when observing the strong densification taking place in many cities (Churchman 2003). The committee evaluating the implementation of the UN Convention on the Rights of the Child acknowledges the general threat of urbanization to children's welfare, particularly in their ability to access spontaneous forms of play and to interact with their surroundings. UNICEF points to the concept of sustainable development as a means to 'boost' child health and children's rights (UNICEF 2013). Taking children's perspectives seriously implies involving children in planning processes and using insights and knowledge accumulated in the field of children's environments studies. Children need to be included in the establishment of sustainable planning regimes as they are directly dependent on the quality of their physical surroundings for their development and well-being (Schultz et al. 2015). We also know that positive place experiences together with persons important to us during childhood have consequences for environmental concern and engagement in environmental issues later in life (Chawla 1998). Working with children in urban planning is one way for adults and children to share their experiences of place and contribute to society's long-term commitment to sustainable development.

The imperative of environmental experiences

The experiences of childhood have a strong influence on our later lives. From the beginning of life, we carry with us not only memories, but also fundamental ways of relating to and understanding the world around us. By attentively making use of and exploring our surroundings we develop ways to use the physical environment for both nourishment and the formation of identity. For our argument we lean on literature in developmental and environmental psychology relating children's environments to the wider issue of sustainable development. Children do have a powerful drive to be included in the life of their communities. Kaj Noschis (2008) describes the need for children to establish their own relationship to the city in order to one day want to play a role as active citizens. He describes how the "physical environment is precisely an occasion to observe, witness and take part in what is happening. And subsequently to reinforce or change it" (ibid., p. 5). Children who get good opportunities to become involved in city life will develop a relationship to their surroundings, which will increase their interest and concern for their community at large.

Noschis describes the city "as a very stimulating environment *for children in particular* because so many things are going on and happen, which children can learn from and build their identity on" (ibid., p. 3, his italics). For a child to establish a relationship to a large-scale urban environment is not an easy thing, however. This was shown in studies comparing the conceptions of the physical environment in children living in different kinds of communities: in small towns in the countryside and in big cities (Nordström 2010). Children living in small communities referred to specific experiences they had in that environment and to people living there, while children in urban settings referred to the surrounding environment in abstract terms. Sometimes the urban children referred to places of their imagination only, like the moon. They did not mention any people. The immediate everyday environment did not seem to carry any special meaning to them. The stories of the children in small communities, on the other hand, clearly manifested feelings of belonging. One way to interpret these differences is that children in small communities more easily relate to their physical and social surroundings and therefore have a richer environmental experience and understanding. Cele's (2013) study of adolescents' use of public places in cities illustrated how the capacity to relate to a larger social and spatial context increases with age. This finding highlights what a challenge it is to make urban areas accessible to all children's environmental needs and the relevance of specifying such ambitions in relation to their age, maturity and competence.

Noschis (2008) stresses the importance of "more frequent encounters between adults and children, as they have important consequences for the priorities when decisions are made as to town planning" (ibid., p.15). Children are important allies in the shaping of a sustainable urban future provided they get access to an environment in which they can develop their competence and commitment. Children's perspectives

on the environment do contain some universal characteristics due to their preferences
for what is sensuous and what affords activity, but their perspectives also depend on
the specific circumstances of their local community.

Children's place in society and in the city park

An early manifestation of acknowledging a child's perspective in Swedish urban planning was evident in the 1890s when it was decided that a play area should be located
at the center of a new urban park, the Vasaparken in central Stockholm (Nolin 1999)
(see Figure 3.1). Until then, play areas had been located at the outskirts of parks,
away from the adult eye and adult activities. The Vasaparken is a symbol of a radically
new attitude to children's role in the public domain, acknowledging children as urban
dwellers and respecting their need to play.

   Later on, in the 1950s, Sweden saw an impressive development of creative and
diverse play areas like adventure playgrounds and 'splash ponds' in our cities, initiated
by influential officials working for parks and by professionals in the field of children's
education. A few of these early playgrounds in the central parts of Swedish cities
remain, and in Stockholm even a number of staffed playgrounds continue to operate.

Child friendly cities before the concept emerged

Generally, children in the Nordic countries still benefit from the child friendly urban
planning that prevailed for several decades during the last century, but to a varying
degree depending on the extent of population growth. Most children in Sweden live in
communities with an average of 30,000 inhabitants. Here many families with children
live in spacious housing developments. The majority live in row houses or single-family
houses, surrounded by a well-distributed network of greenery, with separate lanes for
bikes and pedestrians and with playgrounds and sport facilities adapted for children of
different ages, dispersed throughout the environment (see Figures 3.2–3.5).

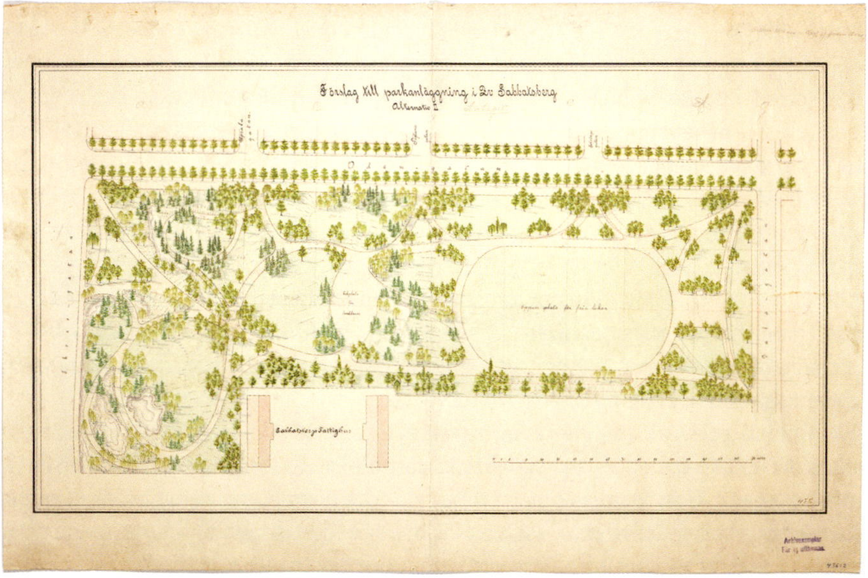

Figure 3.1 A map of Vasaparken in Stockholm from 1897. This park was one of the first parks in Sweden to have centrally located playgrounds. The big open space in the middle of the map says "Open space for free play" and the small space to the left says "Play area for young children" (Source: Stockholm Council)

Figures 3.2–3.5 Staffanstorp. A typical neighborhood from an earlier planning regime with greenways that can be quite plain, but affording children high independent mobility by securing safe routes for transport and easy access to playgrounds and sports facilities (Source: Fredrika Mårtensson)

Recently we investigated children's independent mobility in one such community: Staffanstorp, in the south of Sweden. As many as 78 percent of the 10-year-olds traveled on their own to school by foot or bike and the average levels of daily physical activity were outstanding in comparison with international experience (Johansson et al. 2011). The children's activity diaries showed that many of them enjoy considerable independence traveling on their own to leisure activities or to carry out minor errands, and playing and hanging around with friends in the neighborhood after school. This confirms what we so far have assumed: that children's independent mobility still thrives in smaller communities, even if it has diminished significantly since the 1970s, when it was common that even toddlers were out on their own in housing areas.

The tradition of benefiting from nature

The many benefits of nature for children's play and learning have been a salient theme in Nordic research. In a review of research, Pia Björklid (2005) showed how the indoor environment was framed as problematic due to noise, lack of good lighting, bad indoor climate and other detrimental conditions, while the outdoor environment was usually framed as an environment with expected benefits for children's overall health and development in terms of being spacious places where children can play.

The benefits of nature in housing areas have been the subject of several studies over the decades. These studies have been conducted primarily in large developments from the 1940s to the 1970s. In her dissertation, Pia Björklid (1982) showed that play-grounds were important places for children meeting and forming a community with peers. She also showed that children found their best play opportunities in the natural environment of areas surrounding the playgrounds. A few years later, in a report on the outdoor life of children and elderly people, Ulla Berglund and Ulla Jergeby (1989) showed how outdoor play sessions were a recurring activity in young children's every-day life. Safe and green outdoor environments filled a multitude of functions in the lives of families as places where children would play, recreate and meet other chil-dren and their parents. Studies have continued to demonstrate the benefits of green surroundings to children (Heurlin-Norinder 2005; Jansson 2010; Sandberg 2012).

A strong tradition in child friendly planning

Since the 1980s, Sweden has developed into a more liberal society with less planning regulation than before. Design and planning solutions were quite similar across the country from the 1940s to the mid-1980s, drawing on norms which had developed into a well-established practice of securing children's spaces. Today each municipal-ity decides on its own what building policies to practice and what public spaces to dedicate for children's use, as well as what outdoor facilities to commit for schools and residential land use.

Stockholm once played a leading role in the promotion of good outdoor environ-ments for children. During the present intense economic development in Stockholm, since the early 2000s, there has been and continues to be a strong interest in building and in reserving more land for building, at the expense of children's outdoor environ-ments. The argument is that it is too costly to reserve as much ground for play spaces for children today as had been the custom.

From the 1940s until the early 2000s, Stockholm's children were lucky to grow up in a city with an abundance of open space and extensive green surroundings. There was a group of architects, town planners, politicians and researchers committed to giving children easy access to nature in well-designed residential environments with outdoor playgrounds and play spaces close to their homes, and an overall planning approach which afforded walkable distances to schools. Protecting children from being exposed to the increasing car traffic was also an important issue. Stockholm's child friendly plan-ning influenced the planning standards for the whole country at the time. In landscape architecture it was called 'the Stockholm style', which meant carefully tended nature areas. In addition to well-designed housing areas, children were offered something called 'parkplays', which consist of play spaces with trained staff to take care of the children for a couple of hours, free of charge, every day and to provide children with toys, and even a snack. During this period Stockholm experienced a large number of people moving in from the countryside and the carefully planned and landscaped outdoor spaces served as a means to integrate the many newcomers into the city.

Breaking the tradition of child friendly planning:
the case of Hammarby Sjöstad

Since the deregulation of the planning process in the 1980s, planning and building in Stockholm today happens in different ways on different projects. New approaches to city planning and development reflect the influence of a political majority with strong liberal ideas and commercial interests, as in the case of planning the Hammarby Sjöstad development.

Hammarby Sjöstad is a large residential development designed for 20,000 residents, attractively situated near the center of Stockholm, close to city-district offices. Its construction started in 1998 and will be completed in 2017. As well as meeting an increasing demand for housing, the planners wanted the development to be an international showcase for Swedish competence in environmental technology and 'green' building (Becker 2015). Originally, it was predicted that the development would attract a population of mostly well-off, retired people. However, when the apartment construction was completed, it was apparent that many families were moving in. Families with children will always seek out new housing areas because of their need for more indoor space, and they will also expect outdoor facilities for their children.

Figure 3.6
"Revolt!" Landscape architects in Stockholm making an appeal against bad outdoor environments for children and against the lack of rules to secure children outdoor spaces (Article and photo by Annika Jensfelt, Arkitekten/the Architect, August 2015)

The lack of outdoor space for children in the Hammarby Sjöstad area has caused much criticism from families and given rise to problems for children (Karlsdottir 2012). Efforts have been made to improve the situation by building daycare centers and schools in facilities not originally designed for education. For example, playgrounds have been constructed on rooftops and small areas have been carved out of the limited space available to create tiny play spaces. These ad hoc responses have resulted in crowding in the few and small outdoor places which exist. Parents have reacted by taking their children to play areas outside of the Hammarby Sjöstad area into neighboring housing areas, or by moving away.

The failure of the prestigious Hammarby Sjöstad development to attract and retain families might be one reason why the Stockholm city planning authority has publicly admitted that child friendly planning is important, but when it comes to what constitutes child friendly planning and what will be the implications for each project, it still sees it as a matter of negotiation on a case by case basis. In a few projects, the possibility of requiring child impact assessments (CIAs) has been explored and sometimes successfully realized (see Nordström in this volume).

Public space planning in Malmö inspired by children

The glorious past of children's outdoor spaces in Stockholm, mentioned earlier, was the result not only of bright ideas, but of the determination of many knowledgeable and influential people with a clear political vision inclusive of children. In more recent decades, the city of Malmö has developed an inclusive planning approach, showing an interest in making the urban environment accessible and of good quality for children.

Malmö is a city in the south of Sweden surrounded by farmland, and the city with the least green open space per capita in the country. It was once a gloomy industrial outpost that since the start of the 1990s has been transformed into a vibrant city. Historically it has been known as the 'City of Parks', owing to the early establishment of large public parks such as the Pildammsparken, the site of the Baltic exhibition of 1914. The parks of Malmö are well used by children and their families. Families travel across the city to visit playgrounds. At 'outdoor preschools' children spend the whole day, all year round, outdoors in a park. In one park, Slottsparken, there is a gardener who invites school classes to care for garden lots 'of their own'. Malmö Nature School offers all schools in the community guided tours and advice on how wildlife habitats can support children's play and learning. Since 2010 more than 30 schools have been remodeled as part of a project on schoolyard greening (see Figure 3.7). Numerous research projects on the nature and benefit of green outdoor settings for children have been completed over the years (Grahn et al. 1997; Jansson & Mårtensson 2012; Mårtensson et al. 2009).

One explanation for the successful transformation of Malmö is the active role that planning and architecture have played. Important is a set of major investments: the Øresund bridge connecting Malmö to Copenhagen; the establishment of a university; and a new 'ecological' housing area by the sea (Bo-01, Västra Hamnen). Integrated with all this building, the public open spaces have been upgraded to better meet the expectations and ambitions of the community at large. It is not only the cityscape and the infrastructure that have undergone a transformation; even more importantly, the planning culture has changed.

Figure 3.7 Asphalt
has been replaced
by meadow at this
school as part of a
project of schoolyard
greening (Source:
Märit Jansson)

The joint visionary work of politicians, city landscape architects and planners has
turned physical planning for children and young people into a driving force for local
development. Ten years ago the city was one of the first to develop a long-term strategic program for playground development. In the collaboration between a former
city gardener, Gunnar Ericson, and a young local resident passionate about skating,
grand plans for a large skate park materialized. Over the years, the ways of collaborating with residents have been professionalized and new strategies developed for
integrating social planning with physical planning and for communicating with the
community.

Today the city is internationally recognized for its work on combining advanced
social and ecological sustainability in building design and construction, alternative
energy, and infrastructure systems. In 2010 the city set up a local commission to work
strategically on social determinants of health and well-being. In a country where children's general overall health is ranked sixth in the world, according to UNICEF, the city
of Malmö stands out as atypical. Many of its children are poor, overweight and showing low academic performance, with a third of the population being born in other
countries. An initiative inspired by the work of the World Health Organization, led by
Michael Marmot, resulted in the report *Closing the Gap in a Generation* (2008). An
extensive body of writing and many workshops have been carried out by professionals
in the community and experts from universities, to analyze the local situation and to
make suggestions for the future. One report on children's health includes a chapter on
children's independent mobility (Commission for a Socially Sustainable Malmö 2012b)
and another is a special report on planning titled *The City's Spatial Impact on Health*
(Commission for a Socially Sustainable Malmö 2012a).

There are now a number of planning projects in progress across the city, in which
the municipality is searching for opportunities to use physical planning to help reduce
segregation by supporting empowerment and social cohesion. In one disadvantaged

Figure 3.8 The 'Mat of the Red Rose' is designed to facilitate girls' active use of outdoor spaces and help link the suburb to the rest of the city (Source: Mariana Simici)

district, Rosengård, the plan is to improve pedestrian and cycling infrastructure to create favorable patterns of movement, increased solidarity and expanded social spheres. It presents a vision of a livable and dense city with a good mix of functions and with rich, well-connected, green infrastructure. The perspective of urban green space supporting active living and promoting health is well established in Malmö. Instead of thinking 'house in a park', a motto of Modernist city planning, one now argues for 'neighborhood in a park' and for making infill developments, changing larger roads into smaller-scale streets but keeping 'greenways' with lanes for bikes and pedestrians (Commission for a Socially Sustainable Malmö 2012b).

One of the projects to link the suburb with the city center, just a couple of kilometers away, is the creation of a new type of activity area for children and youth. The aim was to challenge the gendered character of outdoor spaces and especially challenge the dominance of boys using sports facilities. During the summer holiday, girls aged 13–19 years from the migrant population were invited to learn about planning in the municipality and to investigate the potential use of a place as an activity area that would be attractive for girls. The result was a centrally located place at a parking lot by a shopping center, called the 'Mat of the Red Rose' (Rosens röda matta), which consists of a stage with seating and music accessible from one's cell phone through a Wi-Fi system equipped with loudspeakers (see Figure 3.8).

Merits of earlier planning approaches with ongoing value

Nordic children's relatively active lifestyle and related well-being can be ascribed to the child friendly urban planning of an earlier planning regime. With a subsequent general deregulation of planning the quality of outdoor spaces has become a matter for each community and its governance bodies to decide. In this chapter, using examples from two Swedish cities, we wanted to show how children's perspectives on the physical environment can be an inspiration to planning, particularly when it is also sensitive to cultural heritage and expertise.

Children's healthy and happy development requires not only play facilities but possibilities for them to explore the surroundings at large, step by step, on their own terms. The UNCRC can help us take children as urban dwellers seriously and acknowledge the responsibility of planning to safeguard children's free mobility and opportunities for independent action in everyday life.

References

Becker, M 2015, 'Planeringsprocessens betydelse för att skapa barnvänliga bostadsområden—Exemplet Hammarby Sjöstad' [The importance of the planning process to create child friendly communities—the example of Hammarby Sjöstad], Master's thesis, SLU, Alnarp.

Berglund, U & Jergeby, U 1989, *Uteliv: med barn och pensionärer på gård och gata, i park och natur* [Outdoor life: with children and retired people in the yard and street, in the park and nature], Statens Råd for byggnadsforskning, T10, Stockholm.

Björklid, P 1982, *Children's outdoor environment: a study of children's outdoor activities on two housing estates from the perspective of environmental and developmental psychology*, Liber Gleerups, Lund.

Björklid, P 2005, *Lärande och fysisk miljö: En kunskapsöversikt om samspelet mellan lärande och fysisk miljö i förskola och skola* [Learning and physical environment: a survey about the interaction between learning and physical environment in preschool and school], Myndigheten för skolutveckling, Kalmar.

Cele, S 2013, 'Performing the political through public space: teenage girls' everyday use of a city park', *Space and Polity,* vol. 17, no. 1, pp. 74–87.

Chawla, L 1998, 'Significant life experiences revisited: a review of research on sources of environmental sensitivity', *Journal of Environmental Education*, vol. 29, no. 3, pp. 11–21.

Chawla, L (ed.) 2002, *Growing up in an urbanising world*, UNESCO and Earthscan, London.

Churchman, A 2003, 'Is there a place for children in the city?', *Journal of Urban Design*, vol. 8, no. 2, pp. 99–111.

Commission for a Socially Sustainable Malmö 2012a, *The city's spatial impact on health*, Malmö Municipality.

Commission for a Socially Sustainable Malmö 2012b, *Barn hälsa* [Children's health], Malmö Municipality.

Commission on Social Determinants of Health (2008). *Closing the gap in a generation: health equity through action on the social determinants of health. Final Report of the Commission on Social Determinants of Health*. World Health Organization, Geneva.

Heurlin-Norinder, M 2005, *Platser för lek, upplevelser och möten: Om barns rörelsefrihet i fyra bostadsområden* [Places for play, experiences and meetings: children's independent mobility in four dwelling areas], Stockholm University, Sweden.

Jansson, M 2010, 'Attractive playgrounds: some factors affecting user interest and visiting patterns', *Landscape Research,* vol. 35, no. 1, pp. 63–81.

Jansson, M & Mårtensson, F 2012, 'Green schoolgrounds: a collaborative development and research project in Malmö, Sweden', *Children, Youth and Environments*, vol. 22, no. 1, pp. 260–269.

Johansson, M, Raustorp, A, Mårtensson, F, Boldemann, C, Sternudd, C & Kylin, M 2011, 'Attitudinal antecedents of children's sustainable every day mobility' in *Transport and health issues: studies on mobility and transport research*, vol. 3, eds W Gronau, K Reiter & R Pressl, Verlag MetaGISInfosysteme, Mannheim, pp. 55–68.

Karlsdottir, K 2012, 'Children in their local everyday environment: child-led expeditions in Hammarby Sjöstad', Master's thesis, SLU, Alnarp.

Mårtensson, F, Boldemann, C, Blennow, M, Söderström, M & Grahn, P 2009, 'Outdoor environmental assessment of attention promoting outdoor settings for preschool children', *Health & Place,* vol. 15, no. 4, pp. 1149–1157.

Nolin, C 1999, 'Till stadsbornas nytta och förlustande. Den offentliga parken i Sverige under 1800-talet' [For the benefit and pleasure of urban citizens: the public park in Sweden during the nineteenth century], PhD thesis, Stockholm University.

Nordström, M 2010, 'Children's views on child-friendly environments in different geographical, cultural and social neighborhoods', *Urban Studies,* vol. 47, pp. 514–528.

Noschis, K 2008, 'Growing up in the city—an opportunity for becoming aware of urban sustainability issues', manuscript for key-note speech at the Swedish Area group meeting of Researchers in Environmental Psychology, Stockholm University.

Sandberg, M 2012, *'De är inte ute så mycket' Den bostadsnära naturkontaktens betydelse och utrymme i storstadsbarns vardagsliv* ['They are not outdoors that much': nature close to home—its meaning and place in the everyday lives of urban children], University of Gothenburg.

Schultz, ES, Hallberg, J, Bellander, T, Bergström, A, Bottai, M, Chiesa, F, Gustafsson, PM, Gruzieva, O, Thunqvist, P, Pershagen, G & Melén, E 2015, 'Early life exposure to traffic-related air pollution and lung function in adolescence', *American Journal of Respiratory and Critical Care Medicine*, vol. 193, no. 2, pp. 171–177.

UNICEF 2013, *Child well-being in rich countries: a comparative review*, Innocenti Report Card 11, UNICEF Office of Research, Florence.

CHAPTER 4

Envisioning urban futures with children and young people in Australia

Linda Corkery

Introduction

The needs of children and young people living in cities are considerable and extend well beyond parks, playgrounds and skateboard facilities, yet when urban planners and designers consider how best to provide for a city's young residents, these are often the first features that come to mind. Concern for the child, or children, as 'users of the city' is gaining currency for a number of reasons including a shared aspiration among many cities to be more diverse and inclusive, which means children and families must be accommodated and provided for. Further, attracting this demographic mix to live in the city—bringing its attendant social, cultural and economic benefits—will rely heavily on offering access to appropriate and affordable housing, in proximity to good-quality open space, schools, public transport and a safe and amenable public domain.

The headline of a recent *Sydney Morning Herald* news story referred to "Sydney's own Manhattan project". The reporter identified 19 office blocks in the central business

Figure 4.1
Watching street theater in Central Park, New York (Source: Kate Bishop)

district (CBD) scheduled for conversion to high-density residential in the next couple of years. Along with calculating the total number of new residents these projects would bring into the center of Sydney, the article projected an 80.6 percent increase over the next 20 years in the number of residents in the 0- to 17-year-old age group that would reside in central Sydney (Cummins 2015, p. 8). Notwithstanding the impact this would have on the concentration of population in the CBD, a major concern featured in the article was for the provision of early childhood education and long day care centers. This was based on the sensible view that families with working parents will require these services. Nothing was mentioned about the likely character of the housing on offer, impact on existing schools, quality of local streetscapes or the access to public open space, much less nature. Nor was there mention of how the City of Sydney would attempt to discover, from families, children or young people, what their anticipated needs would be.

Sydney's CBD is not the only neighborhood experiencing an increase in the population of families with children. Children are an increasing proportion of the population across the inner city neighborhoods of Sydney as can be seen in the total numbers of 0- to 9-year-olds in the inner Sydney neighborhoods which are showing significant increases just in the years between 2006 and 2011 (Sydney City Council 2006). This also appears to be a trend across all Australian cities.

While there is a perception that most families and children currently reside, or would prefer to reside, in the outer suburbs of Australian cities, there is evidence that more children are living in higher-density settings (Randolph 2006). As has been cited, that is the reality for Sydney and increasingly for other Australian cities, as well. Whitzman and Mizrachi note: "Despite inadequate social infrastructure, it is projected that over 10,000 children aged under 15 will live in the City of Melbourne by 2021, representing a doubling of the child population over 2006 figures" (2012, p. 234).

Figure 4.2 Children need space in the city: Pirrama Park, Sydney (Source: Fiona Robbé)

Figure 4.3
Children in the
city: a different
perspective (Source:
Anirut Thailand/
Shutterstock)

This is not to suggest that growing up in an urban environment is positive or negative—it is simply going to be an increasing reality. As Torres points out: "Questioning whether children should or should not live in cities is a pointless exercise. Instead, the most pertinent question seems to be: How can we make cities better places to grow up?" (2009, p. 6). To answer that question, if the desire is to create family and child friendly cities and communities, we would be wise to enlist the views of children and young people themselves.

Background to the contemporary discussion

While the contemporary concern for the needs of children as users of the city is not new, over the years the social issues and concerns associated with urban childhood have taken on slightly different dimensions. Looking back over the past 40 years, there has been a steady flow of research and writing, starting in the early 1970s with the project undertaken for UNICEF by renowned urban planner and designer Kevin Lynch: Growing Up In Cities (1971–1975). This project tracked the lived experiences of children in nine communities of four countries, including Australia, where the project was based in the Melbourne suburb of Braybrook. Colin Ward's often cited book, *The Child in the City*, was published around this time, as well (1977). Finally, in 1978, the Convention on the Rights of the Child (UNCRC) was introduced in the UN General Assembly (later adopted by the UN in 1989, with Australia ratifying it in 1990).

The UN's International Year of the Child in 1979 was conceived as a means of promoting the proposed UN Convention and itself was the catalyst for a number of other significant initiatives. In New South Wales, an example of this was *Planning with Children in Mind* (1981) by the NSW Department of Environment and Planning. This publication revealed some of the realities of children living in NSW cities and summoned planners and urban designers to focus their attention on the needs of children and young people in their decision-making, beyond simply providing playgrounds and

Figure 4.4
Interacting with the
city environment
(Source: Fiona
Robbé)

schools. Accounting for the needs of children has, historically, been answered by providing the requisite number of parks and playgrounds, for the projected population, distributed according to the current planning standards of the day.

Understanding that children's interaction with the built environment reached further than these designated sites was emphasized by 'The Playful City', a conference convened in Berkeley in 1990. This gathering of academics and practitioners addressed the full range of urban systems and settings that impact the daily lives of children, young people and families, including housing and neighborhoods, marketplaces, transportation, child-serving institutions (childcare, youth centers, schools, cultural facilities, health care) and communication and information systems. All of these settings continue to have a highly significant impact for children, particularly those living in cities—not just playgrounds and parks.

Along with this broadened scope of concern was a focus on engaging with children and young people in genuinely participative modes, as seen in the pioneering work of Roger Hart, Louise Chawla and David Driskell for UNESCO in the 1980s and 1990s (Chawla 2002; Driskell 2002; Hart 1997). Their publications identified exemplary projects around the globe that sought to bring these marginalized age groups into the processes of planning and designing for future environments and systems. The UN Conference on Environment and Development at which Local Agenda 21 was adopted, along with documents ratified at Habitats I, II and III, all repeatedly endorsed the view that "child participation is considered as a key strategy for sustainable development" (Torres 2009, p. 6). And so, the involvement of children and young people in decision-making that would affect their futures was linked to conceptions of sustainable development, rather than being simply a fun thing to do.

Most of this work has evolved under the banner of promoting children's rights as articulated in the UNCRC. The UNCRC also provided the foundation for the Child

Friendly Cities Initiative (CFC), launched in 1996. The international movement to promote children's rights and children's participation in shaping their future environments took hold in Australia in the early 2000s. It was in this context that the NSW Parliamentary Committee on Children and Young People initiated an Inquiry into Children, Young People and the Built Environment in 2005. Several catalysts prompted the Inquiry, including the groundswell of interest and support related to the CFC movement in Australia. It was instigated by both the Chair of the Committee and the then NSW Commissioner for Children and Young People, both of whom were motivated to respond to what children were saying were challenges they were facing in their communities that involved the built environment.

The aims of the Inquiry were to initiate a discussion about how built environment policies and practices impact the lives of children and young people, and contemplate opportunities associated with 'child friendly cities'. It was intended that the findings would "help inform the wider debates within Australia and internationally on child and youth-friendly environments" (Parliament of NSW 2006, p. ix). Fifty-seven submissions were received from academics, professionals and representatives of state, local government and community agencies that provide services for children and young people. The Inquiry culminated in a report released in 2006 which outlined a list of recommendations for the NSW Commission for Children and Young People to oversee and implement. In 2009 a follow-up inquiry was held to review progress on these recommendations, which resulted in another round of recommendations for continuing strategies to raise awareness amongst professionals and public agencies on key issues associated with children, young people and the built environment. This included the seminar series which provided the genesis for this book. (More on the inquiry process is presented in Chapter 12.)

Figure 4.5
Skateboarding in central public spaces is always controversial (Source: Nancy Marshall)

Different kinds of participation

It is important to understand what we mean by 'participation' although it would seem to be a self-evident concept; that is, taking part in something, or being actively involved. However, there are various ways to describe and enact participation, particularly when working with children and young people (Clark & Percy-Smith 2006, p. 1). A special issue of the *Children, Youth and Environments* online journal in 2006 was devoted to the topic of participation, and papers in the issue identified multiple understandings of how children's and young people's participation is interpreted, such as:

- participation as learning and experience
- young people being surveyed as service users to provide their opinions about their level of satisfaction
- participation as a requirement within city planning processes
- a collaborative process of learning and change through dialogue
- participation seen to empower young people and encourage their social action
- as research participants
- facilitating or modeling political involvement, e.g. Australia's National Youth Roundtable held in 2005 (Clark & Percy-Smith 2006, p. 3).

A major concern is that in too many cases, activities that are called 'participation' focus too much on adult priorities rather than those of children and young people (Clark & Percy-Smith 2006, p. 2).

Roger Hart's eight-step ladder of children's participation (Hart 1997), based on Arnstein's (1969) familiar ladder of participation, considers that at the highest form of implementation, participation is child-initiated and directed with decisions shared with adults. At the lower levels of the model, at best, children's participation is regarded as little more than manipulation, decoration or tokenism (Hart 1997).

Seeking a simpler and a greater expression of the possibilities for participation with children and young people, Harry Shier proposed an alternative five-level, three-stage model (avoiding the 'ladder' metaphor) that respects a number of ways children might participate. His model includes a self-assessment for an organization to make regarding its degree of commitment to the process of empowerment. In Shier's (2001) model of participation, there is not a 'peak' level at which children initiate activities on their own, the premise being that children and adults are in partnership as they interact to make decisions.

Shier's five levels of children's participation are as follows:

1 Children are listened to
2 Children are supported in expressing their views
3 Children's views are taken into account
4 Children are involved in decision-making processes
5 Children share power and responsibility for decision-making (Shier 2001, p. 110).

As for adults, Shier's model proposes a three-stage 'pathway' along which individuals or organizations identify their level of commitment and readiness to share decision-making power with children and young people. Organizations, and individuals within them, assess at what stage in the process they are ready to make a commitment. Shier identifies three stages: *openings, opportunities* and *obligations*. At the opening stage, there is an intent to facilitate participation. Perhaps, there is a policy in place that requires participation, but it may/may not proceed until an opportunity arises. This second stage is when the knowledge and resources to facilitate participation are in place. Finally, obligations are established when there is a policy built into the system requiring children's participation and staff are obliged to work with children at a specific level of participation. Shier summarizes his model in this statement: "To fully achieve level five, therefore, requires an explicit commitment on the part of adults to share their power, that is to give some of it away" (Shier 2001, p. 115).

High-level endorsement of participation processes

At the state level, both Victoria and Western Australia have been active in promoting children's participation through their child friendly cities initiatives. For example, the Victorian Local Government Association (VLGA) has produced a toolkit for local government agencies to use in promoting child friendly cities and communities (2014) that not only reminds officials of the commitment to the UN Convention on the Rights of the Child, but also puts forward the Victorian Child Friendly Cities and Communities Charter (CFCC). The Charter elaborates on the UNCRC and articulates a series of principles relevant to the local context. The second principle attends to the issue of participation: "Respect and dignity for children to express their individual opinions, participate in and contribute to decisions about their communities and their wellbeing" (VLGA 2014, p. 4).

In reference to Shier's model, local governments that adopt the CFCC Charter and undertake the steps outlined in the VLGA toolkit would be considered midway on the 'path to participation'; that is, between the stages of *opportunity* and *obligation* (Shier 2001). Full implementation of children's and young people's participation is ultimately enacted at the local government level, in the context of specific projects or planning initiatives.

In Western Australia, the Commission for Children and Young People's publication, *Building Spaces and Places for Children and Young People*, was produced as part of a research project that asked children and young people aged 5–18 years living in the state what they considered important to their well-being. The findings drew on nearly 1,000 responses, and among the key messages about the built environment was this: "They want a built environment that welcomes rather than excludes children and young people. Being acknowledged and listened to and having their ideas taken seriously make young people feel they are respected" (WACCYP 2011, p. 5). The findings were endorsed by the president of the Western Australian Local Government Association (WALGA) and also by the Government Architect, who commented: "Our buildings, places and spaces have an indelible impact on the wellbeing of the young people of our society. We must shape the built environment with children and youth at the very heart of our considerations" (WACCYP 2011, p. 3).

Of all the built environment-related professional organizations, the Planning Institute of Australia (PIA) has embraced the concept of Child Friendly Cities and children's participation most explicitly. PIA's policy on this topic notes that "Planners are in a unique position to directly impact the creation of child friendly cities and communities. PIA supports the characteristics of a Child Friendly City identified by UNICEF" (PIA 2007, p. 2). As per the focus of this chapter, the policy highlights the right of children and young people to be involved in decision-making that affects their lives.

Further, assuming this position in planning has "broad economic, social and cultural benefits . . . and is a long term investment in the life of that community" (ibid.). In other words, this initiative not only addresses children's needs, but potentially has benefits for everyone. As the VLGA document expressed it: "Cities and communities that cater for children, cater for all people" (2014, p. 1).

As a professional institute, PIA itself is not implementing participation activities. In adopting a position statement on child friendly cities, the professional body is publicly communicating its stance on the issue with the expectation that its members will align their professional practice with the values inherent in the statement. This is a significant step that would be excellent to see other built environment peak bodies in Australia emulate. To acknowledge best professional practice in achieving the intent of this policy, in 2012 PIA's New South Wales group introduced a project award for Planning for Children and Young People. This is another way professional institutes can be effective in shifting practice toward more inclusive participation processes—toward the level of *obligation*, to use Shier's terminology.

Overcoming perceived barriers

However, the PIA position statement on CFC acknowledges there remain numerous systemic barriers and challenges to including children and young people's participation in the routine aspects of planning, such as:

1   How can children be involved in decision-making processes, given limited resources and dominance of other issues (such as the ageing population)?
2   How do we counter a perceived growing tendency to design children out of built environments through gated or exclusionary design?
3   How do professionals and those advocating for better decision-making about work-ing with and for children and young people get access to research and information?
4   How do we combat the sometimes narrow sectoralism ('silo mentality') that oper-ates in many state and local government organizations; e.g., where do children's issues fit in a Local Government structure? (PIA 2007, p. 3)

The barriers are not just on the side of public agencies. There are also considerations from the perspectives of the children, young people and their families. For example, as Torres (2009) states, in some cases, family situations may "compromise the ability of parents to support their children in participatory initiatives", which might be the case in areas of low-SES neighborhoods or areas where "few resources remain for 'elective' activities such as involvement in community life" (p. 8). With this in mind, participa-tory activities that are associated with schools may be more successful as there is an institutional structure to support the children's involvement.

The National Youth Affairs Research Scheme (NYARS) undertook an Australia-wide investigation to identify specific barriers that prevent young people from fully partici-pating in their communities. What they discovered included institutional reluctance, perception that participation processes were time and resource intensive, and that the usual means of interacting with their constituents were fairly inflexible. There were also barriers related to young people's attitudes and/or social position that suggested they were unfamiliar with how participatory processes work, or how to interact productively with colleagues from diverse backgrounds. Consequently, they expressed cynicism about participation processes (Bell et al. 2008). The NYARS report offered what they considered the three simple characteristics for a successful participation process with children and young people:

1 It needs to be youth led
2 It is long-term and purposeful
3 It is creative and fun for young people, and uses media such as the internet (NYARS 2008, pp. 64–66).

Three best practice examples of participation in Australia

Over the past 10 years many projects have been undertaken around Australia demonstrating effective ways to invite children's and young people's participation in planning for shared futures. In some cases, these projects have introduced new policies and practices aimed at identifying the remaining obstacles for young residents' voices to be heard in planning and design processes. The Child Friendly Cities program has been an impetus in many of the early undertakings, such as the City of Bendigo, which was the first Australian city to be officially recognized as a child friendly city, and has since inspired other local governments to follow suit. However, one concern is that 'child friendliness' can take on a checklist approach and become a marketing slogan rather than involving genuine participation of children and young people in the planning and design processes. Several exemplary projects that have gained recognition for their innovation are briefly reviewed below.

Tweed Shire Council, NSW

The 2013 NSW PIA Award for Planning for Children and Young People was given to Tweed Shire Council for its *Youth Strategy 'Speak Out' Strategic Plan, 2013–2017*. The

Figure 4.6 Tweed's Youth Speak Out project (Source: Cred Consulting)

youth strategy sits within Council's suite of strategic and operational plans, including the Community Strategic Plan, the four-year Delivery Program, the annual Operational Plan and associated budget, which should ensure its list of actions will not be over-looked. The *Youth Strategy* is an exemplary document, worthy of PIA's recognition, largely because it was produced using a wide range of best practice participatory activities. It is also a great example of both Shier's and the NYARS principles put into practice. These included workshops and surveys, 'vox pops' (short, impromptu videos of person-in-the-street commentaries), a 'Speak Out' website and Facebook page, mail-back postcards distributed to all high school students in the LGA and two forums with local government officers. Council acknowledged the significance of investing time in these activities: "By participating in the planning and delivery of decisions that affect them, young people will have the opportunity to feel more connected to where they live" (Tweed Shire Council 2013, p. 7).

The strategic outcomes that were identified in the process are summarized in the table below. Tweed's 'Young People' . . .:

1   Are valued members of the community and engaged in decisions that affect them
2   Feel proud of where they live, with access to quality spaces and places
3   Are involved in local events and a range of creative, sporting and social activities
4   Have access to a range of education, employment and career opportunities
5   Feel safe and protected from drugs, alcohol and violence
6   Can get around and have access to services and affordable places to live (Tweed Shire Council 2013, p. 10).

Of these six outcomes, the second and final points relate mostly directly to *built* envi-ronment outcomes, while the first one commits the Council to continuing to engage with young people in decision-making regarding the issues that affect them. Each out-come is followed by a detailed list of actions, in some cases up to 18 specific tasks that the Council commits to implementing over the four-year life of the plan. Potentially, this is a powerful document that can be monitored over the years to validate the changes that occur and its overall effectiveness in maintaining an active connection with the children and young people of Tweed Shire. While the product is excellent, the process undertaken to achieve it is worthy of replication.

Stockland, Brooks Reach Development

In 2012, PIA New South Wales initiated a new award for an outstanding project that best demonstrated how children and young people have participated in a project aimed at encouraging their active and creative use of the built environment (PIA 2012). The winner that year was a project in the Illawarra community of Brooks Reach. In creating this new community, Stockland undertook what was considered to be an industry-leading approach to understanding the perceptions and aspirations for the local environment by those who would likely use it most—children. Working with Dr. Karen Malone, the University of Western Sydney's School of Education developed an independent research project in which over 150 local primary school children, aged 5–10 years, were invited to investigate their environment, using cameras and draw-ings, and to participate in a series of workshops and activities between April and July 2011. The children provided their views on what a child friendly neighborhood might

Figure 4.7 Brooks Reach Park (Source: Stockland)

look like. Their submissions were analyzed by a group of Year 5 children and the results informed the brief for the design of a new play environment that Stockland used in commissioning the landscape architects to design it. (A comprehensive discussion of this project is offered in Chapter 1 of this book.)

This is a good model of children as co-researchers, and evaluating it against Shier's model, it is also an example of children's views being taken into account and of their direct involvement in decision-making processes. Stockland committed to more than a tokenistic consultation process with the children, creating and resourcing the processes that enabled their involvement with imagining the qualities of a future residential environment. Finally, the children delivered opinions about the character of a specific feature of the development that would eventually be part of their everyday lives in the new community.

City of Melbourne's Children's Plan and Youth Policy

Social planners in the City of Melbourne undertook the development of their *Children's Plan: Children's Rights, Children's Voices 2010–2013*, committed to taking a child friendly city approach. Working with the University of Melbourne's Centre for Equity and Innovation in Early Childhood, consultations were carried out with children as young as 3 years old, and up to 12 years of age. To capture the needs of children aged birth to 2 years, parents were consulted. For the first time, Melbourne Council could truly claim their *Children's Plan* was "written with children and for children" (Melbourne City Council 2010a, p. 8).

The *Children's Plan* developed seven themes, each one expressing an 'outcome' and a series of specific actions. Themes one and five are particularly relevant to this chapter. Theme one underscores the City's commitment to the rights of children, and in the list of actions, the City undertakes to "give children meaningful opportunities to participation in the design, development, and evaluation of the municipality of Melbourne" (Melbourne City Council 2010a, p. 15). Theme five relates to the natural and urban environment, noting that these settings should be "shaped by children and families, rather than by planners and professionals exclusively" (Melbourne City Council 2010a, p. 23).

A complementary document, *Empowering Young People: Young People's Policy 2010–2013* was produced in parallel with the *Children's Plan*. In that document, the demographic significance of this age group was highlighted: "One third of the City of Melbourne's population is aged between 12 and 25 years, and young people aged 20 to 24 years make up one of the largest overseas-born groups in the municipality" (Melbourne City Council 2010b, p. 2). The *Young People's Policy* identified five goals, the first one addressing participation, leadership and empowerment. The fundamental outcome for this goal was for young people to "actively participate in, and contribute to, the social, cultural, creative, recreational and civic life of the city" (Melbourne City Council 2010b, p. 8).

The *Children's Plan* and the *Young People's Policy* remain active commitments within the City's community services section of its website, while it notes that the more recent document, *Melbourne for All People Strategy 2014–2017*, sets out the ways in which the City of Melbourne will "connect, support and engage people throughout their lives from 0 to 100+" (Melbourne City Council 2014). This document incorporates numerous preceding council policies and strategic plans, including *The Children's Plan: Children's Rights, Children's Voices 2010–2013* and *Empowering Young People: Young People's Policy 2010–2013*. This hopefully signals an approach to public involvement, where children and young people's participation truly becomes a customary way of operating, and moves the City of Melbourne toward the *obligations* stage of Shier's (2001) model.

Conclusions

Ultimately, as planners and designers imagining future urban communities, our ambitions must be to deliver urban environments that boost children's and young people's capacities for future participation as active and engaged citizens. Continuing to plan, design and develop cities solely from the perspective of adult needs runs the risk of creating communities that will not attract and retain the diversity of population we recognize is essential to achieve the balanced social, cultural and economic qualities to which we aspire.

As the preceding project examples demonstrate, children and young people are capable of meaningful participation in planning and decision-making processes. Adults must commit to creating the opportunities for them to participate and commit to sharing the power in the processes of urban governance and management, and visioning urban futures. That includes moving into the highest levels of participation as described by Shier, where children become genuinely involved in decision-making and, where appropriate, share the power and responsibility for the decisions that are made (Shier 2001).

Finally, the 'future generations', of which we too often speak in the abstract—particularly in the context of sustainability—are those children and young people who are part of our everyday lives today. They are capable of contributing to the conversation on planning for shared future environments, especially those that directly impact the quality of their daily lives, e.g. play environments, school grounds, local neighborhoods, community places, transport and safer streets, the public domain. Engagement with children and young people should occur early and throughout the process of planning and design. Importantly, this introduces them to imagining future possibilities, considering the needs of others, sharing community resources, identifying values, understanding the consequences of choosing to take one action over another—all skills that are central to preparing them for an active citizenship in which they take responsibility for the sustainability of their future communities. As Torres comments: "Childhood . . . is a time in which children can build ties with their communities and even transform them . . . [they are] interactive individuals who are both influenced by their living environment and capable of influencing it" (2009, p. 4).

If our ambitions are to deliver high-quality, more inclusive urban environments for everyone, and to bolster children's and young people's capacities for future participation as active and engaged citizens, we must take heed of a closing comment in the Final Report of the NSW Parliamentary Inquiry: "Failure to create child and youth friendly environments will be to the detriment of all society, not just children and young people" (Parliament of NSW 2006, p. 44).

References

Arnstein, S 1969, 'A ladder of citizen participation', *Journal of the American Institute of Planners*, vol. 35, no. 4, pp. 216–224.

Bell, J, Vromen, A & Collin, P 2008, *Rewriting the rules for youth participation: inclusion and diversity in government and community decision-making*, Report to the National Youth Affairs Research Scheme, Canberra.

Chawla, L (ed.) 2002, *Growing up in an urbanising world*, Earthscan, London.

Clark, A & Percy-Smith, B 2006, 'Beyond consultation: participatory practices in everyday spaces', *Children, Youth and Environments*, vol. 16, no. 2, pp. 1–9.

Cummins, C 2015, 'Sydney's own Manhattan project', *Sydney Morning Herald*, April 4–5, p. 8.

De Monchaux, S & New South Wales Department of Environment and Planning & International Year of the Child NSW Steering Committee 1981, *Planning with children in mind: A notebook for local planners and policy makers on children and the city environment*. NSW Department of Environment and Planning, Sydney, Australia.

Driskell, D 2002, *Creating better cities with children and youth: a participatory manual*, UNESCO/Earthscan, London.

Hart, R 1997, *Children's participation: the theory and practice of involving young citizens in community development and environmental care*, Earthscan, London.

Melbourne City Council 2010a, *The Children's plan: children's rights, children's voices 2010–2013*. Available from: www.melbourne.vic.gov.au/CommunityServices.

Melbourne City Council 2010b, *Empowering young people: young people's policy 2010–2013*. Available from: www.melbourne.vic.gov.au/CommunityServices.

Melbourne City Council 2014, *Melbourne for all people strategy 2014–2017*. Available from: www.melbourne.vic.gov.au/CommunityServices.

National Youth Affairs Research Scheme 2008, *Rewriting the rules for youth participation: Inclusion and diversity in government and community decision making*. Available from: http://acys.info/resources/nyars/nyars-reports/

Parliament of New South Wales 2006, *Inquiry into children, young people and the built environment: report No. 8/53*, Committee on Children and Young People, Sydney.

Planning Institute of Australia 2007, 'National position statement on child-friendly communities'. Available from: www.planning.org.au/documents/item/121.

Planning Institute of Australia 2012, *Planning excellence 2012 New South Wales Awards: Nomination Book*. Planning Institute Australia, NSW, Sydney, Australia.

Randolph, B 2006, 'Delivering the compact city in Australia: current trends and future implications', *Urban Policy and Research*, vol. 24, no. 4, pp. 473–490.

Shier, H 2001, 'Pathways to participation: openings, opportunities and obligations', *Children & Society*, vol. 15, pp. 107–117.

Sydney City Council 2006, *Community profiles, 2006–2011*. Available from: www.profile.id.com.au/.

Torres, J 2009, *Children and cities: planning to grow together*, Institut d'urbanisme, Université de Montréal.

Tweed Shire Council 2013, *Youth strategy 'Speak Out' strategic plan, 2013–2017*. Available from: http://static1.squarespace.com/static/54c8492be4b07c97befb5ebc/t/54dbead0e4b0469314182589/1423698640483/TSC04630_Youth_Strategy_and_Action_Plan.pdf.

Victorian Local Government Association 2014, *Child-friendly cities and communities toolkit*, VLGA, Melbourne.

Ward, C 1977, *The child in the city*, Architectural Press, London.

Western Australia Commissioner for Children and Young People 2011, *Building spaces and places for children and young people*, Western Australia Government, Perth.

Whitzman, C & Mizrachi, D 2012, 'Creating child-friendly high-rise environments: beyond wastelands and glasshouses', *Urban Policy and Research*, vol. 30, no. 3, pp. 233–249.

PART 2

RESEARCHING WITH CHILDREN AND YOUNG PEOPLE

This section on participatory research features a series of chapters that demonstrate the potential power and impact of research to shape our views of children and young people in our societies. When long-held ideas become entrenched in professional attitudes, governance instruments and processes, barriers to change can result. This is true for concepts of 'childhood' and 'adolescence'. They continuously shift and change over the generations, and social research contributes to our evolving, contemporary understanding of these stages of human development. Gradually, these ideas percolate through to other sectors such as education, health, community services, urban planning and design—eventually influencing new or revised policies and innovative design that benefit these age groups.

There is powerful potential for research to inform urban planning and design if the links can be made between findings, policy and practice. Currently, however, these links are tenuous: too often research findings do not reach the right audiences. This represents a point of breakdown in the effort to engage children and young people in urban planning and design for their benefit.

Participatory research with children and young people is now widely practiced in many disciplines. Initially, the social sciences pioneered this research; more recently the medical and health sciences have also engaged with it. The authors of the following four chapters represent both the health sector and the built environment design sector, reflecting some of the most contemporary areas of interest within children, youth and environments (CYE) research, including the relationship between nature, the physical environment and children's health and well-being.

In these chapters, children and young people are presented as experts in their own lives with viewpoints that are salient to all social processes, including urban planning and design. The first two chapters summarize the breadth of CYE research in recent decades, identifying the main themes relevant to urban planning and design from children's and young people's perspectives. These chapters by landscape architecture academic Patsy Eubanks Owens and environment behavior academic/researcher Kate Bishop acknowledge the wealth of research that now exists. They also identify barriers that inhibit effective knowledge transfer between researchers and both the policy and practice sectors, which undermines the possibility of this research informing relevant processes such as planning and design. As the authors acknowledge, these challenges are not new but they continue to inhibit the capacity and opportunity for research to be utilized for children's and young peoples' benefit.

(Source: Fiona Robbé)

The chapters by Helen Woolley, landscape architect/researcher from the UK, and Penelope Carroll and Karen Witten, geography academics from New Zealand, extend the discussion to identify and discuss project- and site-specific challenges. Their chapters press the point that children and young people assign significance and meaning to local, accessible urban public space and their participation in its planning and regulation acknowledges and strengthens their civic capacities. These two chapters identify some of the main priorities in participatory research itself, and in urban planning and design processes to which they could be applied.

CHAPTER 5

A place for adolescents

The power of research to inform the built environment

Patsy Eubanks Owens

Introduction

The urban environment is a place where many young people grow up—a place where they make friends, spend time with family, go to school, find a job and learn to be an adult. Yet the importance and provision of these environments in the lives of young people receive little deliberate attention by civic authorities, property owners, designers or others. Instead, young people are left to their own devices to claim urban public spaces for their needs, and their unsanctioned, unauthorized use of these areas is often questioned, contested or banned. However, as this chapter will show, young people need supportive environments for their healthy development and urban environments play a critical role in fulfilling that need.

In recent years, a great deal of research has been conducted that uncovers the places important to adolescents and what makes those places important (e.g., Clark & Uzzell 2002; Duzenli et al. 2010; Owens 1988, 1994). Additional discussion has focused on the exclusion of adolescents from public spaces (e.g., Owens 2002; Woolley et al. 2011). The intent of this chapter is to reframe this prior research so that we might move beyond theoretical discussions to influencing the multilevel decisions that shape the built environment. This chapter is offered as a call to change the status quo, that is, to challenge current perceptions and practices related to adolescents' presence in and use of the built environment, and to inform the creation of more supportive and better places to live. This call is addressed to practitioners in-training as well as the research community and others whose actions impact youth environments. Several questions inform this discussion: what are the factors shaping societal perceptions of adolescents? How can those factors be changed and thereby change the typical response to adolescents' presence in public places? How do certain settings promote positive adolescent development and how can built environments be provided to meet these important needs? How can we translate what we know about the importance of places in adolescents' lives to design and policy actions?

This chapter is organized around three prongs of research: context, content and translation. In this instance, the context refers to the broader societal setting of adolescents' daily lives in urban areas. Examining this setting helps us to understand our research findings more fully and provides direction for translating that research to design and policy response. The content portion of this discussion describes the research on places important to youth. Although individual preferences and experiences should always be acknowledged, research from different disciplines and conducted in varied settings reveals important and consistent findings regarding which places are needed by youth and why. Lastly, the translation of research into action and the role of youth in that change are addressed. The power of this research is most fully realized when it informs the contemporary urban environment.

Daily lives and societal context

In order to understand the urban experience of young people, we need to examine the societal context of these interactions. While the discussion is presented from a US perspective, many of the findings and implications are relevant to other westernized countries and beyond. This context, both historical and contemporary, shapes the relationship adolescents have with their built environment and the relationships others have with adolescents. Further, it informs decisions that directly impact which environments adolescents have access to and the activities in which they can engage. While the underpinnings of this societal context are more complex than can be fully explored here, some of the more salient influences are discussed. These influences include both long-held opinions about the adolescent years and more recent shifts in perceptions of youth and their surroundings. In addition, changes in family structure, environmental concerns and technological advances inform and alter the use and meaning of the built environment for young people.

The long-held general public perception of adolescence as a time of difficulty for the individual and society is well documented (Owens 1997). Adults assume that adolescents will be causing trouble soon even if they are not at the moment. These assumptions contribute to individuals' reactions such as a merchant asking a group of teens to move on, to more comprehensive public reactions such as public policies (i.e., curfew laws, loitering ordinances) and to design decisions that limit adolescents' use of public space (Owens 1997, 2002). This guarded treatment of youth is not universal or uniform. Groups of youth are treated more severely than individuals; boys more

Figure 5.1 Subtle design decisions such as adding stones to a sidewalk discourage a skateboarder, Vancouver, British Columbia (Source: Patsy Eubanks Owens)

Figure 5.2
The addition of
skatestops is a clear
indication that the
activity is prohibited,
Edinburgh, Scotland
(Source: Patsy
Eubanks Owens)

suspiciously than girls; and youth of color more harshly than whites. Even adults who perceive themselves as caring, nonjudgmental and supportive are inclined to cross to the opposite side of the street if they see a group of young people headed their way. The image of youth as troublemakers is not new, but is a recurring message through news reports, television shows and movies.

The urban environment is constantly changing. Some of these changes result in restrictions to the use of public areas by youth, while others provide legitimate activities for young people. Currently, many urban open spaces in the US and abroad are held and managed by private owners. This increase in privately held public land has been due in part to cities requiring developers to provide publicly accessible land as a condition of project approval. In some instances, these owners have and often use their authority to restrict access to a space. This trend echoes the same issue and discussions associated with shopping malls. Whether in downtown locations or the suburbs, shopping malls are a frequent and favored venue of adolescents. While some governments have ruled the shopping mall is a public space that must be open to anyone, others have restricted the use of these places by young people (e.g., Owens 2002).

Just as these changes to property ownership and management impact the use of urban areas by youth, changes in commercial uses influence where young people can be found in the city. Earlier generations of youth typically found temporary refuge at fast food establishments. The purchase of a small fries and soft drink was the inexpensive price of a place to sit for a while, meet friends or use the restroom. Today, the ubiquitous coffee shop provides an alternative stopping place and frequently has the added bonus of sidewalk seating.

In addition to these public perceptions of youth and changes in the urban landscape, the family context can impact a young person's knowledge of and relationship with the area outside of her home. Many youth in westernized societies are the products of an upbringing quite different from earlier generations. The prominence of two-career couples and continuous news cycles sharing extreme stories of abductions have contributed to a fear of harm to children and increased restrictions on youth access to outdoor settings and over-scheduling of their lives (e.g., Louv 2005). From an early age, many children are now enrolled in after-school activities in an effort to 'keep them out of trouble', play is relegated to predetermined dates and playmates, and randomly exploring and playing is frowned upon and sometimes declared illegal (see, for example, recent police citations against parents for allowing their children to walk home from the park unescorted, or the public outcry in response to a mother letting her nine-year-old son ride the subway alone, Skenazy 2015). The ability for youth to seek healthy, developmentally appropriate adventures has been stunted and, along with that, knowledge of and attachment to their community has decreased. For many youth, the ability to learn about a place and its residents through exploration and interactions is missing.

Environmental issues such as global warming, climate change, reliance on petroleum products, population growth and recycling also inform how young people feel about where they live. Youth from many different countries have cited the importance of addressing these environmental issues in their communities (Chawla 2002). Likewise, youth in some studies have lamented the loss of agricultural land to housing developments and questioned the future of where they live (Owens 1988).

Lastly, the everyday lives of contemporary youth revolve around electronic devices and this interaction has changed how, when and with whom youth use public spaces. This generation has a new set of interests and distractions spurred by their mobile phone applications and internet connections. Entertainment is immediate and varied. Communication with friends is constant. While not totally lost, the random meeting of friends at the mall on a Friday evening (which was a common occurrence for many young people during the 1970s and 80s), is often replaced by a complicated orchestra of text messages to determine when and where to meet, and what to do. A seemingly endless array of movies and music online also offers free or inexpensive entertainment options that in turn mean that these youth may not elect to enter the public realm for these activities.

These broader societal issues need to be considered when examining the places important in adolescents' lives since they impact which places are available for youth to use, what activities they are allowed to engage in, when they are allowed to be in the public realm and which places they choose to use. In particular, places where adolescents spend their leisure time are often public places, and these are the settings where they are subjected to scrutiny from adults or deliberately excluded. A fuller understanding and respect of this societal context is important since it impacts both the young person's experience and the built environment.

The importance of place

Research over the last three decades has revealed consistent findings regarding the public places important to adolescents, why these places are important and the things they do while in these places. These places have been identified and examined using several different frameworks: the land use or place types (commercial, residential, recreational, educational) (e.g., Owens 1988, 1994; Korpela 1991); the affordances actualized in these settings (socializing, being alone, place for play) (e.g., Clark & Uzzel 2002; Duzenli, Bayramoglu & Özbilen 2010); or the benefits such places provide to adolescents' development and well-being (relationship building, restoration, empowerment) (e.g., Clark & Uzzel 2006; Faber Taylor et al. 2002; Kaplan 1995; Korpela et al. 2002; Passon et al. 2008).

Young people are frequent occupiers of the public landscape. Whether in North or South America, Europe, Australia, Africa or Asia, their daily lives often involve traversing these areas as they travel between home and school, meet their friends after school and on weekends, seek entertainment and, for some, journey to work. Just as important as understanding the types of places adolescents frequent, understanding the role of these places and the accompanying activities in an adolescent's development is essential. While the role of the physical environment in the development of young children has been well researched and documented, and has informed the design of children's playgrounds for many years, our understanding of its role in adolescents' development is less understood or appreciated (Clark & Uzzell 2002, 2006; Duzenli, Bayramoglu & Özbilen 2010).

An examination of the affordances sought by adolescents in the public realm in the context of their known developmental tasks, or the developmental affordances,[1] provides important insight into the connections between place and well-being. An examination of existing research through this developmental affordance lens reveals many ways that the physical environment can either support or hinder healthy adolescent development. Four of the most salient and positive roles of the built environment for adolescent development that are found in public areas are discussed.

Satisfying social relationships

Informal observations and common knowledge confirm that young people like to be with their friends (e.g., Fitzgerald et al. 1995; Owens 1988, 1994) and to hang out in downtown areas and other commercial settings (e.g., Duzenli, Bayramoglu & Özbilen 2010; Hopkins 1991). These older youth are often seen in groups of friends, seemingly wandering aimlessly and raising the concern of adults, merchants and even other youth. Such downtown settings include public plazas, parks and street corners as well as places of business. The criteria for which places make the best ones in which to hang out include places to sit, lean or perch, and significantly, where no one asks them to leave.

An important task of adolescence is to develop satisfying social relationships. Young people need places and opportunities to get together with their friends and to make new friends. Through the interactions with these peers, adolescents begin to acquire social competence, build their self-esteem and develop their self-identity. These social relationships are needed for youth to develop into psychologically healthy adults (Larson & Richards 1989). When getting together with their friends, youth make many decisions—what time to get together, where to meet, what to do and who to ask along. Through these practice sessions, they learn how to get along with others and how to make group decisions.

However, hanging out with friends and the accompanying developmental tasks are in conflict with the societal context described earlier. Public settings such as urban plazas and businesses provide places for young people to gather, but this is often viewed as an inappropriate activity for the space. Many adults see this 'hanging out' as an unproductive use of youths' time while in actuality the young people are engaging in a very productive developmental task.

Figure 5.3 Young people finding a place to gather under a highway overpass in Vancouver, British Columbia (Source: Patsy Eubanks Owens)

Figure 5.4 Urban shopping areas provide a place for young people to meet their friends, Pasadena, California (Source: Patsy Eubanks Owens)

Restoration

We also know that many adolescents seek out places where they can be alone, or alone with a close friend (e.g., Korpela 1991; Owens 1988). These places are less visible, but no less important. In many communities youth seek places that fulfill this need in the public realm. For many urban youth, home environments are not conducive to the quiet, solitary activity of sorting through problems, making decisions or thinking about their future. Youth in these situations seek public places they can claim for quiet reflection or building more intimate relationships. Places used for these purposes often include natural elements, such as trees, grass and flowers, or views.

Figure 5.5 Finding nature and a place for restoration in the city, The High Line, NYC (Source: Patsy Eubanks Owens)

Adolescence is a critical time for the individual to develop his or her self-identity. Erikson (1956) describes adolescence as a time of growth from self-consciousness and self-doubt to self-certainty. During adolescence, the young person needs to learn to be comfortable with being alone and productively use the time for reflection (e.g., Larson & Richards 1989). In addition, numerous research studies have linked these 'get away' environments with reduction of stress and attention restoration (Kaplan & Kaplan 1989; Kaplan 1995; Ulrich et al. 1991; Ulrich 1984).

There also appears to be a strong link between the presence of nature and the ability of a place to help youth develop self-discipline and become restored (Faber Taylor, Kuo & Sullivan 2002; Korpela, Kyttä & Hartig 2002; Owens & McKinnon 2009). Likewise, prospect refuges—those places where they can look out, but not be seen—

provide places where youth can get away and figure out their place in the world (Owens 1988). However, for urban youth, these types of places can be difficult to find (Ladd 1978). Along with these places not being very prevalent, young people can be discouraged from traveling or being alone in the city. Concerns for safety prompt parents to limit a young person's exploration of the city and to make sure they always know where their children are.

Managing free time

Adolescents need to develop an ability to spend time on their own and to find enjoyment and satisfaction in activities of their own choosing (Larson & Richards 1989). The common and frequent adolescent cry of "I'm bored" is a symptom of their struggle to learn how to use unstructured time. This unstructured time can be spent participating in recreational activities which researchers have shown can help to build character, encourage teamwork and raise self-esteem in youth (Kirshnit et al. 1989).

When describing their free time, youth often describe the recreational activities in which they participate. These include organized sports, individual pursuits and commercial recreation such as bowling and roller-skating as well as more passive activities such as listening to music. As noted earlier, in an effort to make sure their children stay busy and out of trouble, many parents 'over-schedule' their offspring. What was once free time becomes anything but that. Many youth have limited to no time that is not committed to specific obligations.

Figure 5.6 Skateboarding in public plazas, such as on Pier 7 in San Francisco, is a common recreational activity in cities (Source: Patsy Eubanks Owens)

Figure 5.7
Participating in the
weekly farmer's
market teaches
these youth skills
while giving
them a role in
their community,
West Sacramento,
California (Source:
Yaminah Bailey)

Empowerment and social responsibility

An individual begins to more fully develop a sense of belonging to a community outside of their family during the adolescent years. Nightingale and Wolverton (1993) note that adolescents need opportunities to develop their role in society. Participation in the larger society can help youth with the developmental tasks of identity formation, building social competence and developing social responsibility, whereas removing youth from broader community activities limits their opportunities for learning how to communicate and cooperate with others.

For adolescents, this support can occur in any of the settings where they spend time including the urban environment. These places and the interactions youth experience there can play an important role in making young people feel either welcome or unwelcome, and it is often the latter. Along with the general societal connotations associated with youth and the resulting negative responses, formal and deliberate actions, such as public policies and design practices, often seek to ban or limit adolescents' use of public spaces (e.g., Owens 2002). Conversely, some research has shown that the presence of a welcoming merchant can make young people feel like they belong in a community (Childress 2000). Opportunities for engaging in their community are appreciated by youth when available. San Luis Obispo youth participating in an unpublished study noted that they had meaningful experiences—"helping to shape the future of youth", "[it will] make a difference in kids' lives" and "did something for someone unfortunate".

Moving forward

Understanding the societal context in which youth grow up and applying the findings of prior research are first steps in addressing the shortcomings of the built environment to provide supportive environments for adolescent development. How we translate and communicate that research to produce more knowledgeable practitioners, shift public perceptions, create welcoming public places and encourage engaged and healthy youth is the next challenge. Research can be a powerful tool for designers, planners, policy makers and others in the creation and protection of environments that support healthy adolescent development as well as toward informing the public discourse. While this body of research has seen substantial expansion over the last three decades, the sharing of that knowledge has been limited, and the translation into design and policy even less.

Practitioners and players

Those on the front lines of adolescent environment work include academic researchers, design and planning professionals, youth-serving organizations and policy makers. Making sure that these players have access to the current research and thinking on youth environments is critical. Reaching each of these audiences requires unique strategies.

Since researchers on adolescents and their environments come from varied fields, articles are often published in diverse and discipline-specific journals. While some journals, such as *Children Youth Environments*, attract authors and readers from multiple disciplines, many are restricted to particular academic fields. Even in academic settings, young researchers beginning their quest for information on youth environments often believe that little is known about the topic and too often their academic advisor is also unfamiliar with the body of work. Publications, such as this book, might help to reach this broad audience and serve to build a cross-disciplinary base of knowledge. Likewise, building upon existing youth environment networks, such as the Environmental Design Research Association's Children Youth Environment network, will strengthen a shared understanding of the existing body of research.

Academic publications are seldom read by anyone other than researchers conducting related work, therefore other publishing venues such as practitioner-focused journals and popular press publications should be targeted. Sharing research through these outlets gets the information more directly to those who can effect change. Reaching these audiences through non-print media is also important. Opportunities for other dissemination such as radio, television and social media are abundant. The need for providing more hospitable and nurturing environments for our young people is a compelling story and needs to be shared. For those advocating for youth environments, this information is often needed to convince adults that most youth behavior in public spaces is normal and, more importantly, necessary rather than a problem.

Public perception

At the crux of addressing adolescents' needs in the built environment is reframing society's perceptions and expectations of young people's engagement in public environments. The attention needs to shift from how young people disrupt and disturb urban life to the positive role public places can have in adolescent development. Through increasing society's understanding of the negative impacts of current approaches, such as youth exclusion, the potential for creating more supportive places and processes becomes possible. Without this change in perception, adolescents will continue to have difficulty in finding places to meet their needs, and efforts to limit young people's use and presence in public places will likely persist and expand.

While shifting broad public opinion may be difficult, enlisting design and planning practitioners as well as public policy makers in the effort is an immediate and manageable goal. Reframing the view of adolescents' use of public space within these professions could have direct impacts on decisions related to the built environment, as well as influence the mind-set of others. Well-informed practitioners have an opportunity to advocate for creating or maintaining places that meet these adolescent needs. In addition, they are in a position to educate their clients (both the paying client and the public) about the benefits of such youth-supportive places.

Other potential partners in this effort are youth-serving organizations such as schools, youth centers and clubs at the local, regional, state and national levels. Adults associated with groups such as 4-H, Girls and Boys Clubs, and Boards of Education are typically interested and invested in the well-being of young people. Often these organizations focus on programming activities to keep youth busy, but are unaware of the full spectrum of influence they could have on youth development.

Researchers need to share their findings with these groups or, preferably, enlist them as research partners. Providing supportive built environments is within the capabilities of such groups as well as the ability to be effective proponents of such environments and leaders in reframing societal views of youth.

Places and policies

Although we can continue to refine our understanding of the role and impact of various environments on the use, enjoyment and benefits of places to adolescents, we have ample evidence to advance changes in our current public environments. For the creators of public spaces, this research has the potential to inform their understanding of the role these environments play for youth and how design and policy decisions facilitate positive experiences for them.

From the obvious implications of school and school district policies to those at the city and regional scale, research indicates that these decisions often dictate whether or not the unique needs of youth are addressed. For example, youth in West Sacramento identified aspects of transportation and recreation planning that warranted attention. Bus routes designed for downtown workers caused problems for youth trying to get from school to other parts of town. Likewise, conventional park planning ignored their desires for recreation beyond sports fields (Owens 2010).

While policy decisions can have broad implications for youth-inclusive places, design decisions are critical in the development of places that encourage use by this age group and thereby legitimize their activities. In particular, a rethinking of our street, park and school design is important to ensure that these environments optimize opportunities for youth to develop satisfying social relationships, engage in restorative activities and build their sense of social responsibility and community belonging. These considerations have significant potential for changing traditional design recommendations.

Participation and power

Lastly, young people should be involved in the research concerning their environments and in the design decisions related to them. Youth involvement in these decisions

Figure 5.8 Youth participated in a PAR process where they identified important aspects of their community, San Luis Obispo, California (Source: Patsy Eubanks Owens)

has many positive ramifications including producing more supportive places and contributing to their successful journey to adulthood. Many processes have been clearly documented for the inclusion of youth in decision-making processes (e.g., Driskell 2002; Hart 2008) while their role in research is relatively less explored (e.g., Owens et al. 2011).

Research methods often focus on the academic researcher identifying the questions they want answered, determining how to get those answers and analyzing the finding. One method that challenges that approach is participatory action research (PAR). In particular, the PAR method is noteworthy for its effectiveness in engaging young people, promoting their voice and building their capacity as active citizens. As partners in the research, young people have the opportunity to inform the questions being asked and how the data is interpreted. Through the process, young people can become invested in the work as well as becoming powerful and effective disseminators of the findings.

Involving youth in decisions also has potential benefits to the development of the young person. Passon, Levi and del Rio (2008, p. 74) note that "The city and its network of public spaces become an important scenario where teenagers develop their personalities and social roles. This is why participation of teenagers in the planning and design of the built environment and of their own places is so important, and why teenagers as a social group should participate in making decisions that affect their community". Youth appreciate and desire the opportunity to be involved in their community. Learning how to make decisions, how to engage with others and how to be part of a community are important tasks of the adolescent. Engagement of young people in these processes is an investment in the future by helping to foster contributing and productive members of society.

Conclusion

The built environment is an important setting for the healthy development of young people. Research shows that places to be with friends, to be alone, to make decisions and to feel like they belong are among the developmentally supportive roles the physical setting can play for adolescents, yet a concerted and widespread effort to provide such environments is lacking. Instead, research shows that many young people are frequently unwelcome in or excluded from public spaces. Understanding this societal context is an important precursor to addressing the creation and management of supportive environments. Conducting and sharing research can help shift the perception of adolescents in public settings as troublemakers to one that recognizes them as legitimate users of these areas. Likewise, the inclusion of young people in conducting research, sharing findings and initiating change can be a powerful and effective means to producing an accurate accounting of the role the physical environment plays in their lives and to a successful translation of research into positive changes to the public realm.

Note

1   *Developmental affordance* is a term developed by the author to describe the link between affordances of places and the developmental tasks associated with them. A developmental affordance may be perceived, consciously or unconsciously, and may or may not be actualized by the individual or group for the completion of the specific tasks relating to the psychological or sociological growth of the individual.

References

Chawla, L (ed.) 2002, *Growing up in an urbanising world*, Earthscan Publications/ UNESCO Publishing, London.

Childress, H 2000, *Landscapes of betrayal, landscapes of joy*, State University of New York Press, Albany.

Clark, C & Uzzell, DL 2002, 'The affordances of the home, neighbourhood, school and town center for adolescents', *Journal of Environmental Psychology*, vol. 22, pp. 95–108.

Clark, C & Uzzell, DL 2006, 'The socio-environmental affordances of adolescents' environments' in *Children and their environments: learning, using and designing spaces*, eds C Spencer & M Blades, Cambridge University Press, Cambridge, pp. 176–195.

Driskell, D 2002, *Creating better cities with children and youth: a manual for participation*, Earthscan, New York.

Duzenli, T, Bayramoglu, E & Özbilen, A 2010, 'Needs and preferences of adolescents in open urban spaces', *Scientific Research and Essay*, vol. 5, no. 2, pp. 201–216.

Erikson, E 1956, 'Ego identity and the psychosocial moratorium' in *New perspectives on juvenile delinquency*, Department of Health, Education and Welfare, Washington, DC, pp. 1–23.

Faber Taylor, A, Kuo, FE & Sullivan, WC 2002, 'Views of nature and self-discipline: evidence from inner city children', *Journal of Environmental Psychology*, vol. 22, pp. 49–63.

Fitzgerald, M, Joseph, AP, Hayes, M & O'Regan, M 1995, 'Leisure activities of adolescent school children', *Journal of Adolescence*, vol. 18, no. 3, pp. 349–358.

Hart, R 2008, *Children's participation: the theory and practice of involving young citizens in community development and environmental care*, Earthscan, New York.

Hopkins, J 1991, 'West Edmonton mall as a center for social interaction', *The Canadian Geographer*, vol. 35, no. 3, pp. 268–279.

Kaplan, S 1995, 'The restorative benefits of nature: toward an integrative framework', *Journal of Environmental Psychology*, vol. 15, pp. 169–182.

Kaplan, R & Kaplan, S 1989, *The experience of nature: a psychological perspective*, Cambridge University Press, Cambridge.

Kirshnit, CE, Ham, M & Richards, MH 1989, 'The sporting life: athletic activities during early adolescence', *Journal of Youth and Adolescence*, vol. 18, pp. 601–615.

Korpela, KM 1991, 'Adolescents' and adults' favorite places' in *Environment and social development: proceedings of the East-West colloquium in environmental psychology*, eds T Niit, M Raudsepp & K Liik, Tallinn Pedagogical Institute, Tallinn, pp. 76–83.

Korpela, K, Kyttä, M & Hartig, T 2002, 'Restorative experience, self-regulation, and children's place preferences', *Journal of Environmental Psychology*, vol. 22, pp. 387–398.

Ladd, FC 1978, 'City kids in the absence of . . .' in *Humanscape: environments for people*, eds R Kaplan & S Kaplan, Duxbury Press, North Scituate, Massachusetts, pp. 77–81.

Larson, R & Richards, M 1989, 'Introduction: the changing life space of early adolescence', *Journal of Youth and Adolescence*, vol. 18, no. 6, pp. 501–509.

Louv, R 2005, *Last child in the woods: saving our children from nature-deficit disorder*, Algonquin Books, Chapel Hill, North Carolina.

Nightingale, EO & Wolverton, L 1993, 'Adolescent rolelessness in modern society', *Teachers College Record*, vol. 94, no. 3, pp. 472–486.

Owens, PE 1988, 'Natural landscapes, gathering places, and prospect refuges: characteristics of outdoor places valued by teens', *Children's Environments Quarterly*, vol. 5, no. 2, pp. 17–24.

Owens, PE 1994, 'Teen places in Sunshine, Australia: then and now', *Children's Environments*, vol. 11, no. 4, pp. 292–299.

Owens, PE 1997, 'Adolescence and the cultural landscape: public policy, design decisions, and popular press reporting', *Landscape and Urban Planning*, vol. 39, no. 2–3, pp. 153–166.

Owens, PE 2002, 'No teens allowed: the exclusion of adolescents from public spaces', *Landscape Journal*, vol. 21, pp. 156–163.

Owens, PE (ed.) 2010, *Youth voices for change: opinions and ideas for the future of West Sacramento*, Center for Regional Change, University of California, Davis.

Owens, PE & McKinnon, I 2009, 'In pursuit of nature: the role of nature in adolescents' lives', *Journal of Developmental Processes*, vol. 4, no. 1, pp. 43–58.

Owens, PE, La Rochelle, M, Nelson, AA & Montgomery-Black, KF 2011, 'Youth voices influencing local and regional change', *Children, Youth and Environments*, vol. 21, no. 1, pp. 253–274.

Passon, C, Levi, D & del Rio, V 2008, 'Implications of adolescents' perceptions and values for planning and design', *Journal of Planning Education and Research*, vol. 28, pp. 73–85.

Skenazy, L 2015, 'I let my 9-year-old ride the subway alone and got labeled the "world's worst mom"', *The Washington Post*, January 16. Available from: www.washingtonpost.com.

Ulrich, RS 1984, 'View through a window may influence recovery from surgery', *Science*, vol. 224, pp. 420–421.

Ulrich, RS, Simons, RF, Losito, BD, Fiorito, E, Miles, MA & Zelson, M 1991, 'Stress recovery during exposure to natural and urban environments', *Journal of Environmental Psychology*, vol. 11, pp. 201–230.

Woolley, H, Hazelwood, T & Simkins, I 2011, 'Don't skate here: exclusion of skateboarders from urban civic spaces in three northern cities in England', *Journal of Urban Design*, vol. 16, no. 4, pp. 471–487.

CHAPTER 6

Utilizing research for the benefit of children's lives in cities

Acknowledging barriers and embracing change

Kate Bishop

Introduction

In keeping with the philosophical approach of this book which values children and young people themselves as key members of any society, this chapter positions research that articulates and analyzes children's experience as a vital resource for city planning and design. Children have perspectives on the world which adults cannot have and adult designers and planners cannot do without if they are to design cities that truly embrace the needs and nature of the children and young people who live there. This chapter will summarize some of the persistent and relevant themes in research on children in city environments, and it will explore some of the stumbling blocks in the process of designing cities with and for children, including not only our failure to draw on the vast evidence base created in research with children and young people in design and planning practice, but also the limitations of historic conceptualizations of children, childhood and adolescence, and their continuing and embedded impact on social attitudes towards children.

Figure 6.1 Group of boys on Sproul Plaza, Berkeley, California (Source: Nancy Marshall)

Children's experience in all areas of life, including their environmental experience, has received greater attention in research as the needs of children and adolescents are better understood and given greater social value. Since the United Nations Convention on the Rights of the Child (UNCRC, 1989), and the introduction of the rights-based approach to children's participation, there has been a steady increase in types and definitions of participatory research with children and youth. Many contemporary social researchers now begin with the assumption that childhood and adolescence have an intrinsic social status and value that commands recognition and respect, and that they need to be understood as particular entities in themselves, with their own cultures and not merely as part of a larger continuum of development (Corsaro 2005; Prout & James 1990). This research represents a large body of work at this point but it is not well utilized at present by policy-makers, planners and designers in their decision-making processes, and therefore it is not able to benefit children and young people as it might. Greater recognition of what research recommends and greater acceptance of the duty within the built environment professions to apply it for children's benefit is needed. The responsibility for this rests with researchers, practitioners and policy-makers alike.

Planning cities with children and young people in mind

Most of the world's children and young people will grow up in urban contexts from this time forward. This is a sobering thought, as we know little at this point about how to design a nourishing urban habitat that consistently supports human beings' well-being, let alone what this environment should look like for two of the most impressionable groups of our populations. We would probably say that many of our

Figure 6.2
Children in an urban environment (Source: Adrian Boddy)

Figure 6.3 Climbing a retaining wall, Calgary, Canada (Source: Nancy Marshall)

design and planning decisions to date, influencing the nature of the built form of cities, are not ideas that we should repeat. Indeed, both design and planning are always moving on; often rejecting much of what has gone before in favor of the new, which means that a large component of any built solution will always be experimental. It is both a virtuous and a lamentable process as its social impacts can be crude and unintended or highly successful.

This leads to the question: why should we draw attention to the needs of children and young people in city planning and design in particular? The answer responds to the continued powerlessness of children and young people in social processes. Children and young people still need champions in all social processes, including urban design and planning, to ensure that the nature of their needs is met or even considered (Chawla 2002).

As Churchman (2003) states, "we can with a high degree of certainty assert that, on the whole, cities are not planned and managed with children in mind" (p. 101). Instead, children's environmental needs are usually relegated to three traditional environments: their homes, schools and recreational settings such as playgrounds and skate parks (Churchman 2003). In recognizing this, the aim is not to devalue these formal environments in children's lives; indeed, together they still represent the places in any community where children spend the majority of their time (see Freeman & Tranter 2011). The aim is to draw attention to the inherent limitations of this conceptualization and the lost environmental consideration for children that it represents.

Adults need to acknowledge our habit of compartmentalizing children and childhood, youth and adolescence, environmentally and socially in ways that inevitably limit how we design and plan inclusive city environments for them. Dividing children's and adolescents' lives into a series of prescribed functional zones and activities does not necessarily lead to comprehensive solutions which fully support children's developmental, educational and/or recreational needs in cities. The city is a shaper of children's lives socially and physically, and children and youth have rights to the whole city that are rarely reflected in these approaches.

Adolescents, in particular, comprise a social subgroup which is poorly served by this tradition of grouping environmental experience based on age. They are major users of public space, but the historic conceptualizations of functional environmental provision for this age group are usually inadequate as they do not acknowledge adolescents' use of public space as legitimate (Childress 2004; Owens 1988, 1997, 2002). Instead many societies problematize their normative behavior and seek to control it so that it fits within the society's notions of the correct spatial allocation for adolescence. Many communities identify the colonization of public areas by young people as a social problem, identifying it as a troublesome outcome needing to be controlled rather than recognizing this as an expression of environmental need by this age group that should be embraced in urban planning processes. As Iveson (2006, p. 49) describes it, "both exclusionary and inclusionary responses to the 'problem' of young people in cities are frequently mobilized on behalf of a vision of social control, in which difference is reduced to deviance, conflict is reduced to disorder, and 'the community' is reduced to 'the compliant'". We fail to recognize how central access to public space is for this age group in most communities (Iveson 2006).

Designing cities that are inclusive of children and adolescents is becoming more and more of an imperative. In the last 10 years, in particular, interest in the implications of children's environmental experience has greatly increased in the research of most of the social science and health science disciplines. This is largely due to changes in social attitudes to childhood, the perceived loss of environmental opportunities in urban settings and increases in the prevalence of health problems such as obesity and mental illness within the populations of many developed nations (Feng et al. 2010; Jackson 2003; Papas et al. 2007). Increasingly, disciplines such as medicine, which have not traditionally recognized the role of the physical environment in people's health outcomes, are acknowledging that the physical environment influences many positive outcomes that they care about, such as community health. This has produced new areas of interdisciplinary research concerned with the nature and quality of the urban built environment for promoting healthy life styles, physical activity and

Figure 6.4
Adolescent boy
playing a piano in
a plaza in Boston
(Source: Nancy
Marshall)

Figure 6.5 Boys out riding the streets of Inuvik, Canada (Source: Kate Bishop)

community well-being (e.g., Giles-Corti & Donovan 2002; Giles-Corti 2006; Wood et al. 2010). The experience of children and youth has been one of the areas targeted in this burgeoning field of research (Crawford et al. 2008; Giles-Corti et al. 2009; Hume et al. 2009).

Exploration of the persistent themes in research relevant to children's experience of cities

In this brief chapter it is not possible to do justice to the wealth of research that exists on children's urban environmental experience, and recently it has been well summarized in other texts (see Freeman & Tranter 2011). In this section of the chapter, the most persistent themes that have emerged in the last decade and earlier in research on children's urban experience will be discussed briefly.

Major social themes with environmental implications:

1 Children's increasingly poor health, namely the issues of increased childhood obesity and mental health problems. Physical activity is seen as part of the remedy for both conditions, which has implications for both children's social and physical environments (Crawford et al. 2008; Giles-Corti et al. 2009; Hume et al. 2009).
2 Increased social risk aversion, which manifests in parental attitudes to risk and children's capacity for independence. Society is increasingly risk averse, which impinges on children's freedoms, independent mobility, capacity to build neighborhood knowledge and connections (Dohmen et al. 2012; Mackett et al. 2007; Tandy 1999).
3 Increased reliance on technology, which has both negative and positive impacts on childhood and children's engagement with their social and physical environments (Hutchby & Moran-Ellis 2001).
4 Diminishing self-directed time and increasingly structured childhoods (Tranter & Sharpe 2007). Although this takes many forms, one of the most public examples

is in the US where a number of states have banned recess at school because they cannot quantify the value of informal playtime in children's education. This has provoked a long-running debate across many sectors involved in children's health, welfare and development (American Academy of Pediatrics 2013).

Major environmental themes with social implications:

1   Child-blind planning and built forms. This discussion emerges from the challenges associated with increasing urban densification and the increase in high-density living in most major cities as a solution to the need for more residential space. Child-blind planning refers to the lack of consideration of the presence of children in these high-density developments in terms of environmental provision for additional areas and amenities to support children's everyday needs outside their homes (Easthope & Tice 2011; Gleeson & Sipe 2006).
2   The need for child friendly communities. Interest in child friendly communities has grown in recent years in response to health considerations including the need for increased physical and, preferably, outdoor activity to combat the rise in obesity. Addressing child friendliness in relation to the physical environment means addressing environmental characteristics such as traffic calming devices, street design, opportunities for play, access and safety which support children's independent mobility (Thompson & Capon 2012).
3   Diminishing space and use of space. Children's urban territories and spaces are shrinking. They have been for a while in response to increased residential pressure in many societies. Informal, undeveloped spaces are rare in most urban neighborhoods today. This has happened slowly and the implications for children and young people have largely gone unrecognized. Children have lost access to what was a traditional type of environmental opportunity in cities and the loss of this kind of environment has not necessarily been replaced by an increase in formal, sanctioned spaces for children and young people (Freeman & Tranter 2011; Moore 1997).

Figure 6.6 Playing hide and seek in the Botanic Gardens, Brooklyn (Source: Kate Bishop)

4 Children are losing contact with nature in urban settings (Louv 2005; Ward-Thompson et al. 2008). Again, this is largely due to the pressures on urban neighborhoods described in the previous point. Natural settings—backyards, small local parks, vacant lots—where children would normally play near home are becoming scarcer in cities, or they are too removed from residential areas for children to access them independently. There are many implications associated with less contact with nature but one of the most pressing is associated with poorer psychological health (Mayer et al. 2009).

To understand the implications of the listed themes, they must be considered together as forming a picture of contemporary urban childhood; and the picture is troublesome. They paint one of an increasingly isolated childhood, lived in formal, probably private spaces most of the time, with limited independence and freedom to explore and experience their wider social and environmental contexts. They paint one of a pressured, goal-driven childhood with little freedom and time for self-direction. They paint one of poorer mental and physical health and psychological well-being.

If this is to become the average childhood around the developed world, then the onus is on adults as designers and planners of cities to understand children's contemporary social and environmental experience, as the implications for their health and well-being is profound. Working without reference to this large body of research is like working with our heads in the sand. As professionals we must engage with the reality of the situation surrounding children's lives and be sure to do what we can to redress imbalances where the environment is implicated.

We also need to be sure we are not working from any imagined notion of childhood which romanticizes its nature as this also lets children and young people down. The reality of any modern urban childhood is complex and comprised of real needs.

Figure 6.7 Playing in a fountain, Vancouver, Canada (Source: Kate Bishop)

Not engaging with this, as it is understood in research, represents missing a glaring opportunity to make productive contributions to children's lived experience.

The picture of a modern urban childhood also indicates the need to revise our understanding of children's environmental needs beyond the limitations of the three traditional environments associated with childhood. If we are to make productive contributions to children's and young people's lives through their environmental provision, we have to recognize the value and worth to them of the vast amount of environmental opportunity that sits outside these three environment types in any urban setting and be sure, when designing public spaces for example, that we have capitalized on the opportunities of each site for children and young people as far as we can.

Utilizing research

One of the themes of this book centers on discussing points of breakdown that occur in built environment processes which have the potential to compromise the ultimate effectiveness and suitability of the environment for children and adolescents. One of the first points of breakdown is that we do not draw on the available evidence base to inform design and planning practice and policy which affects children's experience of cities. Many arguments are offered as to why this does not happen much. For example, it is not easy for practitioners to access this information; it is not written in a way that easily translates into policy or design practice; it is considered of low priority in the scheme of a larger project.

The point of breakdown being acknowledged here is that research findings about children and young people's experience of the city are not sufficiently valued. Children rarely experience being included in civic processes, such as participating in planning consultations or community design workshops. It follows, therefore, that research concerning their lived experience is also undervalued, ignoring a wealth of insights into children's lives that it provides. With the introduction of participatory research in recent decades we now have a bank of evidence from children's and young people's perspectives, alongside adults' interpretations of their lives, that can usefully inform design and planning practice and associated policy. However, in reality this, too, rarely happens.

In 2009, the NSW Commission for Children and Young People and the Australian Research Association for Children and Youth (ARACY) held a think tank on the Australian experience of participatory research with children and young people. Participants included leading researchers from around Australia with expertise in this type of research. As part of the day-long discussion, the group identified four major points of action: build capacity of children; build understanding and knowledge of gatekeepers; build knowledge and capacity of researchers; increase the influence of research (ARACY & NSW CCYP 2009). Most of these points are concerned with the facilitation of this type of research itself—not surprising, as it is a difficult and time-consuming form of research. The final recommendation concerns the need to facilitate knowledge transfer from one sector where the research is completed to another where it can be implemented. The need for greater knowledge transfer is certainly recognized by researchers but they are often not skilled at reaching audiences to report on the outcomes of their work. Similarly, the design and planning community may like to learn more about research findings but they do not necessarily know how to access it. The process of knowledge transfer represents an additional process for both groups which is not easily managed, and as a result it does not often happen effectively. This is a major point of breakdown as it means that salient findings from research do not reach the audiences who could incorporate them into policy or build them into practice.

The limitations of our conceptualization of children, childhood and adolescents

In addition to the failings of our wider social *processes* which have implications for children and young people, we need to take stock of which *messages* are passing through the many social filters applied to any subject in our societies and to identify what is working and what is not. Of the three key areas that are addressed by the UNCRC (1989), including children's rights to protection, provision and participation, it is easy to say that the third area has managed to penetrate social psyches and social values the least. The greatest barriers to the inclusion of children and youth in any culture, socially and spatially, are attitudinal. The social norms surrounding the value and acceptance of children and childhood, and of youth and adolescence, condition the social processes of planning and design. This reflects Sanoff's (2010) discussion that physical environments are an expression of the society that builds them and that they are as much a social phenomenon as they are a physical one. As Sanoff states, all that we do as members of any society is conditioned by the culture of that society and it follows that designing and planning for children and young people is no exception.

The argument here is not that children and young people are not valued by their societies. It is that the framework of social attitudes and beliefs about children, childhood and adolescence and the competence of these ages is a collection of limited and outdated reference points, historically established, which impedes change and the embrace of better social processes, inclusive of children and young people. At present, attitudes towards children and young people as groups in society are sufficiently conflicted to derail the prospect of delivering good built environments for urban children before any particular project brief is written or addressed. The significance of these

Figure 6.8 Children engaged in research (Source: JAS Jugend-Architektur-Stadt e.V., Essen)

conflicted views and the potential impact on children's experience is profound and no doubt undermines children's consistent inclusion in social processes.

Urban planning and design is value-laden and assumptions made about young people, whether articulated or not, shape their inclusion or exclusion in these processes, and shape the decisions about what will be provided for them in their communities. For example, if children and adolescents are viewed as vulnerable and as having limited competence, as opposed to being competent, active, social citizens, this will influence the opportunities they are given for participation and inclusion in the community's governance and social processes such as planning and design. Community perceptions surrounding children and adolescents are the most powerful drivers influencing environmental provision for them.

Some of the interesting questions to ask are: why are we so resistant to the idea of embracing children's competence and legitimate participation in our social processes? And how intentional is that resistance, or is it just habit? Part of the answer may rest in the history and evolution of the social concepts of children and childhood. Both are relatively modern concepts, emerging in the seventeenth century and becoming increasingly associated with the values we give these concepts today during the eighteenth and nineteenth centuries (Ariès 1962). The conflicting conceptualizations that surround childhood, children and adolescence today have been present in the social construction of these concepts since their inception. In relation to children, specifically, the familiar view of them as being either 'devils' or 'angels' has been running concurrently since the earliest acknowledgment of childhood as a distinct stage of human development (Ariès 1962). These historic views of children and childhood, which we are still using now, are inadequate and their continuing and embedded impact on social attitudes are some of the influences that lead to inadequate social recognition.

In addition to these two persistent views of children, a third one, introduced earlier in the chapter, has been added by childhood sociology in the last 25 years, reflecting a rights-based approach: the view that children are competent social actors in their

Figure 6.9
Gathering young people's view on the built environment (Source: JAS Jugend-Architektur-Stadt e.V., Essen)

own lives (Corsaro 2005; Prout & James 1990). This signals an elevation in the status of children to "human beings rather than human becomings", as aptly summarized by Qvortrup et al. (1994, p. 4). It is an alternate view to the idea that children are passive recipients of adults' decisions. Such an understanding of children's competence and agency provides a new and positive expectation of the social input from children and young people which participatory research has helped to reveal.

Adolescence is a much more modern social construct, emerging in the twentieth century (Nilan et al. 2007), but as with children and childhood, an early conceptualization of it as a troubled time of life, full of turmoil and aberrant behavior has persisted and remains powerfully present in social attitudes towards this age group today.

Participatory research recognizes the need to give children and young people the opportunity to define themselves in research, rather than continually be defined by adults and their assumptions about childhood (Grover 2004). However, this view of children's competence and status, now commonly accepted in children's research, is still struggling to be recognized in other forms of professional practice, including planning and design. A conscious social effort is required to reject outdated reference points for children, childhood and adolescence by policy-makers and design and planning practitioners, to afford children and young people much greater access to community development processes, which have so much potential to affect their lives.

Those of us who champion children's participation and children's rights know how embedded the earlier social conceptualizations of children and their status are. We continue to persist in advocating for the recognition of children's competence because the society that we want to live in is one that values all citizens equally and expresses this through its social structures and processes.

Conclusion

After years of working with children and young people in research and in design, I know that their involvement in any project concerning their lived experience greatly enriches the research findings or the design solution. Children and young people are competent, capable contributors to any research or design process and we need to embed and embrace their right to participate in our social processes more conscientiously than we do at present.

We also need to draw much more insight from research and, in particular, participatory research with children and adolescents for our conceptualizations of who children and adolescents are at any point. Likewise, participatory research can also assist in identifying what aspects of contemporary childhood or adolescence have implications for their environmental provision and for urban design—but it will only be of value if we make it available and draw on it. We know that children and adolescents use and value spaces and places differently to adults and we must take this seriously if we wish to create nourishing cities for children and young people in an increasingly urbanized world.

References

American Academy of Pediatrics 2013, 'The crucial role of recess in school', *Pediatrics*, vol. 131, no. 1, pp. 1–8.
Ariès, P 1962, *Centuries of childhood: a social history of family life*, Vintage, New York.

Australian Research Association for Children and Youth & NSW Commission for Children and Young People 2009, *Involving children and young people in research*, ARACY and the NSW Commission for Children and Young people. Available from: www.aracy.org.au/publications-resources/area?command=record&id=73&cid=6.

Chawla, L (ed.) 2002, *Growing up in an urbanising world*, UNESCO and Earthscan, London.

Childress, H 2004, 'Teenagers, territory and the appropriation of space', *Childhood*, vol. 11, no. 2, pp. 195–205.

Churchman, A 2003, 'Is there a place for children in the city?', *Journal of Urban Design*, vol. 8, no. 2, pp. 99–111.

Corsaro, WA 2005, *The sociology of childhood* (2nd ed.), Pine Forge Press, Thousand Oaks, California.

Crawford, DA, Timperio, AF, Salmon, JA, Baur, L, Giles-Corti, B, Roberts, RJ, Jackson, ML, Andrianopoulos, N & Ball, K 2008, 'Neighborhood fast food outlets and obesity in children and adults: the CLAN study', *International Journal of Pediatric Obesity*, vol. 3, no. 4, pp. 249–256.

Dohmen, T, Falk, A, Huffman, D & Sunde, U 2012, 'The intergenerational transmission of risk and trust attitudes', *Review of Economic Studies*, vol. 79, no. 2, pp. 645–677.

Easthope, H & Tice, A 2011, 'Children in apartments: implications for the compact city', *Urban Policy and Research*, vol. 29, no. 4, pp. 415–434.

Feng, J, Glass, TA, Curriero, FC, Stewart, WF & Schwartz, BS 2010, 'The built environment and obesity: a systematic review of the epidemiologic evidence', *Health & Place*, vol. 16, no. 2, pp. 175–190.

Freeman, C & Tranter, P 2011, *Children and their urban environments: changing worlds*, Earthscan, London.

Giles-Corti, B 2006, 'The impact of urban form on public health', paper prepared for the 2006 Australian State of the Environment Committee, Department of the Environment and Heritage, Canberra. Available from: www.deh.gov.au/soe/2006/emerging/publichealth/index.html.

Giles-Corti, B & Donovan, RJ 2002, 'The relative influence of individual, social and physical environmental determinants of physical activity', *Social Science & Medicine*, vol. 54, no. 12, pp. 1793–1812.

Giles-Corti, B, Kelty SF, Zubrick, SR & Villanueva, KP 2009, 'Encouraging walking for transport and physical activity in children and adolescents: how important is the built environment?', *Sports Medicine*, vol. 39, no. 29, pp. 995–1099.

Gleeson, G & Sipe, N (eds) 2006, *Creating child-friendly cities: reinstating kids in the city*, Routledge, London.

Grover, S 2004, 'Why won't they listen to us? on giving power and voice to children participating in social research', *Childhood*, vol. 11, no. 1, pp. 81–93.

Hume, C, Timperio, A, Salmon, J, Carver, A, Giles-Corti, B & Crawford, D 2009, 'Walking and cycling to school: predictors of increases among children and adolescents', *American Journal of Preventive Medicine*, vol. 36, no. 3, pp. 195–200.

Hutchby, I & Moran-Ellis J (eds) 2001, *Children, technology and culture: the impact of technologies in children's everyday lives*, Routledge Falmer, London.

Iveson, K 2006, 'Cities for angry young people? from exclusion and inclusion to engagement in urban policy' in *Creating child friendly cities: reinstating kids in the city*, eds B Gleeson & N Sipe, Routledge, Oxon, UK, pp. 49–66.

Jackson, RJ 2003, 'The impact of the built environment on health: an emerging field', *American Journal of Public Health*, vol. 93, no. 9, pp. 1382–1384.

Louv, R 2005, *Last child in the woods: saving our children from nature-deficit disorder*, Algonquin Books, Chapel Hill, North Carolina.

Mackett, R, Brown, B, Gong, Y, Kitazawa, K & Paskins, J 2007, 'Children's independent movement in the local environment', *Built Environment*, vol. 33, no. 4, pp. 454–468.

Mayer, FS, Frantz, CM, Bruehlman-Senecal, E & Dolliver, K 2009, 'Why is nature beneficial? the role of connectedness to nature', *Environment and Behavior*, vol. 41, no. 5, pp. 607–643.

Moore, RC 1997, 'The need for nature: a childhood right', *Social Justice*, vol. 24, no. 3, pp. 203–221.

Nilan, P, Julian, R & Germov, J 2007, *Australian youth: social and cultural issues*, Pearson Education Australia, Sydney.

Owens, PE 1988, 'Natural landscapes, gathering places, and prospect refuges: characteristics of outdoor places valued by teens', *Children's Environments Quarterly*, vol. 5, no. 2, pp. 17–24.

Owens, PE 1997, 'Adolescence and the cultural landscape: public policy, design decisions, and popular press reporting', *Landscape and Urban Planning*, vol. 39, no. 2–3, pp. 153–166.

Owens, PE 2002, 'No teens allowed: the exclusion of adolescents from public spaces', *Landscape Journal*, vol. 21, pp. 156–163.

Papas, MA, Alberg, AJ, Ewing, R, Helzlsouer, KJ, Gary, TL & Klassen, AC 2007, 'The built environment and obesity', *Epidemiology Review*, vol. 29, no. 1, pp. 129–143.

Prout, A & James, A (eds) 1990, *Constructing and reconstructing childhood*, Falmer Press, London.

Qvortrup, J, Bardy, M, Sgritta, G & Wintersberger, H 1994, *Childhood matters: social theory, practice and politics*, Avebury, Aldershot, England.

Sanoff, H 2010, *Community participation methods in design and planning*, John Wiley & Sons, New York.

Tandy, CA 1999, 'Children's diminishing play space: a study of intergenerational change in children's use of their neighborhoods', *Australian Geographical Studies*, vol. 37, no. 2, pp. 154–164.

Thompson, S & Capon, T 2012, 'Heathy built environments: putting children first', *New Planner*, March, pp. 22–23.

Tranter, P & Sharpe, S 2007, 'Children and peak oil: an opportunity in crisis', *International Journal of Children's Rights*, vol. 15, pp. 181–197.

Ward-Thompson, C, Aspinall, P & Montarzino, A 2008, 'The childhood factor: adult visits to green places and the significance of childhood experience', *Environment & Behavior*, vol. 40, no. 1, pp. 111–143.

Wood, L, Frank, LD & Giles-Corti, B 2010, 'Sense of community and its relationship with walking and neighbourhood design', *Social Science & Medicine*, vol. 70, no. 9, pp. 1381–1390.

CHAPTER 7

Being ourselves

Children and young people sharing urban open spaces

Helen Woolley

Introduction

It is well understood that access to urban open space can make a significant contribution to the quality of the daily lives of children and young people, as acknowledged by Beunderman, Hannon, and Bradwell (2007). Open space is valued for its ability to "support active lifestyles; support personal development and emotional wellbeing; facilitate learning about wider society; encourage positive attitudes to nature and sustainable development and foster citizenship and participation in decision-making" (pp. 29–30). However, this is not fully understood and not well supported in the planning, design and management of cities. Since Beunderman et al.'s report for *Play England* in 2007, two general elections in the United Kingdom have resulted in the removal of policy structures which had the potential to have a positive influence on children, young people and public open space.

This is of particular importance to the UK, where in the first decade of the twenty-first century various national and international indicators revealed that many children have a poor quality of life. A UNICEF report on children's well-being in developed countries in 2007 ranked the United Kingdom at the bottom of the table, while other indicators point to the increase in obesity levels in children (National Audit Office 2012). During this time academic researchers have continued to explore issues surrounding children, young people and public open space, giving voice to children and seeking to reaffirm that positive experiences in the outdoor environment can enhance children's and young people's health and daily lives.

This chapter will begin with a definition of urban open space before drawing on research from the UK published during the last five years which has sought to understand some of the issues relating to children and young people's activities in public space including play, walking, gathering with friends and skateboarding. The research discussed comes from different disciplines including health, sport, children's geographies, psychology and landscape architecture, providing insight from the perspectives of different academic disciplines. The final reflections will include suggestions for a movement towards more child friendly outdoor environments in the cities of the UK.

Domestic, neighborhood and civic urban open spaces

First some clarification of terms is needed. Beunderman et al. (2007) use the terms *public realm* and *public space* interchangeably to mean both outdoor and indoor public spaces. This chapter is focused on the wide range of open spaces which are outdoors, some of which may be either public or privately owned (see, e.g., Madanipour 2003; Minton 2006). In earlier research it has been suggested that, from the perspective of end users rather than planners, these open spaces can further be classified as being domestic, neighborhood or civic (Woolley 2003). These three categories encompass a variety of different open spaces, both public and private.

The constructed neighborhood open spaces that children use, and that society expects children to use, are playgrounds, skate parks and school playgrounds. Other neighborhood open spaces include parks, streets, city farms and incidental spaces. Domestic open spaces that children might use include gardens and areas in which housing is located. Civic open spaces that are also accessible to young people, such as town and city centers, can include commercial, health, education, transport and recreational spaces (Woolley 2003), but society tends to see these as adult spaces.

It has been suggested that beyond the three dimensions of home, school and playgrounds, young people are often invisible in the fourth dimension of public open space, and that token additional spaces are provided which do not adequately meet the needs and desires of young people (Matthews 1995; Matthews et al. 1998; Matthews et al. 1999). In addition, many of the constructed open spaces which children are expected to use can be of limited play and experiential value (Woolley & Lowe 2013).

Children's use of urban open space in established housing areas

Many definitions and understandings of play exist (e.g., Cole-Hamilton et al. 2002; Lester & Russell 2008), but the term *active play* appears to stem from a medical context where it is understood as unstructured physical activity which takes place outdoors in a child's free time (Veitch et al. 2006). Active play is particularly important with respect to the health agenda for children in England because it is an important type of physical activity for children (Department for Children, Schools and Families 2008; National Audit Office 2006).

Within the agenda of children's health, a key piece of recent research explored active play for children aged 10–11 years from different socioeconomic backgrounds, in urban and urban-rural fringe locations in the city of Bristol in the southwest of England. A total of 77 randomly selected children from four primary schools accepted the invitation to be involved in focus groups, each group including four to eight boys and girls. The children were asked to discuss motivations and supporting and/or limiting factors to their participation in active play in the outdoor environment (Brockman et al. 2011). Although the focus of this research was not on the physical environments themselves, the importance of different urban open spaces was clearly highlighted. Socializing and being with friends was a primary motivator for the outdoor activities discussed by the respondents while the benefit of being away from adult control, rules and structured activities was also appreciated (Brockman et al. 2011).

The spaces reported as valued by children in this research included the domestic open space of cul-de-sacs—short streets with a dead end or no exit at one end—which were frequently mentioned by boys as being a good place to play football. Beyond the cul-de-sac, some of the boys had a field they could also go to, moving from a domestic to a neighborhood open space. Other easily accessible green spaces in the neighborhood were also popular with both male and female respondents. For

Figure 7.1 A typical cul-de-sac in Bristol where football might be played (Source: Rowan Brockman)

several children it was important that these open spaces were close to home, if not right outside the front door, so that friends could call after homework was finished. Neighborhood open spaces of parks, together with fields and hills, were repeatedly mentioned as being important for play and meeting up with friends (Brockman et al. 2011). So although no detail is provided of the character of these open spaces, it is clear that their provision and existence close to home is important for supporting regular use and providing opportunities for going outside, being physically active and keeping fit, healthy and happy.

   Such opportunities for using domestic and neighborhood open spaces were limited by the well-known and often reported parental concerns involving social and physical fears of strangers and traffic. Many of these were understood as being reasonable by the children and were acknowledged as having little impact on the children's active play. One factor supporting the active play of many of these children was technology; specifically, cell phones. Although phones are sometimes maligned with respect to children's play, many of the children reported that getting permission to play in the different types of open spaces was facilitated by the fact that they had a phone, enabling them to contact parents or for parents to contact them (Brockman et al. 2011). Many of the children and young people in this study regularly played in their nearby domestic and neighborhood open spaces.

Figure 7.2 A typical
neighborhood park
in Bristol (Source:
Rowan Brockman)

Children's use of urban open space in expanding housing areas

Further research has explored the experiences in outdoor environments of slightly older children and young people aged 9–16 years, in the context of four urban and urban-rural fringe areas associated with the development of a growth area in the south of England where new housing was being built. Some of the developments were in self-contained areas in rural settings, making them village-like. Between 2005 and 2009, 30,000 new houses were built in the growth area, with the intention that facilities such as playgrounds, hangouts and multi-use games areas would also be constructed. However, these were not all delivered on time, and some were not provided at all because of the slowdown in housing construction following the 2008/9 international economic downturn. Walking was encouraged throughout the growth area by the provision of pedestrian paths linking public open spaces. The research focused on four development areas within the greater growth area, each with differing demographics and approaches to planning, design and implementation (Horton et al. 2014).

The research revealed that children were limited in moving around the area without an adult taking or accompanying them on journeys to locations such as school, shops, leisure and recreation activities, and beyond the neighborhood. All the children identified a physical boundary outside of which they were not allowed to go without an

Figure 7.3 A path that children chose for walking around the area (Source: Sophie Hadfield-Hill)

adult. This was pronounced for 20 percent of the respondents who were not allowed to go unaccompanied when moving more than 50 meters from home. The spatial boundary in these new developments was fixed by parents considering factors such as the edge of the development, busy roads, their knowledge and friendship networks and areas where parents considered that 'unsafe' people might be present. However, within these boundaries the territories included a variety of neighborhood open spaces which were closely associated with the activity of walking, often on long and repeated routes. These routes sometimes explored the perimeter of an individual's given boundary, but they also were often focused on the location of friends' houses. Beyond this there were a number of neighborhood open spaces, not specifically designed for children and young people, including courtyards, alleyways and street corners that were highly valued (see Figure 7.4). In addition, drainage channels were used by some of the participants. So for the 80 percent of children and young people whose parents allowed their independent movement beyond 50 meters from home, a variety of neighborhood open spaces were appreciated and used in their daily walking routines around the community (Horton et al. 2014).

As with active play, walking in and through these open spaces had a clear social focus, which was possibly at the heart of the experience for the children and young people (Horton et al. 2014). An additional spatial dimension was reported as occurring when one group's walking route coincided with that of different groups, providing an expanded social experience. As with the Bristol research, some of these social experiences were not positive and this often involved older children or young people. Such experiences were avoided by physically moving away to another space.

Figure 7.4
A street corner
in the new
development
(Source: Sophie
Hadfield Hill)

Figure 7.5
A courtyard supports
children's play in the
new development
(Source: Sophie
Hadfield-Hill)

Children's and young people's exclusion from urban open space

Despite the fact that public open spaces can provide many positive opportunities for children and young people, there are times when not only parental controls but also controls by other parts of society limit children's use of public open space. One such mechanism introduced in the UK in 1999 was Anti-Social Behavior Orders (ASBOs), giving police the power to move people on who were perceived as being a nuisance and exclude them from public open spaces. In some areas, ASBOs have often been used to exclude young people from specific open spaces (Millie 2009). This sets the context for research undertaken in a large city in the south of England which focused on a locale the police had identified as an Anti-Social Behavior (ASB) 'hotspot'. Young people aged between 12 and 16 years were recruited through youth clubs to participate in focus group discussions. The youth clubs were selected because they were located near sites that had been designated as dispersal zones in the previous two years or were one of the ASB 'hotspots'. A total of 41 young people took part in 10 focus groups, and as with some of the previously reported research, the physical characteristics of the open spaces used were not the focus of the discussion; rather, the focus was on the regulation of the open spaces and the experiences of young people who had been excluded (Gray & Manning 2014).

For the most part, the respondents accepted that it was appropriate for there to be some control in public urban settings, and that in some instances, having the police around made them feel safer, particularly the girls. In admitting this, some individuals revealed that, being a little older now, they understood the need for police to exert control in these spaces and if told to move on or not hang around in an area, they would comply. Most of their dealings were with the police, but on occasion they also involved parents, other adults and members of the community, who were encouraged to keep an eye on these places.

The participants commented about situations where they felt there had been inappropriate control of public open space. One person described an incident where a police officer asked a group of young people sitting on a park bench what they were doing. Their response was: "sitting here", "just talking" . . . "we're not doing nothing". The police officer didn't think this was a reasonable answer and asked them to move on (Gray & Manning 2014, p. 647). This everyday experience of just sitting and chatting with friends, not doing anything wrong, was deemed not acceptable.

As the researchers note, young people in public space are often, by virtue of their age, regarded as 'out of place'. In the case of the ASB legislation, they become subject to routine surveillance and frequently being asked to account for their activities and behavior, even when that is "just sitting here". Amongst the young people themselves, there were contrasting views on how much regulation is required and what is appropriate, especially where the actions of a few might result in reduced freedoms for others of the same age. The researchers comment: "these young people's accounts reflect and reproduce widely held ideological arguments about young people as being both 'at risk' and 'the risk' in public spaces" (Gray & Manning 2014, p. 651).

Excluding skateboarders from civic space

One specific group, predominantly young males, who are often excluded by society from particular civic spaces is skateboarders (Beal 1995; Borden 2001; Karsten & Pel 2000). Skateboarders often choose to use civic open spaces in city centers which are usually surrounded by commercial, retail or government buildings. These open spaces are popular with skateboarders because they are known to be great skating spots and easy to access. The landscape elements provide opportunities for the tricks

Figure 7.6 Peace Gardens, Sheffield. The handrail and sitting wall details designed to prevent skateboarders using the area (Source: Helen Woolley)

that skateboarders like to undertake (Woolley & Johns 2001). Research in three cities in the north of England has revealed the reasons and mechanisms that support the exclusion of skateboarders from civic urban open spaces. This research involved focus groups with skateboarders as well as interviews with designers and managers of civic open spaces to provide a multidimensional perspective on the issue of skateboarding in these cities (Woolley et al. 2011).

One of the main reasons that skateboarding is not deemed appropriate everywhere is because of the potential for damage to street furnishings, paving and other urban elements, and the associated repair costs for the community. These environmental concerns, together with other social concerns, have resulted in legal, social and physical controls on skateboarders' use of specific civic open spaces. Frequently the approach is to 'design out' skateboarders using elements such as bull-nosed edges to seats and walls, textured paving and obstructive handrail details. Retrofitting areas with anti-skate devices on walls and benches can also be implemented once it is apparent that skateboarders are using specific elements in a civic open space. Legal controls often take the form of a by-law excluding skateboarders from specific open spaces or areas of a town or city center and these are often reinforced by the social control of local wardens or ambassadors (see Figure 7.7). Another physical control on skateboarding is the provision of skate parks which relegates skaters to a specific area in the community. These skate parks can form part of a larger strategy comprising legal, physical and social controls (Woolley et al. 2011).

It is clear that some of the open spaces that children and young people choose to use in cities can have controls imposed on them, not just by parents but also by society in the design and management of specific open spaces.

Figure 7.7
Sheffield City
Centre Ambassadors
(Source: Helen
Woolley)

Reduction in use of urban open space over generations

Research set in a northern city in the UK explored differences in use of open space across three generations of two families, using structured interviews and maps with grandparents, parents and children (Woolley & Griffin 2014). The findings revealed dramatic changes in the five dimensions of unaccompanied distance, types of outdoor spaces visited, activities undertaken, number of companions in the outdoors and mode of travel to outdoor spaces, reflecting earlier cross-generational findings from other parts of the world (Gaster 1991; Karsten 2005; Kinoshita 2009; Skår & Krogh 2009; Tandy 1999).

Children in the study were only allowed up to 115 meters from their door without an adult where they could play with a friend or a couple of other people, in the garden or on the grass outside. This contrasts with their grandparents' experience of being allowed to travel unaccompanied by adults to a wide range of public places and open spaces including shops, fields, woods and a dam where they went with groups of friends and siblings, sometimes meeting other larger groups. The variety of open spaces used by the parents, and particularly the grandparents, was wide ranging and included many well beyond the constructed open spaces of playgrounds. Over the three generations, the number and type of open spaces used by the children dramatically decreased, as did the number of companions they would go with and meet, together with the number and variety of activities they would undertake (Woolley & Griffin 2014).

Towards child friendly open spaces

These studies from different disciplines cannot be assumed to be generalizable but bringing them together gives a range of insights and provides the pixels to construct a picture, even if blurred and patchy, of some of the contemporary issues for children and young people in public open spaces in England. First, a range of qualitative methods was used to develop these understandings of activities in different spatial settings. Interviews, focus groups, maps and walkabouts all provided opportunities for in-depth exploration of the issues. The locations for undertaking the research were carefully considered so they would be convenient for the children, not the researchers. On more than one occasion schools were used to access children's opinions, as well as youth clubs, community events and word of mouth. All techniques were used to achieve a broad set of participants.

Second, although not all of the pieces of research focused on the type, nature and character of the open spaces the participants were using, it is clear that a wide range of spaces was being used where this was allowed. Such public open spaces included cul-de-sacs and other incidental spaces immediately outside or close to homes, and open spaces further away but within the neighborhood including courtyards and fields, domestic and neighborhood open spaces. Within these public open spaces specific elements, such as footpaths and benches, facilitated children's and young people's activities and opportunities to meet and gather.

These findings reflect those of research undertaken in housing areas in England as long ago as the 1960s and 1970s, where it was identified that children not only used playgrounds but also played well beyond the playgrounds on roads and pavements, paved and grassed areas, wild and planted areas, walls, fences and garage roofs, and walked on paths around housing estates. Paths were identified as of particular relevance for the activities of walking, cycling and meeting people (Allen et al. 2005; Department of the Environment 1973; Hole 1996).

A third issue to emerge from the research informing this chapter is that of the level of acceptance by some children and young people of the constraints that adults put on them and their use of public space. Indeed, the examples discussed reveal that there is sometimes agreement and an understanding of the reasons for these constraints, though there is no evidence to say if this is the case with skateboarders. This has some resonance with the early definition of 'home-range' where it was acknowledged as being negotiated between child and parent (Hart 1979).

The fourth and final issue to emerge from the research reviewed in this chapter is the supportive role of technology. Technology is sometimes perceived as a detractor to children's activities in public open spaces; however, at least two of the pieces of research clearly showed that technology in the form of cell phones has become an essential part of daily life providing a communication tool for parents and children, allowing some level of freedom for children and the ability for parents to call a child home.

It is clear that there are ways that cities can provide public open spaces of different types which can support children and young people to be themselves and participate in activities including active play, walking, sitting, skateboarding and exploring. To do this a variety of public open spaces are needed at the domestic, neighborhood and civic levels which go beyond the limitations of the constructed spaces of playgrounds and skate parks. This should be considered and implemented by those who plan, design and manage cities.

Conclusion

Political support is needed for the planning stage so that a variety of public open spaces—not only well-designed playgrounds—that can purposively accommodate children and young people can be included in development plans. In this way a vision for a child friendly outdoor environment in a city can be set. The vision can then be taken up by developers who work within a city plan to ensure that a child friendly approach is used and such developers can work with children, in a process facilitated by suitably experienced academics and professionals with experience of using qualitative methods to engage children and young people in imagining the design of public spaces they would enjoy.

Once the vision of a child friendly city has been re-affirmed in this way, designers, particularly enlightened landscape architects, architects and engineers, can put the vision into practice in the way that designs are brought together, formed and built. Such professionals should be carefully chosen to ensure they have a good understanding of a child friendly approach or should be given a very clear brief as to what this means. In addition, the way public open spaces in cities are managed can also contribute to or detract from the vision of a child friendly city. Such management includes town center management schemes where wardens, ambassadors, police and others in authority can strongly influence children and young people's use of open spaces. It also includes those who manage housing areas, both privately owned and managed, and publicly owned or social housing areas, where often there are many poor-quality open spaces.

If these providers are not trained to understand the importance of children and young people being able to use public open spaces, but only perceive them as a nuisance, then that can destroy the child friendly city vision, no matter how well the planning and design processes have been executed. These approaches should apply to new cities, newly built areas within existing cities, the regeneration or refurbishment of existing cities and the ongoing management and small-scale design changes that can take place in cities. If a vision is set for cities to have child friendly outdoor environments and this vision is fulfilled by these different parts of society then the benefits suggested by many, including Beunderman et al. (2007), can be achieved. This will take many different people engaging in the process, including children, young people and parents.

References

Allen, C, Camina, M, Casey, R, Coward, S & Wood, M 2005, *Mixed tenure twenty years on—nothing out of the ordinary*, Chartered Institute of Housing for the Joseph Rowntree Foundation, Coventry, UK.

Beal, B 1995, 'Disqualifying the official: an exploration of social resistance through the subculture of skateboarding', *Sociology of Sport Journal*, vol. 12, pp. 252–267.

Beunderman, J, Hannon, C & Bradwell, P 2007, *Seen and heard: reclaiming the public real with children and young people*, Play England and Demos, London.

Borden, I 2001, *Skateboarding, space and the city: architecture and the body*, Berg, London.

Brockman, R, Jago, R & Fox, KR 2011, 'Children's active play: self-reported motivators, barriers and facilitators', *BMC Public Health*, vol. 11, no. 46. DOI:1186/1471-2458-11-461.

Cole-Hamilton, I, Harrop, A & Street, C 2002, *Making the case for play: gathering the evidence*, Children's Play Council, London.

Department for Children, Schools and Families, Department for Culture, Media and Sport 2008, *The play strategy*, DCSF Publications, Nottingham. Available from: http://webarchive.nationalarchives.gov.uk/20130401151715/http://www.education.gov.uk/publications/eOrderingDownload/The_Play_Strategy.pdf.

Department of Environment 1973, *Children at play*, Her Majesty's Stationery Office, London.

Gaster, S 1991, 'Urban children's access to their neighborhood: changes over three generations', *Environment and Behavior*, vol. 23, no. 1, pp. 70–85. DOI:10.1177/0013916591231004.

Gray, D & Manning, R 2014, '"Oh my god, we're not doing nothing": young people's experiences of spatial regulation', *Journal of British Social Psychology*, vol. 53, pp. 640–655. DOI:10.1111/bjso.12055.

Hart, R 1979, *Children's experience of place*, Irvington Press, New York.

Hole V 1996, *National building studies research paper 39: children's play on housing estates*, Her Majesty's Stationery Office, London.

Horton, P, Christensen, P, Kraftl, P & Hadfield-Hill, S 2014, '"Walking . . . just walking": how children and young people's everyday pedestrian practices matter', *Social and Cultural Geography*, vol. 15, no. 1, pp. 94–115. DOI:10.1080/14649365.2013.864782.

Karsten, L 2005, 'It all used to be better? different generations on continuity and change in urban children's daily use of space', *Children's Geographies*, vol. 3, no. 3, pp. 275–290. DOI:10.1080/14733280500352912.

Karsten, L & Pel, E 2000, 'Skateboarders exploring urban public space: ollies, obstacles and conflicts', *Journal of Housing and the Built Environment*, vol. 15, pp. 327–340.

Kinoshita, I 2009, 'Charting generational differences in conceptions and opportunities for play in a Japanese neighborhood', *Journal of Intergenerational Relationships*, vol. 7, no. 1, pp. 53–77. DOI:10.1080/15350770802629024.

Lester, S & Russell W 2008, *Play for a change—play, policy and practice: a review of contemporary perspectives*, Play England, London.

Madanipour, A 2003, *Public and private spaces of the city*, Routledge, London and New York.

Matthews, H 1995, 'Living on the edge: children as outsiders', *Tijdschrift voor economische en sociale geografie*, vol. 86, no. 5, pp. 456–466. DOI:10.1111/j.1467-9663.1995.tb01867.

Matthews, H, Limb, M & Percy-Smith, B 1998, 'Changing worlds: the microgeographies of young teenagers', *Tijdschrift voor Economische en Sociale Geografie*, vol. 89, no. 2, pp. 193–202.

Matthews, H, Limb, M & Taylor, M 1999, 'Reclaiming the street: the discourse of curfew', *Environment and Planning A*, vol. 33, pp. 1713–1730.

Millie, A (ed.) 2009, *Securing respect: behavioral expectations and anti-social behavior in the UK*, The Policy Press, Bristol.

Minton, A 2006, *What kind of world are we building? the privatisation of public space*, The Royal Institution of Chartered Surveyors, London.

National Audit Office, Health Care Commission, Audit Commission 2006, *Tackling obesity—first steps*, The Stationery Office, London.

National Audit Office 2012, *An update on the government's approach to tackling obesity*, NAO Publications, London. Available from: www.nao.org.uk/wp-content/uploads/2012/07/tackling_obesity_update.pdf.

Skår, M & Krogh E 2009, 'Changes in children's nature-based experiences near home: from spontaneous play to adult-controlled, planned and organized activities', *Children's Geographies*, vol. 7, no. 3, pp. 339–354. DOI:10.1080/14733280903024506.

Tandy, C 1999, 'Children's diminishing play space: a study of intergenerational change in children's use of their neighborhoods', *Australian Geographical Studies*, vol. 37, no. 2, pp. 154–164.

LIVERPOOL JOHN MOORES UNIVERSITY
LEARNING SERVICES

UNICEF 2007, *Child poverty in perspective*: *an overview of child wellbeing in rich countries*, UNICEF Innocenti Research Report 7, New York.

Veitch, J, Bagley, S, Ball, K, Salmon, J 2006, 'Where do children usually play? a qualitative study of parents' perceptions of influences on children's active free play', *Health and Place*, vol. 12, no. 4, pp. 383–393.

Woolley, H 2003, *Urban open spaces*, Spon Press, London.

Woolley, H & Griffin, E 2014, 'Decreasing experiences of home range, outdoor spaces, activities and companions: changes across three generations in Sheffield in north England', *Children's Geographies*, vol. 13, no. 6, pp. 677–691. DOI:10.1080/147 33285.2014.952186.

Woolley, H & Johns, R 2001, 'Skateboarding: the city as a playground', *Journal of Urban Design*, vol. 6, no. 2, pp. 211–230.

Woolley, H & Lowe, A 2013, 'Exploring the relationship between design approach and play value of outdoor play spaces', *Landscape Research*, vol. 38, no. 1, pp. 53–74. DOI:10.1080/01426397.2011.640432.

Woolley, H, Hazelwood, T & Simkins, I 2011, 'Don't skate here: exclusion of skateboarders from urban civic spaces in three northern cities in England', *Journal of Urban Design*, vol. 16, no. 4, pp. 471–487. DOI:org/10.1080/13574809.2011.585867.

CHAPTER 8

Children as urban design consultants

A children's audit of a central city square in Auckland, Aotearoa/New Zealand

Penelope Carroll and Karen Witten

Introduction

The well-being of children living in cities is increasingly compromised by changes to the built environment, risk-averse parenting practices and wider societal attitudes. In cities already designed predominantly for adults and cars, residential densification threatens to further reduce environmental opportunities for children. Children are increasingly confined to the "semi-fortified space of home" (Kearns & Collins 2006, p. 108), driven to and from school and adult-supervised activities and deemed 'out of place in public space' (by design, decree and safety concerns). Gleeson and Sipe (2006) write of 'toxic' cities which fail to nurture children. There is emerging recognition that children's needs must be considered by urban planners, and that children are competent enough and should be consulted (Freeman & Aitken-Rose 2005; Graham & Fitzgerald 2010). However, urban planners have been slow to take into account the specific needs of children—and slower still to include them as part of public consultations or planning decision-making (Freeman & Tranter 2011). The UNICEF Child Friendly Cities initiative (2010) has been gaining momentum and is helping spearhead children's participation in urban planning (Fotel 2009). However, as Shier (2001) notes, 'participation' can vary from children merely being listened to at one end of the continuum, to children sharing power and responsibility for decision-making at the other, and there are few examples of the latter.

A 2015 children's audit of the redevelopment of an Auckland (Aotearoa/New Zealand's largest city) central city square, facilitated by the authors in partnership with Auckland Council Community Development and Design Office staff, provides a useful model for participatory planning with children. Feedback and suggestions from a reference group of children aged 7–13 years involved with the audit/consultation informed the proposed final design of the square. The success of the process has led to intentions to incorporate children's audits into design briefs for future redevelopment projects.

In this chapter we outline the process of the Freyberg Square children's audit/consultation—a first for Auckland Council—and consider connections between research, policy and practice which created it. We reflect on how the rhetoric of 'putting children and young people first' and seeking children's participation might become embedded in planning policies to produce a truly child friendly city.

Background

Children need to be physically active and socially interactive for their present-day well-being, and good health outcomes later in adulthood (Carroll et al. 2015; McDonell 2007). Being independently mobile—that is, out and about without adult supervision—is also important to promote a sense of place and belonging (Christensen 2003), and gives children opportunities to learn social skills and competencies (Lennard & Crowhurst Lennard 1992). If children are able to safely engage with their neighborhood environments, their independence, resilience and social competence are enhanced and the whole community benefits.

In current urban planning practice, children's use of the public realm is largely relegated to child-specific destinations such as playgrounds, swimming pools and libraries. Their presence is seldom anticipated or even welcomed throughout the city. Restricting children's opportunities to play and socialize outdoors places their physical, emotional and cognitive development at risk (McDonell 2007; Spencer & Woolley 2000), and the long-term social sustainability of our cities is in question (Carroll et al. 2015).

In 1993, when New Zealand ratified the 1989 United Nations Convention on the Rights of the Child, it committed to acknowledging a raft of children's rights, including the right to play, to move safely through the public realm, and to speak out and be heard on matters which affect them. In 1997 UNICEF launched a framework for the participation of children in urban planning with its Child Friendly Cities initiative. This followed the 1996 UN Conference on Human Settlements which declared the well-being of children to be the ultimate indicator of a healthy habitat. These UN initiatives have signaled a shift from the view of children as adult 'becomings', with a focus on their need for care and protection, to a broad consideration of children's lived experiences and a view of children as already full citizens, capable of participating in civic decision-making (Freeman & Tranter 2011; Percy-Smith & Burns 2013).

Auckland Council's stated aim to "put children and young people first and consider their wellbeing in everything that we do" (Auckland Council 2012b, p. 78) mirrors this shift. It stops short of committing to the formal requirements of the Child Friendly Cities agenda; however, in the Auckland City Centre Masterplan (Auckland Council 2012a), the blueprint for redevelopment of the central business district (CBD), 'inclusiveness and child-friendly' are guiding principles. Furthermore, since February 2015, Waitemata Local Board (the city's local board responsible for the CBD) has committed to the formal requirements of the Child Friendly Cities agenda. These include children's meaningful participation in decisions which will affect them.

Auckland is Aotearoa/New Zealand's largest and fastest-growing city. The population of 1.4 million—300,000 of them children—is expected to reach 2 million in the next 30 years. To accommodate this growth, Auckland has committed to develop a more compact city, which has the potential to profoundly impact children's everyday lives including their access to public open space and places to play.

Researching with children

Our 'Kids in the City' research was spurred on by the need to ensure that children are considered and their voices heard in densifying Auckland (see kidsinthecity.ac.nz for details of our team's child-related projects). Underpinning this research is an understanding of childhood as both a biological phenomenon and a social construct. This acknowledges developmental imperatives, as well as considering children as experts and agents in their own lives—and potential agents of change in the wider environment (Kellett 2014; Percy-Smith & Burns 2013).

In Kids in the City (2010–2014) we worked with 253 children aged 9–12 years across nine Auckland neighborhoods, investigating their neighborhood experiences and relationships between urban design attributes, safety perceptions and children's levels of independent mobility and physical activity (Carroll et al. 2015). Findings highlight the extent to which children's and parents' fears restrict access to the public realm. They provoke questions about the extent to which children's rights to play and move about safely have been disregarded in urban design and planning practice.

As a follow-on pilot project in 2013, six children aged 10–12 years who had previously participated in Kids in the City conducted their own research with peers on 'living in the city'. Each child came up with a research question and was mentored through data collection, analysis, presentation and dissemination of their findings to Auckland Council. Council's interest in the 'Children-Researching-Children' pilot suggested possibilities for future child-led research in the urban planning arena.

Children's voice

In some spheres children have come to be recognized as 'experts' on their own lives and agents in their own right (Casas et al. 2013; Christensen & James 2000), who have "a valuable contribution to make to social and political life" (Graham & Fitzgerald 2010, p. 135). Evidence suggests when their voices *are* heard—that is, when they are involved in program design and research to inform policies—policies are more likely to successfully meet their needs (Tisdall & Bell 2006). Yet children remain marginalized, their voices seldom heard or their perspectives considered in the urban planning arena (Freeman & Tranter 2011). Understanding the everyday experiences of children living in the city and contributing their voice to urban planning has been a focus of our Kids in the City research.

There is increased interest, internationally and in Aotearoa/New Zealand, in children's participation in local government decision-making (Freeman & Tranter 2011; Percy-Smith 2010). However, this has largely been motivated by a desire to "'do something' . . . rather than any deeper desire to confront the marginalized position of young people in society and local government" (Freeman & Aitken-Rose 2005, p. 375). Commissioning a children's audit for the Freyberg Square redevelopment confronts this.

Children's audit/consultation

We were approached in May 2015 by Auckland Council's Community Development team to carry out a child friendly audit of Freyberg Square: in the first instance, an audit of the current square and adjacent community facility, and later of the proposed redevelopment design.

Dating from the 1870s, the square is an open, paved space incorporating a cascading water feature, benches and historic steps. It is adjacent to the Pioneer Women's and Ellen Melville Hall, a community center built in 1963, but separated by a vehicle access lane. The redevelopment, part of the Central City Masterplan, will remove the access lane, enlarge the square and connect it with the community center, which is also being redeveloped. Since 1946, the area has commemorated WWII hero Lord

Freyberg, with a statue added in 1976. The current design dates from the mid-1990s and is now in need of refurbishment.

Figure 8.1 Current design of Freyberg Square, Auckland, New Zealand (Source: the authors)

The project design brief called for the creation of "a world class place that is a distinctive, safe and popular destination, where locals and visitors choose to frequent and linger" (Auckland Council 2015, p. 6). With increasing numbers of families with children living in inner city apartments and a lack of nearby outdoor spaces for children to safely play and interact (Carroll et al. 2015), Freyberg Square is an important public space not just for adults, but for children as well. Yet there was no mention of incorporating affordances for children in the briefing documents.

The children's audit of the square was an afterthought which evolved from a combination of several general factors, including Auckland Council's stated commitment to 'put children and young people first'; dissemination of Kids in the City research findings highlighting the perspectives of Auckland children; 'child friendly' champions amongst Council staff and Local Board members; and Waitemata Local Board's commitment to Child Friendly City accreditation. Council's Community Development team wanted to showcase the value of child impact assessments (to fulfill strategic requirements) and identified the square's redevelopment as an opportunity to do this. Discussions between researchers and Council staff led to initial ideas of a child impact assessment evolving into a 'child friendly audit', a first for Auckland Council.

Methods and findings

The audit was conducted in partnership with Council staff from Community Development and Council's Design Office. After the ethical approval was obtained through Massey University, six children who had previously participated in Kids in the City and Children-Researching-Children were invited to take part, along with an additional five younger children. The six girls and five boys ranged in age from 7 to 13 years. Three workshops were held between June and August in 2015.

First workshop: June

The preliminary workshop was conducted in Freyberg Square itself and the adjacent hall. Information from Council about the proposed upgrade and what the design team wanted to learn from a 'child friendly audit' preceded children's exploration of the space.

Figure 8.2 and Figure 8.3 Children explored the square and took photographs (Source: the authors)

Children took photographs and considered what they liked/disliked and why, where and what they would play, and whether they felt safe. They evaluated ground surfaces, seating, a water feature, tree and the statue of Lord Freyberg. They leapt, jumped and cart-wheeled through the space; climbed the tree, the water feature, the bank and the stairs; slid/hid in the grass on the bank; balanced on ledges and sat on the benches. Back inside the hall, their observations were elicited during group discussion. They were asked to further investigate specific features of particular interest to Council—the seating, the statue, the water feature and tree—and how they might engage with these. The children's ideas were forwarded to the Design Office team in a report prepared by researchers and many were incorporated into the redevelopment design (see *Third workshop*).

Second workshop: July

In a follow-up workshop, a photo-voice exercise with photographs taken during children's on-site investigation and group discussion generated additional suggestions for a more child friendly Freyberg Square. The team was interested to discover how the audit may have fostered prerequisites for a child friendly environment such as agency, a sense of safety and a positive sense of self (NSW Commission for Children and Young People 2009).

In terms of agency, children felt they had a right to be consulted about changes in the city, and appreciated being consulted about Freyberg Square. Children and adults had different views and different needs, they said, and children felt their input could make public spaces better for a wide range of people: 'Kids usually have more creative ideas, interacting with things'. Most said they felt safe because the square was 'close to buildings, and with shops around . . . not hidden away'; and they approved of the plan to close off access to cars, which they also thought would increase safety. Children's positive self-image is seen to be fostered when they feel welcomed in public spaces (NSW Commission for Children and Young People 2009). To them Freyberg Square at present did not appear welcoming; it looked drab and uncared for and rubbish made it feel unwelcoming, they said. More color and fun things to do, regular maintenance and a 'welcome to the square' sign were suggested. Children also came up with creative ideas to better integrate the square and the community center.

Third workshop: August

Once Council's draft design was complete, the children met again on-site with researchers and two Council staff. The Council's draft design was presented showing the children where and how their ideas/feedback were incorporated—some specifically, and other ideas informing functional elements of the space in a way that worked for children and adults alike.

Table 8.1 contains examples of children's ideas which fed into the draft design followed by comments from the Project Leader.

Other suggestions designers took on board included signage explaining the significance of Lord Freyberg; drinking fountains (including positioning one where those in wheelchairs could reach it); art work; and bean bags, balls and other equipment which could be stored inside the hall and used out in the square. "A lot of the things

Figure 8.4 Part of the new concept design responding to children's audit of the existing square (Source: Auckland Council)

"The water feature was the first thing I saw and the first thing I went to. It was an interactive feature – it wasn't just taking up a chunk of space. It was fun climbing to the top."

"A group of kids could have like a scavenger hunt around the statue and it could be like an adventure."

"I like the water, how it comes down, the noise it makes."

"A drinking fountain."

"I'd come on a warm day with one of my friends, scooter around, go up into the tree, play on a playground – and I'd probably feed the birds."

"No cars should be allowed to drive in."

AERIAL PERSPECTIVE

Table 8.1 Children's and Project Leader's comments.

Children's comments	Project Leader's comments
Access to the statue of Lord Freyberg:	
"The statue is nice to touch because it is smooth"	"Some kids said that they wanted to touch him and it would be fun to play around him, so we made sure that we . . . provided access up to and around the statue."
Being able to play amongst the plants on the bank and access areas above the square:	
"It's fun to play in the bushes"	"They talked about how they would really love to do a treasure hunt or to play in the plants and access some of the out of bound areas, and so we worked in a discovery trail."
Climbing and being up high:	
"It just feels good to sit up high"	"That was quite an easy one to work into the design . . . we provided many different places of stairs and terraces so that children felt like they could be up high at many different points within the space."
The water feature:	
"I liked how you could jump around the fountain"; "If someone in a wheelchair wants to touch the water they have to lean over"	"The water feature is much more organic now in form than it was in the previous design. You can walk over it, you can be in it, you can step through it on little stepping stones . . . and you can easily touch it."
Climbing trees:	
"You could have a ladder so kids could easily get up"	"They loved being able to climb the trees. That helped solidify the fact that we thought Pohutukawa [a climbable New Zealand native] would be a good species."

they came up with were reinforcing ideas that we had, so it made us feel like we were heading in the right direction" (Project Leader 2015, pers. comm., September 9).

   After the draft design had been presented, children worked outside in the square imagining specifics of the design and writing their thoughts on plans provided. They also commented on plans for the refurbished hall and suggested 'child friendly' activities.

Figure 8.5 and Figure 8.6 Children evaluate specific aspects of the draft design (Source: the authors)

Children's feedback on the audit process

Feedback from the children on the audit process indicated the workshops enabled them to participate meaningfully and gave them a vehicle for expressing their views. All of the children said they had been able to say what was really important for them: "Everyone got time to speak" (girl, 10 years). Opportunities to also write ideas down meant less confident children were also 'heard': "We didn't need to talk about our ideas if we weren't confident or comfortable enough—we could write our ideas and thoughts" (girl, 13 years).

Interacting with the site helped them formulate ideas: "I liked the outdoor interaction" (boy, 11 years); "Exploring the area made it easier to come up with ideas of what to do with the area" (girl, 13 years). The photo-voice exercise was also helpful for this: "Taking photos and writing down what we liked and what we didn't like was a good part of the process" (boy, 11 years).

All the young participants felt children had a right to be involved in re-shaping their city, and that their ideas were important and added value: "I liked that our ideas were brought into consideration and placed in the final design" (girl, 13 years). They all said they would willingly participate again in a similar audit: "It was super fun" (girl, 8 years); "I liked the style of this consultation" (boy, 12 years).

Outputs of value

The report on the audit prepared for Council was seen as 'really important' by Council staff because it provided a collective response from the children, gave legitimacy to their views and showed how the audit had informed and strengthened the final draft design. It also showed such an audit was 'doable': "It's actually been extremely useful . . . I would definitely be an advocate for following this process again on another project" (Project Leader 2015, pers. comm., September 9). In addition, the report provided 'tangible evidence' of consultation with children for the Waitemata Local Board, in line with their commitment to attaining Child Friendly City status. Children subsequently presented a montage of their photographs and captions created from the photo-voice exercise in the second workshop to the Board at their October meeting.

Managing a productive research-to-policy interface

With an emphasis on the need for 'evidence-based policy', it is interesting to reflect on the Freyberg Square children's audit in terms of the value of a productive research-to-policy interface, particularly given a statement by the City Centre Design and Delivery Manager (pers. comm. 2015, September 23), of the vital role of our Kids in the City research: "You were able to allow children's voices to be heard on how they perceived the urban environment. It was very powerful and demanded attention and reaction. I can't imagine we would have responded in the way we have if we had not gained an appreciation your work brought to us". Our research was fortuitously timely and relevant, both generating and providing support for Auckland Council's political commitment to 'put children and young people first'.

Different models of research-to-policy processes range from simple instrumental and linear models to more complex discursive models which take into account the policy context and political considerations (Fafard 2008; Nutley et al. 2007). Whatever the model, it is useful to consider modes of transfer (from researchers to policy-makers) and different stages—agenda setting, policy formulation, decision-making, policy or policy evaluation—at which research may have an impact (Burton 2006). It is also useful to differentiate between *conceptual* uptake, that is, changing ways of thinking about an issue, and *instrumental* uptake, where there is direct input into policy. Arguably, our Kids in the City research has had an impact at several stages, including agenda setting, policy formulation, decision-making and policy implementation, with the Freyberg Square audit a concrete outcome. It has contributed to both conceptual and instrumental changes, and helped create child friendly champions amongst local government policy-makers and practitioners. It is an example of a productive, well-managed researcher/policy-maker/practitioner relationship, and illustrates the value for civic organizations and researchers of building research/policy/practice relationships to broker research knowledge transfer and help facilitate desired changes in the community.

A way forward to facilitate a more 'child friendly' Auckland City

What could assist the current impetus towards ensuring the rights and participation of children are incorporated into planning for a more compact Auckland? Key informant interviews with Council staff and the Waitemata Local Board suggested the following:

- Cultivate child friendly champions within the research community and the political and bureaucratic arms of Council
- Develop best practice guidelines for child friendly design in the Auckland Design Manual which currently only deals with open space
- Undertake more Auckland-specific research to persuade Council and staff that:

  - Children have developmental needs, which the design of the built environment can either facilitate or hinder
  - A city that works for children works for everyone, and while the rationale for a more compact city is transport, energy and infrastructure sustainability, social sustainability is also vital (Carroll et al. 2015)
  - Children are experts on their own lives and have the right to be consulted as citizens, and have rights to the public spaces of the city

- Carry out more child friendly audits to persuade Councilors and staff of their value and to have them become a mandatory part of any redevelopment project because:

  - Children add value to the design process because they see things in novel ways
  - Children's input makes the design stronger: "The whole concept is stronger because it's had input from the children around what they would like in the space, how they'd use it, what could be improved" (Project Leader 2015, pers. comm., September 9)

- Such audits are 'doable'
- Endorse Council's stated child friendly aims more explicitly and demonstrate their integration into planning and review processes.

While there is a strong momentum here and elsewhere towards more child friendly cities and children's inclusion in urban design and planning, there are competing discourses for the 'branding' of cities—and child friendliness is just one of them. For instance, when the Freyberg Square draft design (including input from the children's audit) was released for public consultation, press reports on the proposed redesign of the square touted for another discourse: 'Let's have something smart, cool, urban and urbane' (McKay 2015). There was also a backlash from local traders, because they felt children's perspectives had been specifically considered and their perspectives had not. "Public space projects are massively challenging as there are so many interest groups. We have similar challenges from Mana whenua [Maori with authority in a place, based on ancestral links] who do not feel we are sufficiently responsive to their story . . ." (City Centre Design and Delivery Manager 2015, pers. comm., September 23).

Despite the challenges to privileging a child friendly city discourse, the City Centre Design and Delivery Manager says he cannot imagine the current momentum being derailed. But it could be diluted. "We need to bring the evidence base to the table. And we need to be able to benchmark our successes and build on the Freyberg Square audit, providing compelling reasons for doing it elsewhere" (City Centre Design and Delivery Manager 2015, pers. comm., September 23). Compelling reasons include children's right to be consulted and evidence that the participation of children adds value to the design process, and that a city which works for children works for everyone. The Freyberg Square audit can be used by child friendly city champions to build capacity and momentum as well as illustrate what can be achieved by engaging children in the planning process.

Conclusion

Relevant research can inform and strengthen existing policies. It can also, over time, shift thinking, shape aspirations and galvanize advocacy to change policies and practice. For instance, research on the everyday lives and needs of children has led to reconceptualization of childhood and recognition of children's agency and children's rights. This in turn has lent weight to the argument that children have a right to participate in decision-making on matters important to their lives. In the current example, regular sharing of research findings with receptive Auckland Council staff has contributed to a recognition that children live everywhere in the city; they need spaces to play and explore, spaces that are scarce in the city center; and urban planning has a role as facilitator in creating public spaces that welcome children. Freyberg Square is one such space. Following the audit, designers took the children's feedback on board and incorporated elements encouraging exploration and play into Council's draft redesign for the square.

This case study is an example of research providing local evidence to support a more child friendly agenda, and helping produce changes to both policy and practice in urban planning. It has built on decades of international research which produced a conceptual shift in the way children are viewed, that is, as citizens with rights and capabilities as change agents; and highlighted the need for urban planners to also consider the well-being of children living in cities designed predominantly for adults. Building good researcher/policy-maker/practitioner relationships facilitates knowledge transfer and assists in furthering causes such as the participation of children in decisions which affect their well-being.

Figure 8.7
Children's audit team (Source: the authors)

Involving children in the redesign of Freyberg Square has not only facilitated a more child friendly, welcoming space, with affordances for play and exploration; the process of the audit itself has been child friendly. Children's right to participate was recognized, and their sense of agency, safety and positive sense of self—all child friendly indicators—were enhanced through the process. Their ideas were taken seriously and it was accepted that children's experiences, needs and desires differ from adult assumptions of these.

Feedback from the children's reference group and Council staff, along with the research team's observations, confirm the effectiveness of the audit process and the outcomes in progressing the child friendly city agenda in Auckland. By instigating the child friendly audit of Freyberg Square, Auckland Council can 'walk the talk' of the Auckland Plan. Ongoing research and communication will help advance the process. The links between our Kids in the City findings and the Freyberg case study underline the crucial importance of building researcher/policy-maker/practitioner relationships.

Acknowledgments

Heartfelt thanks to Aira, Angeline, David, Dustin, Elizabeth, Fergus, Jaden, Jennifer, Jessica, Julian and Scarlett for their willingness to participate.

References

Auckland Council 2012a, *Auckland city centre masterplan*, Auckland.
Auckland Council 2012b, 'The Auckland plan'. Available from: www.aucklandcouncil.govt.nz/EN/planspoliciesprojects/plansstrategies/theaucklandplan/Pages/theaucklandplan.aspx.
Auckland Council 2015, *Project design brief: Pioneer Women's and Ellen Melville Hall and Freyberg Square upgrade*, Auckland.
Burton, P 2006, 'Modernising the policy process: making policy research more significant?', *Policy Studies*, vol. 27, no. 3, pp. 173–195.

Carroll, P, Witten, K, Kearns, R & Donovan, P 2015, 'Kids in the city: children's use and experiences of urban neighbourhoods in Auckland, New Zealand', *Journal of Urban Design*, vol. 20, no. 4, pp. 417–436. DOI:10.1080/13574809.2015.1044504.

Casas, F, Gonzalez, M, Navarro, D & Aligue, M 2013, 'Children as advisers of their researchers: assuming a different status for children', *Child Indicators Research*, vol. 6, pp. 193–212.

Christensen, P 2003, 'Place, space and knowledge: children in the village and the city' in *Children in the city, home, neighbourhood and community*, eds P Christensen & M O'Brien, Routledge Falmer, London, pp. 13–28.

Christensen, P & James, A 2000, 'Introduction: researching children and childhood: cultures of communication' in *Research with children: perspectives and practices*, eds P Christensen & A James, Routledge, London, pp. 1–8.

Fafard, P 2008, *Evidence and healthy public policy: insights from health and political sciences*, National Collaborating Centre for Healthy Public Policy, Montreal.

Fotel, T 2009, 'Marginalized or empowered? street reclaiming strategies and the situated politics of children's mobilities', *Geography Compass*, vol. 3, no. 3, pp. 1267–1280.

Freeman, C & Aitken-Rose, E 2005, 'Voices of youth: planning projects with children and young people in New Zealand local government', *Town Planning Review*, vol. 76, no. 4, pp. 375–400.

Freeman, C & Tranter, P 2011, *Children and their urban environment: changing worlds*, Earthscan, London.

Gleeson, B & Sipe, N 2006, 'Reinstating kids in the city' in *Creating Child Friendly Cities*, eds B Gleeson & N Sipe, Routledge, London, pp. 1–10.

Graham, A & Fitzgerald, R 2010, 'Children's participation in research: some possibilities and constraints in the current Australian research environment', *Journal of Sociology*, vol. 46, pp. 133–147.

Kearns, R & Collins, D 2006, 'Children in the intensifying city: lessons from Auckland's walking school buses' in *Creating child friendly cities: reinstating kids in the city*, eds B Gleeson & N Sipe, Routledge, London, pp. 105–120.

Kellett, M 2014, 'Images of childhood and their influence on research' in *Understanding research with children and young people*, eds A Clark, R Flewitt, M Hammersley & M Robb, Sage, Los Angeles, pp. 15–33.

Lennard, H & Crowhurst Lennard, S 1992, 'Children in public places: some lessons from European cities', *Children's Environments*, vol. 9, no. 2, pp. 37–47.

McDonell, J 2007, 'Neighborhood characteristics, parenting, and children's safety', *Social Indicators Research*, vol. 83, no. 1, pp. 177–199.

McKay, B 2015, 'Bill McKay: New design for Freyberg Place misses the mark', *New Zealand Herald*, September 15. Available from: www.nzherald.co.nz/nz/news/article.cfm?c_id=1&objectid=11512951.

NSW Commission for Children and Young People 2009, *Built4kids*, NSW Commission for Children and Young People, Sydney.

Nutley, S, Walter, I & Davies, H 2007, *Using evidence: how research can inform public services*, Policy Press, Bristol.

Percy-Smith, B 2010, 'Councils, consultations and community: rethinking the spaces for children and young people's participation', *Children's Geographies*, vol. 8, no. 3, pp. 107–122.

Percy-Smith, B & Burns, D 2013, 'Exploring the role of children and young people as agents of change in sustainable community development', *Local Environment*, vol. 18, no. 3, pp. 323–339.

Shier, H 2001, 'Pathways to participation: openings, opportunities and obligations', *Children & Society*, vol. 15, no. 2, pp. 107–117.

Spencer, C & Woolley, H 2000, 'Children and the city: a summary of recent environmental psychology research', *Child: Care, Health and Development*, vol. 26, no. 3, pp. 181–197.

Tisdall, E & Bell, R 2006, 'Included in governance? children's participation in "public" decision making' in *Children, young people and social inclusion: participation for what?* eds E Tisdall, J Davis, M Hill & A Prout, Policy Press, Bristol, pp. 103–119.

UNICEF 2010, *Child and youth participation resource guide*. Available from: www. unicef.org/adolescence/cypguide/resourceguide_planning.html.

PART 3

INSTRUMENTS WITH IMPACT

Legislation and policy

Policies and legislation, rules and regulations all define the constraints and set the parameters that surround any built environment setting. Some laws and policies control built environment outcomes intentionally, and sometimes unintentionally, for children and young people. As presented in these four chapters, sometimes this is a benefit for children and young people, but sometimes it undermines their opportunities to access and *use* the built environment.

When a state-level political process addresses the issue of children, young people and the built environment in a way that is well resourced and results in recommendations to be actioned, then considerable ground can be gained politically, environmentally and socially. This was the case of the NSW parliamentary inquiries described in Corkery's and Bishop's chapter. Importantly, the issue is given public prominence and remains on the political agenda for a long time, and at a high level; in this case, a number of years. This example illustrates the importance of having children's champions in strategic political positions to ensure that significant issues reach and remain on political agendas.

Helen Woolley's chapter makes a similar point, although her UK campaigners are grassroots champions. They are determined that specific issues are elevated to political agendas and acted upon. Although not in quite the same position of political power, Woolley's examples make the case for demonstrating how people power can have significant political sway. However, issues championed in this way are always more vulnerable to dismissal.

Maria Nordström's chapter also illustrates this vulnerability. She discusses the experience of using a Swedish policy instrument called a Child Impact Assessment, or CIA, designed to support the consideration of children's interests in urban planning and design projects, but implemented at the discretion of local municipal authorities. In her examples, once again it is the insistence of the local community that ensures positive outcomes for children. Another example of the power of passionate individuals to bring about change, and another illustration of just how vulnerable these successes are, in Swedish society in this instance.

Law academic Cathy Sherry discusses the impact of by-laws—part of a uniquely Australian property title instrument called strata title. By-laws have intentional and unintentional capacity to limit children's use of common space in medium- and high-density housing developments in Australia. Sherry draws attention to how powerful these seemingly benign, often community-drafted, pieces of legislation are if applied

(Source: Ben Danks)

to the letter of the law. Her examples illustrate how they can be used by residents to regulate the behaviour of neighbors—and their children—particularly when applied strictly, often in ways that unreasonably limit young people's use of common areas for the ordinary activities of childhood, such as playing or just simply hanging out.

CHAPTER 9

Accommodating children's activities in the shared spaces of high-density and master-planned developments

Cathy Sherry

Introduction

When we consider the impact of the built environment on children and whether facilities meet their needs, we are usually examining public open space—public parks, streets, wild spaces, outdoor malls. Public open space is essential for children in cities for two clear reasons: the space is *open*, allowing activities and a sense of freedom that is prohibited in the smaller, indoor spaces which abound in cities; and it is *public*, meaning that, at least theoretically, it is accessible by anyone and everyone.

It is easy to assume that open space in cities has always been public, but that is not necessarily the case. The great public parks of Europe typically began life as private royal hunting grounds; London's squares were almost all built as private gardens

Figure 9.1 Central Park, New York (Source: Kate Bishop)

accessible only by adjoining landowners (Summerson 1978), and this model was replicated overseas in developments like Gramercy Park in New York. However, the growth
of civil, democratic society from the seventeenth century onwards forced the aristoc-
racy to share their open urban spaces with the public and provided incentives for the
construction of new public open space. Central Park in New York was audacious, not
just in its scale and form, but in its commitment to provide recreational space for the
diverse population of the city (Miller 2003).

In London, during World War II, the iron railings of private squares were removed
to be used for ammunition, causing George Orwell to celebrate that "the squares
lay open, and their sacred turf was trodden by the feet of working-class children, a
sight to make dividend-drawers [ground landlords] gnash their false teeth" (Orwell
1944). In the post-War period, many railings were not replaced, leaving the squares
permanently accessible to the public. In Australia, strong government commitment
to freehold housing meant that private open space was always rare, and during the
twentieth century, suburb after suburb was developed with parks, playing fields and
bushland, in public ownership and accessible by all.

Commitment to public open space grew throughout the twentieth century, possibly
reaching its zenith in the 1970s. By the 1980s doubts began to grow about the ability
of government to fund a range of public services, from health to schools to parks and
other open space, and in an attempt to fill the gap, policies of privatization were implemented in the United Kingdom, the United States and to a lesser extent in Australia.

Privatization affected urban governance and the delivery of development and
construction projects in four main ways: contracting out, public-private partnerships,
service shedding and 'club forms'[1] of service delivery (Warner 2012). While the first
two are relatively common in Australia today, and the third remains rare, the fourth—
club forms of service delivery—is on the rise. This is the form of privatization that is

Figure 9.2
A typical, publicly
owned and
freely accessible
recreation space
in an Australian
suburb (Source: Kate
Bishop)

most likely to impact the availability of public open space for children, particularly in residential settings.

Privatization of open space through 'club forms of service delivery' has occurred in Australia as a result of a shift in residential development from freestanding houses in largely unregulated subdivisions, to medium- and high-density developments and master-planned estates. Changes in residential development have primarily been driven by state government urban consolidation policies, intended to combat suburban sprawl. However, the legal form used for new developments—strata and community title—has privatizing effects.

This chapter will begin by setting out the law in relation to high-density and master-planned estates in Australia. The law, more specifically property law, is significant because it determines the public or private nature of open space; and if the latter, who can use that space and how. By examining the law we can also identify some of the unintended and unanticipated social consequences of high-density and master-planned development. The chapter will then explore the predicted versus actual presence of children in high-density and master-planned estates, and the consequent provision or lack of provision of space for children's outdoor activities. Then, two specific case studies will be presented on the effect that legal form, in particular privately written by-laws, can have on children's activities in shared spaces. The chapter will conclude by discussing the necessity for planners, governments and courts to be more mindful of the profound social effects on children who reside with their families in privatized development.

The legal structure of apartments and master-planned estates

While it may seem counterintuitive, to explain the privatization of open space in Australia we have to start with high-density residential development. This is because high-density apartments are a rapidly increasing proportion of the housing market, and because even when new housing remains low- or medium-density, developers frequently use the same legal form that they use for high-density construction. That is, low-, medium- and high-density housing in Australia is increasingly being constructed as strata or community title.

Strata title—like condominiums in the United States, sectional title in South Africa, unit titles in New Zealand and the commonhold in the United Kingdom—allows the subdivision of buildings into individually owned freehold apartments and collectively owned common property. Common property is typically halls, foyers, lifts, gardens and car parks. Both individual apartments and common property are regulated by by-laws. These are not public law, like council by-laws, but rules chosen and agreed to by private citizens, specific to each building. By-laws are initially chosen by developers, who can either use 'model' by-laws included in the state's legislation, or bespoke by-laws drafted by their lawyer. Either way, with appropriate majority vote, by-laws can subsequently be changed by a building's body corporate, the governing body made up of all owners (not tenants). There is little legislative restriction on the content of by-laws in most states, with the only requirement that they relate to individual apartments or common property in some way (Sherry 2013). By-laws typically regulate noise, garbage disposal, parking and pets. But they can also be more detailed and intrusive: for example, regulating window coverings, balcony furniture and, importantly for our purposes, how and where children can play, with or without supervision.

Strata title legislation was first enacted in Australia in the early 1960s to facilitate apartment construction. By the late 1960s, Australian property developers wanted to be able to expand into the kind of master-planned estates they had seen in America: low-rise housing with small private yards, quiet cul-de-sac streets and commonly owned facilities, maintained and run by a private association of owners, a 'homeowner association' (McKenzie 1994). However, a divergence in the common law of Australia and United States made it impossible to create the necessary legal structures (Sherry 2014) and so developers pressured governments to solve the problem by extending the strata title legislation to low-rise subdivisions. This allowed for the subdivision of sub-urban areas into individually owned housing lots and collectively owned open space and infrastructure, all governed by a body corporate administering privately written by-laws, just like an apartment complex. Queensland was the first state to facilitate developers' desires, with legislation in the early 1970s, and other states eventually followed suit (Sherry 2014). In New South Wales, these subdivisions are known as 'community title'.[2] While some community title estates are low-rise housing, some contain a mix of low-, medium- and high-density, while others are a conglomeration of high-density strata schemes.

This new form of residential development has been adopted enthusiastically by developers and governments alike. Developers are eager to use community title, as extensive collectively owned property like pools, gyms and country clubs can be advertised as 'exclusive', 'prestigious' or 'resort-style living'. Low-rise developments are frequently marketed to families, with a neo-traditional emphasis on community, friendships and education.

Governments are enthusiastic about community title because it is a form of privatization through 'club service delivery', noted above. The body corporate is effectively a 'club' which people join by acquiring property in the estate. They have access to the assets of the club, such as roads, parks, sewers, bushland and sporting facilities, as well as services, such as telecommunications, social organization and street landscaping services, relieving government of the obligation to provide these goods publicly. Community title not only removes initial infrastructure costs from the public purse, but almost all costs in perpetuity, because all assets are privately owned, maintained and insured. The theory that has been propounded in the United States, although never explicitly in Australia, is that purchasers can 'shop' between different private residential estates, choosing the one that best provides the services and facilities they desire (Buchanan 1965; Foldvary 2002; Tiebout 1956).

The spread of community title in Australia is arguably privatization by stealth. The legal structure is extremely complicated and research suggests that many purchasers do not understand the complexity of the title they are buying (Goodman & Douglas 2010). It is likely that many purchasers do not appreciate the significance of these documents, nor do they fully understand that they have to collectively manage all open space, pay for it and insure it, although their use will be circumscribed by any developer-made or collectively agreed rules. While local and state governments are no doubt aware of the privatizing effect of community title and the benefit to their bottom lines, government has arguably not appreciated the social, economic and political consequences of privatized estates. This is consistent with research on 'privatopias' in the United States, where it has been argued that homeowner associations have created a host of unanticipated problems in urban management (McKenzie 1994, 2011).

One of the most significant problems in the United States, which is also present in Australia (Sherry 2013), is a failure by government and the judiciary to anticipate the implications of allowing private citizens to govern their neighbors via bodies corporate. Those implications are, first, that traditionally unregulated space within the home and minimally regulated public space outside the home have both become subject to detailed rules that govern behavior and use. Second, those rules are written by private citizens with no expertise in governance or land use, and no compulsion to act other than in their own interests.[3] Surveying half a century of privatized residential development in the United States, McKenzie (2011, p. 14) concluded that

> [one] point cannot be overemphasized: the entire institution of common interest housing rests on the volunteer directors, yet they are unpaid, untrained, often unqualified, and almost entirely unsupported by the governments whose work they are often doing.

This point is equally applicable to Australia. While strata and community title developments might be created by professional planners and approved by governments with reference to community needs, any open or recreational space that has been created for children's well-being will ultimately be privately owned and controlled by a body corporate, made up of citizens with no expertise in child development and no legal compulsion to consider children's well-being when writing rules for the use of shared open space. The two case studies presented below will illustrate this phenomenon, whereby the intended benefits of open space for children can effectively be nullified by private regulation restricting use.

Figure 9.3 Boys playing football in a common area (Source: Govorov Pavel/Shutterstock)

The presence of children in strata and community title developments

The extent to which children are impacted by the privatizing effects of strata and community title depends on their presence in these forms of housing. Low-rise community title estates on the urban fringe, like ordinary residential subdivisions in the same areas, are planned for and marketed to families with children, who continue to express strong preferences for freestanding, low-density housing (Yates 2001). As a result, there are significant numbers of children in these estates. For example, the new, predominantly community title residential developments on the northern end of the Gold Coast in Queensland are known as 'Nappy Valley' because of the exceptionally high numbers of young children.

Children's presence in strata title apartments is more complicated. Unlike Europe, where high-density housing estates were planned specifically for families, particularly in the post-War period, apartments were never considered ideal or even acceptable housing for families in Australia. Some low- and high-density apartments were built in the public housing sector in the twentieth century, but government remained equivocal about their benefits (Butler-Bowdon & Pickett 2007). In the much larger private housing sector, apartments constituted a minority of housing stock and were never planned or marketed to families (Butler-Bowdon & Pickett 2007).

In the late twentieth century, pursuant to state urban consolidation policies, apartment construction in Australia's largest cities boomed; however, this coincided with declining fertility and a sharp increase in smaller households. As a result, it was assumed that new apartment stock would be taken up by sole-person and couple households and that families would remain in the low-rise suburbs. As Woolcock et al. (2010, p. 183) note:

> Planners are planning for cities to accommodate singles, couples and the elderly. As far as the planners are concerned, family housing is already oversupplied in this new ageing city and needs little encouragement. As a consequence, contemporary strategic planning has almost become child-blind, with the new higher density centres being built essentially for the childless in mind.

'Child-blind' planning of new apartments is a continuation of a long-standing pattern in Australian apartment construction. While planners have been correct in anticipating a continued preference for low-rise, freestanding housing by families, the preference is not universal, nor can all families make choices that are consistent with their preference. As a result, there are increasing numbers of children living in apartments in Australian cities. For example, Easthope and Tice (2011) found that between 2001 and 2006, the proportion of couple families with children in the new high-density residential areas on Sydney's redeveloped Olympic site jumped from 13 percent to 31 percent, while the proportion of couples without children fell from 46 percent to 36 percent. Nearby, in a new high- and medium-density residential development called Liberty Grove, families with children now constitute the largest group on the estate, including a significant proportion of families in which one or both parents were born in China, Korea or India (Randolph et al. 2005). In addition to new developments, there are families with children living in Sydney's aging apartment stock, built in the pre- and post-War period. These families are predominantly low-income, recent migrant families with young children, renting their homes (Randolph 2006).

As Sydney's apartment stock, both old and new, was built without children in mind, the physical form of apartment buildings typically fails to meet children's needs. First, apartments are overwhelmingly one or two bedrooms, with larger three- or four-bedroom family apartments a rarity. Second, few have any outdoor play space. Many apartment buildings in Sydney were built by small builders, block by block, on former single housing sites, with little planning control (Butler-Bowdon & Pickett 2007). Consequently, buildings typically take up the entire site, with open space only left for cars.

The exception to this general rule are the new medium- and high-density developments that have been constructed on large disused industrial or infrastructure sites, pursuant to policies of spot densification. While these apartments remain overwhelmingly one and two bedroom, buildings have been more rationally positioned in relation to each other, with significant open space and facilities in between. Liberty Grove, the new residential development noted above, has two swimming pools, two tennis courts, a gymnasium, a basketball court, two playgrounds, two large parks, four small parks and a community hall serving a total population of 2,000 in 760 apartments.

While these contemporary apartment developments are a vast improvement on the largely unplanned construction of buildings on discrete, single housing blocks, the legal structure of these developments can present significant impediments to the use of open space and facilities. The individual apartment blocks are strata title and thus internally regulated by private by-laws, and the entire estate is invariably community title, making the parks and sporting facilities private, not public property, also regulated by by-laws. All of these by-laws can be written by the developer and subsequent community, with no reference to children's well-being.

Figure 9.4 Liberty Grove (Source: Hazel Easthope)

Case studies on by-laws restricting children's activities in shared spaces

It is axiomatic that play, in the broadest sense of the word, is essential to children's well-being and optimal development. There is a direct relationship between physically active play and children's health (Gleave & Cole-Hamilton 2012), particularly as a factor in avoiding childhood and adult obesity (Reilly & Kelly 2011). Play is essential for cognitive development, contributing to vocabulary, problem-solving skills, self-confidence, motivation and awareness of others. Imaginative play is crucial for lateral and creative thinking, and risk-taking play minimizes anxiety (Gleave & Cole-Hamilton 2012). In addition to playgrounds, children need private play spaces, away from parents' supervising eyes; private cubby houses, secret trees, even alleys are important for children to develop mastery over their own lives (Lester & Russell 2010). Finally, children need 'community play', that is, play in public spaces, which aids the formation of friendships and networks as well as helping children to learn the rules of social life in order to navigate unfamiliar environments and to develop public trust (Gleave & Cole-Hamilton 2012).

It is equally axiomatic that children must have *somewhere* to play and as noted above, in strata and community title developments, as well as their overseas counterparts, that space will be private property. It may be the private space of their own home which, if it is an apartment, is likely to be small with little or no outdoor space. Alternatively, the play space will be the collectively owned, but equally private property, of the strata or community scheme. All of that private property will be regulated by private by-laws.

Figure 9.5 Tear Drop Park, New York City (Source: Linda Corkery)

Kingsdene Mews

The litigation in *The Owners of 111 The Broadview Landsdale—Survey Strata Plan 38894 v Colavecchio* [2004] WASTR 15 (*'Colavecchio'*) provides a clear insight into the power that by-laws have to compromise children's play. The site of the dispute was Kingsdene Mews, a low-rise strata title estate in Perth, Australia with common-property grassed nature strips and a circular cul-de-sac road around a central lawn and garden. The grassed pavements and center lawn and garden were ideal open play space for children, and the cul-de-sac road was safe for riding bikes or skateboards. However, the by-laws for Kingsdene Mews included a blanket ban on children playing on *any* common property. While model by-laws often prohibit children playing in areas that might pose dangers, this by-law even prohibited children playing on the grassed pavements or central lawn. It prohibited all play, whether active or passive.

A resident owner alleged that a tenant's 8- and 10-year-old children had damaged gardens and made undue noise on common property and within their own yard. Ten owners supported the application and 10 opposed it, with the evidence of each camp revealing conflicting perceptions of appropriate use of property and varying perception of children's needs. Those supporting the application claimed to have been 'plagued' by the bouncing of basketballs, shouting and screaming, along with the playing of tennis on grassed areas, as well as repeated playing of popular songs. Other support-ers of the application complained about the children riding their bikes, chasing each other, and laughing and talking loudly. Opponents of the application argued that the children of the tenants "did nothing that any children their age could and should not have been doing". They noted that private yards were small, that it was reasonable for children to use the common property as a result, and that noise was an inevitable part of "children's healthy play" (*'Colavecchio'* 2004, p. 39).

The application was dismissed, but only because the evidence was conflicting and it was not clear if an owner could be fined for tenants' actions. There was no con-sideration of whether by-laws limiting or banning children's play might be harmful and should be disallowed as a result. In fairness to the decision-maker, the legislation gave him no power to consider the effect of private by-laws on children's, or anyone else's, well-being. Australian legislatures have assumed that it is entirely beneficial for communities to choose their own rules and have consequently placed few limits on communities' or developers' powers to write by-laws (Sherry 2013).

However, as the case demonstrates, developers and communities do not always choose wisely;[4] they can create rules that are inimical to children's well-being. With three-bedroom homes located in a suburban cul-de-sac, the development was clearly intended for families and public planning law would have required sufficient open space for recreation. However, as a strata title development, all of that space was privately owned and its benefits could be nullified by the private by-law-making power.

The case also highlights that choices about the multiple and conflicting uses of open space must be made. The complainants valued the open space for its visual amenity, while the children, and presumably their parents, valued the space for physi-cal recreation and socializing. The strata title legal structure allowed the developer (and subsequent owners with sufficient support) to determine which use prevailed, with no requirement to consider the objective value of each use and whether play, with the social, cognitive, physical and emotional benefits it provides to children, should be weighted higher.

Liberty Grove

Figure 9.6 Entrance to Liberty Grove (Source: Hazel Easthope)

The conflicting uses and benefits of open space are also evident in Liberty Grove, another community title scheme. Liberty Grove is a large master-planned estate, containing 12 medium- to high-density strata schemes, as well as extensive common property comprising pools, tennis and basketball courts, playgrounds and multiple parks.

Liberty Grove's by-laws include limited regulation of common-property open space. They reasonably ban 'organized' sports without written approval of the Executive Committee, and require children under 12 years to be accompanied by an adult in the pools.

Figure 9.7 Liberty Grove shared public space (Source: Hazel Easthope)

Figure 9.8
Overlays of internal
regulations (Source:
Hazel Easthope)

Not being a gated community, the by-laws also require the body corporate to allow members of the public to use the 'public open space' and 'communal open space' for 'passive recreation'. This provision was included as a condition of development consent and cannot be altered without the local council's approval, indicating that at least in the public planning stage and in relation to non-residents, the local council was mindful of the potential effect of by-laws on the use of open space. However, with little legal limit on a body corporate's power to alter other by-laws, in 2010 a reference to the *Liberty Grove Community Policies Handbook* was added to Liberty Grove's by-laws.

The *Handbook* provides that "Children under 13 must be accompanied and supervised by an adult at all times while using any of the community facilities on the estate" and "Supervision of children must be carried out by an adult resident of age 21 or older" (*Liberty Grove Community Policies Handbook* 2011, p. 7). The change was most likely inspired by liability concerns and a desire to reduce insurance premiums—insurance being a substantial burden of owning private property. The change no doubt met the needs of adults who could still use the space freely, at less cost, but not families and children. A group of 10- or 12-year-olds are not allowed to shoot hoops at the basketball court, kick a ball around the parks or play tag without supervision. As the by-law refers to 'using' any community facility, they are not even permitted to sit on the grass and talk. If their 20-year-old sister offered to watch them, this would not be sufficient, and the same applies to their non-resident grandfather. Liberty Grove has a privately imposed vehicle speed limit of 20 km an hour and even a cautious parent would likely let their 10- or 12-year-old go to the local park unsupervised. However, this is impermissible as a result of rules created by their neighbors.

Unlike the public planning process which addresses social needs and includes an objective of providing "convenient open space and recreational opportunities for the residents of multi-unit housing projects" (Liberty Grove DCP 2007, p. 10), there is no legal compulsion for the private body corporate to consider these issues or weigh the proven benefits of outdoor activity for children when creating rules regulating shared open space in the development. Despite the fact that parks and sporting facilities are essential for active play when children live in apartments, the body corporate is free to limit children's outdoor activities. Strata and community title legislation does not require the ever-growing number of bodies corporate to consider children's well-being when creating by-laws, nor does it allow courts or tribunals to review and repeal by-laws on the basis that they are harmful to children. As long as a community agrees to the by-law by appropriate majority, it is valid.

Conclusion

This chapter has documented the privatization of open space in Australia through the increase in medium- to high-density residential development. Although primarily motivated by policies of urban consolidation, the legal form of these developments—strata and community title—inevitably creates privately owned open space which will be regulated by private by-laws.

Owing to planners' assumptions that children will not live in high-density apartments, most strata schemes are built with negligible amounts of shared open space, let alone areas designated for children's use. However, even when development occurs on large master-planned estates and recreation space is included in accordance with public planning law, private by-laws can nullify the benefits of that space for children. There is almost no limit on the content of by-laws in most states and by-laws can and do ban or restrict children's activities. Further, because of simplistic assumptions by legislatures about the benefits of collectively and/or voluntarily agreed community rules, courts and tribunals are given no power to invalidate by-laws on the grounds that they are inimical to children's and thus the wider community's well-being.

If Australian cities continue to pursue policies of urban consolidation, we are going to have to think more critically and deeply about their impact on children. Planners and government will need to appreciate the consequences of the legal form that is being used to consolidate cities. Strata and community title do not simply pack more housing into smaller spaces, they are a form of 'club service delivery' and give private citizens the power to regulate their neighbors. Legislatures and courts are going to have to confront the reality that there are limits to the benefits of voluntarily chosen private rules. While it makes sense for people to control their own environment, given unlimited power to do so choices can be made that harm others. Finally, conflicts and choices in relation to land use are inevitable and if we value the well-being of children we need the legal means to prioritize children in those conflicts.

Notes

1   'Club goods theory' has its genesis in James Buchanan's seminal article, 'An economic theory of clubs' (Buchanan 1965). Buchanan was attempting to create a calculation for the optimal size of a club (that is, a voluntary group of people), to provide private goods or services. His ideas were taken up by economists, legal and public policy writers interested in the benefits of collective private, rather than public provision of goods and services.

2   While terminology varies around the country and across the globe, the term 'community title' will be used here to refer to master-planned estates with common property and a governing body corporate. 'Community title' is the equivalent of homeowner

associations or common interest developments in the United States. It is essential to differentiate these developments from master-planned estates that do not have any governing body or enforceable by-laws; these are still common in Australia.

3   In New South Wales, for example, courts have confirmed that when voting on a body corporate, individual owners are entitled to vote in their own interests: *Houghton v Immer (No 155) Pty Ltd* (1997) 44 NSWLR 46, 52-3.

4   The clearest demonstration of the harm that can be caused by unrestrained private regulation of land are the racially restrictive covenants that were endemic in the United States in the twentieth century, limiting land ownership and occupation to 'people of the Caucasian race' (McKenzie 1994, pp. 67–78).

References

Buchanan, JM 1965, 'An economic theory of clubs' *Economica 1*, vol. 32, no. 125, pp. 1–14.

Butler-Bowdon, C & Pickett, C 2007, *Homes in the sky*, Melbourne University Publishing, Carlton, Victoria.

'Colavecchio' 2004, *The Owners of 111 The Broadview Landsdale—Survey Strata Plan 38894 v Colavecchio* [2004] WASTR 1, [1]-[51].

Easthope, H & Tice A 2011, 'Children in apartments: implications for the compact city', *Urban Policy and Research*, vol. 29, no. 4, pp. 415–434.

Foldvary, F 2002, 'Proprietary communities and homeowner associations' in *The voluntary city: choice, community, and civil society*, eds DT Beito, P Gordon & A Tabarrok, University of Michigan Press, Ann Arbor, Michigan, pp. 305–338.

Gleave, J & Cole-Hamilton, I 2012, *A world without play: a literature review*, Play England, London, UK.

Goodman R & Douglas K 2010, 'Life in a master planned estate—community and lifestyle or conflict and liability?', *Urban Policy and Research*, vol. 28, no. 4, pp. 451–469.

Lester S & Russell W 2010, *Children's right to play: an examination of the importance of play in the lives of children worldwide*, Working Paper No. 57, Bernard van Leer Foundation, The Hague, The Netherlands.

Liberty Grove Community Policies Handbook, 2011. Available from: www.libertygrove.net.au/policies.

McKenzie, E 1994, *Privatopia: homeowner associations and the rise of residential private government*, Yale University Press, New York.

McKenzie, E 2011, *Beyond Privatopia: rethinking residential private government*, Urban Institute Press, Washington, DC.

Miller, SC 2003, *Central park: an American masterpiece*, Abrams, New York.

Orwell, G 1944, 'As I please', *Tribune*, 18 August.

Randolph, B 2006, *Children in the compact city: Fairfield as a suburban case study*, City Futures Research Center, Sydney, Australia.

Randolph, B, Holloway, D & Ruming, K 2005, *Social outcomes of residential development, Sydney Olympic Park, stage 1: local area analysis*, City Futures Research Center, Sydney, Australia.

Reilly JJ & Kelly J 2011, 'Long-term impact of overweight and obesity in childhood and adolescence on morbidity and premature mortality in adulthood: systematic review', *International Journal of Obesity*, vol. 35, pp. 891–898.

Sherry, C 2013, 'Lessons in personal freedom and functional land markets: what strata and community title can learn from traditional doctrines of property', *University of New South Wales Law Journal*, vol. 36, no. 1, pp. 280–315.

Sherry, C 2014, 'Land of the free and home of the brave? the implications of United States homeowner association law for Australian strata and community title', *Australian Property Law Journal*, vol. 23, pp. 94–121.

Summerson, J 1978, *Georgian London*, Penguin Books, London.
Tiebout CM 1956, 'A pure theory of local expenditures', *Journal of Political Economy*, vol. 4, no. 5, pp. 416–424.
Warner ME 2012, 'Privatization and urban governance: the continuing challenges of efficiency, voice and integration', *Cities*, vol. 20, Suppl. 2, pp. S38–S43.
Woolcock, G, Gleeson, B & Randolph, B 2010, 'Urban research and child-friendly cities: a new Australian outline', *Children's Geographies*, vol. 8, no. 2, pp. 177–192.
Yates, J 2001, 'The rhetoric and reality of housing choice: the role of urban consolidation', *Urban Policy and Research*, vol. 19, no. 4, pp. 491–527.

CHAPTER 10

Every Child Matters

Policies and politics that influence children's experience of outdoor environments in England

Helen Woolley

Introduction

Policy frameworks have a major impact on practice in different areas of society, including the urban outdoor environments that children use or might use in their daily lives. In England, policy is set at a national level by government, is sometimes accompanied by funding programs and delivery mechanisms, and is then interpreted and implemented by local authorities and practitioners. Whether any outcomes fully reflect the original intention of a policy and the policy-makers may depend on the instruments of funding, delivery organizations and the commitment of specific individuals who remain vulnerable to changes in political priorities.

In recent years, the most significant change in English policy relating to children took place following the election of the (New) Labour government in 1997, with the introduction of the Sure Start program for early childhood, and then the Every Child Matters agenda (Department for Education 2003), which was driven by child protection issues. Prior to Every Child Matters, a range of policies existed which could influence children's use of outdoor environments, including travel to school, home zones, anti-social behavior orders, green and open spaces, and play policies (Woolley 2006). Two sectors have predominantly championed the view that society should support child friendly outdoor environments: the play sector and the green and open spaces sector. Neither of these are statutory services, which means that unlike the statutory services of education and housing, local authorities are not legally bound to provide or nominate a budget for them. Nevertheless, these two sectors have driven the development of policy and generated funding for a range of programs which have sought to provide more child friendly outdoor environments in England, building on parts of the Every Child Matters agenda. This chapter will explain two key policy areas—travel to school and home zones—which existed prior to and during the development of Every Child Matters; and will then discuss the influence of the green and open spaces and play sectors in the first decades of the twenty-first century. In exploring these two particular sectors, the aim is to illustrate how important passionate activists have been in the development of policy at the national level, and how this has impacted outdoor environments for children in England.

Two key policies: Travel to school and home zones

Travel to school

Walking to school is one way that children can experience and learn about their urban environments on a daily basis. For many years the number of children walking to both primary and secondary schools in England decreased: between 1971 and 1990 the number of 7- and 8-year-olds allowed to walk to school by themselves reduced from 80 percent to 9 percent (Hillman & Adams 1992). In response, and with a desire to reverse this trend, a number of policy interventions have been put in place over a period of years. These included a *Transport White Paper* (Department of the Environment, Transport and the Regions 1998) and a *Travel to School Initiative* (TSI) (Department for the Environment, Transport and the Regions 2010), the latter accompanied by a USD240 million program for School Travel Plans and School Travel Advisors. The aim has been to reduce the numbers of children being driven to school by encouraging safer routes for walking and cycling and increasing the use of public transport. In some, mostly rural, locations where land is more available, new safe routes to schools were developed.

Initiatives in urban areas included construction of bicycle shelters and distribution of high-visibility vests for children to wear on 'walking buses', where parents escort a group of children, picking them up along the way to school. No overall significant changes could be identified in numbers of children walking to school as a result of the TSI; however, the national policy and associated funding was instrumental in motivating schools to take up the walking to school agenda (Department for Transport 2012). The conclusion seems to be that, despite a range of policy and associated funding initiatives over a period of years, there has been no great increase in the number of

Figure 10.1
Children walking and cycling to school has been encouraged by various policies (Source: Helen Woolley)

children walking to school in England. This deprives children of experiencing their neighborhood and developing confidence in moving around a familiar environment.

Home zones

The places of play for children in residential areas include courtyards, communal gardens, parks, nearby wild areas, car parks, garage roofs and sidewalks (Woolley 2007). The street is another place where children will play if the road design, traffic patterns and neighborhood culture allow them to (Woolley 2003). During the last 50 years, some housing developments and social norms have not supported this and a campaign for home zones was led by the Children's Play Council and SUSTRANS (SUStainable TRANSport). Key aims of the home zone concept are that priority should be given to social activities, including children's play, rather than cars, and this is expressed in the design of the physical environment. Lobbying resulted in the government introducing a Home Zone Challenge Fund of USD46 million in 2001, providing for the retrofitting of streets in a number of existing housing areas.

The process of developing home zones was particularly important in this program with an expectation that communities would be involved throughout the process. The resultant schemes did not always include specific pieces of play equipment but often provided a safe space within a street where children could play. In some schemes there were concerns about teenagers being on the streets (Department for Transport 2005) and this was seen as a social problem rather than the result of a lack of alternate facilities for teenagers. A London Home Zone scheme was initiated in 2004 when legislation was in place but funding opportunities were not available nationally. Projects took longer than expected, due to the challenges of involving communities, and they were resource intensive. Despite this, some benefits were identified which included a stronger sense of community, children playing more in the street and adults considering that the streets can be safe places for children's play (Gill 2007).

Figure 10.2 Staiths Home Zone in Gateshead in the northeast of England shows that play can be accommodated (Source: Mike Biddulph)

The two policy areas of travel to school and home zones were mainly driven by people in the play or transport sectors. The home zone approach of shared surfaces and priority for pedestrians, including supporting children's play in the outdoor environment, was also supported by academics and practitioners. These two policy areas continue to be implemented to some extent but only where there is a local desire. Other policy issues affecting children's outdoor environments have followed in the two sectors of green and open spaces and play, and the discussion will now turn to these.

Activists to researchers: the green space sector

In the final years of the twentieth century and the first decade of the twenty-first, both the green and open space sector and the play sector promoted children's outdoor environments in England. Reflecting on these years, it is evident that there were similarities in the processes and activities of both sectors. Driven by passionate activists, they were committed to gathering evidence and developing policy which underpinned funding programs and instruments for delivery. But eventually, major changes resulted in the removal of policies, leaving the passionate activists without frameworks for action.

Urban parks and green spaces support many opportunities for children's outdoor play and the decline of these open spaces during the latter half of the twentieth century stimulated lobbying among park managers and others who were passionate about the benefits that such spaces and facilities provide. There was also concern that funding to this sector had declined over a period of years. It was as if politicians and society had forgotten the many benefits of urban parks and green spaces. In 1999, many of these green space activists came together to form the Urban Parks Forum, later called Green Space. It soon became clear that a lack of evidence was a serious barrier to policy development and investment. This lack of research evidence was initially addressed from two directions, one of which was internal and the other external to the urban parks and green sector.

Demos, a think tank which addresses social issues, became convinced of the importance of urban green spaces through their work on cities. They undertook a comprehensive research project resulting in the publication *Park Life* (Greenhalgh & Worpole 1995). This study explored some of the issues of use, perception, safety, and management of neighborhood and town parks, and specific types of urban open spaces, including commons, cemeteries, school playing fields, children's playgrounds, allotments, urban woodlands and abandoned wasteland. Suggestions for improvements included placing urban green space on the government's emerging urban regeneration agenda, and channeling investment into these urban assets from the National Lottery, which had been established by the Conservative government in 1993.

Another key piece of research undertaken within the sector resulted in the *Public Park Assessment* (PPA) (Urban Parks Forum 2001), which provided data measuring two main issues: the declining quality of urban parks and green spaces and the decrease in funding available to the sector. Quality of urban green space was reported to have declined in nearly 40 percent of the stock, while a cumulative underspend of USD2 billion during the preceding 20 years was identified.

As the twentieth century drew to a close, both investigations provided baseline evidence to support the lobbying efforts of activists and professionals, who urged the government to acknowledge the value of urban outdoor environments for society, and particularly for children. The importance of urban parks in supporting children's outdoor play was also acknowledged by a government Select Committee on Town and Country Parks in 1999. One response was that the National Lottery, through its Heritage Lottery Fund, established the Urban Parks Program (UPP), which invested over USD1 billion in urban parks and green spaces in its first 18 years (Neal 2014). Within the first 10 years of the UPP, the most frequently funded aspect of park regeneration was playgrounds.

Activists to researchers: the play sector

During the twentieth century the play sector in England included many voluntary organizations and individuals. The Children's Play Council (CPC), established in 1988, sought to raise awareness of the importance of children's play and the need for better play opportunities and services. Like the green space sector, the play sector was driven by individuals and groups who were passionate about the importance of children's play but lacked the evidence to support their claims that play was important in children's daily lives. In response to this, the CPC, in partnership with others, assembled evidence on how children benefit from play opportunities and how such benefits can be supported in play services and spaces. National government supported the publication of the evidence in the document *Best Play* (CPC 2000).

Soon after this the CPC joined forces with the New Policy Institute, another policy think tank. They produced two publications consisting of research findings, reviews of relevant local authority policies, submissions from play workers, outputs from consultation activities with children and parents. Using this material, they drafted policies and proposed strategies for ways forward (Cole-Hamilton & Gill 2002; Cole-Hamilton et al. 2002). Based on the mounting evidence, in mid-2001 the National Lottery pledged USD300 million for the improvement of children's play opportunities, confirming a general election commitment made by the Labour party.

Concurrently, the CPC published *More than Swings and Roundabouts* (CPC 2002), a guide for creating new or improving existing outdoor environments. CPC aimed to expand the consideration of children's outdoor environments beyond that of designated playgrounds. The advisory group for the guide was not restricted to people from the play sector; there were individuals and representatives from local authorities and non-governmental organizations from the green and open space sector. This was the beginning of a productive collaboration between the two sectors.

Evidence to policy: the establishment and structure of CABE Space

In the late 1990s, the national government established an Urban Taskforce to explore how and where 4 million new homes could be accommodated. The Taskforce's report touched on the issue of urban green spaces but did not focus on them (Department for the Environment, Transport and the Regions 1999). Ongoing lobbying using the evidence base from the *Park Life* study, the PPA publications, and the Select Committee into Town and Country Parks, pressured the government to acknowledge the need to address the provision of urban parks and green spaces, along with more housing. The government responded by establishing an Urban Green Spaces Taskforce that included experts and practitioners from both the green space and the play sectors, continuing their collaboration.

One of the Taskforce's recommendations was the establishment of a national agency that would address the urgent questions of green space and urban park provision. CABE Space was subsequently established in 2003 as an advisory agency on outdoor environments, situated within the original organization: the Center for Architecture and the Built Environment (CABE). CABE Space was funded by the Office of the Deputy Prime Minister, elevating these issues to a new level in national government (Office of the Deputy Prime Minister 2002a). CABE Space's staff and advisors included some of those passionate activists mentioned earlier. They worked with local authorities to support the development of green and open strategies, another recommendation from the Urban Green Spaces Taskforce. A number of the advisors were selected in 2006 to work with Play England to support the development of play strategies for all of England.

Alongside the Urban Green Spaces Taskforce and establishment of CABE Space, other relevant planning and funding activities occurred. Most notable was the revision to *Planning Policy Guidance 17 Open Space, Sport and Recreation* (PPG17), shifting the balance of active sport and recreation to acknowledge the many benefits of informal urban green spaces, particularly for children (Office of the Deputy Prime Minister 2002b).

Evidence to policy: the establishment of Play England

The Director of the Children's Play Council was seconded to work alongside the Minister for Culture to develop a strategy for the expenditure of the USD300 million that had been pledged by the National Lottery for children's play. *Getting Serious About Play* (Department for Culture Media and Sport 2004) was published three years after the lottery funding was pledged. A revision to the workings of the National Lottery resulted in further delays and in 2006, five years after the money was pledged, the BIG Lottery launched a USD240 million initiative for children's play, providing three funding streams. One stream supported the establishment of Play England within the National Children's Bureau through March 2011. The second stream was for the development of *Planning for Play* (CPC 2006), and the establishment of Play England with staffed offices in the nine English regions. The third stream of funding was directed towards volunteer and community organizations. By this time, CABE Space advisors were experienced in supporting local authorities to develop strategies, and it was expected that this experience would feed into the development of play strategies.

Building on the Every Child Matters agenda, the Labour government did something unique in 2007: it confirmed the importance of play in their policy agenda by introducing the first ever national Play Strategy for England (Department for Children, Schools and Families 2008). In doing this, the government

Figure 10.3
The National Play Strategy, 2008 (Source: Department for Culture, Media and Sport)

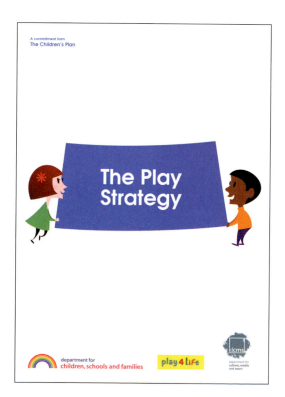

Figure 10.4
A playground in a housing area improved under the government's Play Pathfinder program (Source: Helen Woolley)

asserted their intention to make England the best place in the world for children to grow up. The strategy was accompanied by a USD360 million funding program between 2008 and 2011 for the creation of new and/or improved outdoor public play spaces and environments. The money was allocated to local authorities. Play England provided project services and support to the local authorities. Two key publications accompanied the program, providing guidance on design (Shackell et al. 2008) and on the risks and benefits inherent in play (Ball et al. 2008).

Ultimately, the program that had the most potential for cultural change towards child friendly outdoor environments was the Play Shaper program. Play Shaper aimed to deliver training for built environment professionals—that is, planners, landscape architects, architects and park managers—together with police, local authorities and their partners, to create more child friendly environments and communities. The Play Shaper program was funded for two and a half years between 2008 and 2011 and led by Play England in partnership with Playwork Partnerships and SkillsActive (Day et al. 2011).

Activists, evidence, policy, funding sources and service users: key components to child friendly spaces

A series of key components can be identified as being important through the process of improving the situation for child friendly outdoor environments in England in the first decades of the twenty-first century. These key components can be identified as *activists*, *evidence*, *policy*, *funding sources* and *service users*. These have driven the agenda in both the urban parks and green space and the play sectors. Alongside these drivers have been the *delivery organizations*: CABE Space for the green space sector and Play England for the play sector.

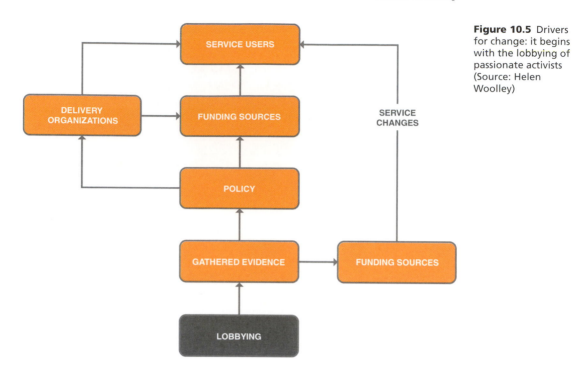

Figure 10.5 Drivers for change: it begins with the lobbying of passionate activists (Source: Helen Woolley)

Activists: passionate about their sector

The first key component that makes anything happen is an energetic and committed group of individuals and organizations—sometimes voluntary, sometimes paid—who remain completely dedicated to the aims of their sector and the benefits it provides, both directly for children and indirectly to society as a whole. Both sectors had these.

Gathering evidence to support the development of policy, funding and delivery organizations

The way to attract political attention in government is to use evidence. In both scenarios discussed, this was supported by each sector using partners within and external to their sector. Within each sector this brought together a variety of individuals, voluntary organizations, local authorities, non-governmental organizations and small commercial companies. During this evidence-gathering stage contributors from outside of each sector included think tanks, the National Lottery and some government departments. In both sectors, the findings and recommendations led to the development of national policy and mechanisms for implementing the policy. For the urban parks, green and open space sector, this resulted in the establishment of CABE Space.

The play sector had an established evidence base, but the funding it hoped to leverage from the National Lottery was delayed for several years. When the funding was forthcoming, one thing it did was to support the establishment of the delivery organization, Play England. The lottery funding was followed by a significant policy in the Children's Play Strategy and a large funding program directly from government. Reflection on this process also reveals an important link between the two sectors.

Users: impact on children in the urban built environment

The final piece of the story should relate to the children who use these urban environments and the impact of these policies and programs on their experiences and opportunities. There is no one piece of evidence that reveals whether the actions and outcomes of the activists, research, policy or funding have resulted in either more child friendly outdoor environments, or an increased use of those environments. There are, however, indicators of what these processes have achieved through evaluations of specific processes and outcomes, mainly generated by the play sector. An interim review of the work of CABE Space (National Audit Office 2006) focused mainly on the issue of green and open space strategies and did not address children's outdoor environments.

Various evaluations were undertaken of the work that took place under the auspices of Play England. The introduction of play rangers, facilities and improvements to spaces through the BIG Lottery Children's Play Program were generally well received, although concerns were raised about the ongoing sustainability of these services with only a few of the projects identifying ongoing revenue sources or social enterprises as a way forward (Smith & Day 2011). In addition, some of the new and improved outdoor play spaces would not have taken place without the Children's Plan policy and associated funding program (Frearson et al. 2013). Play England also influenced a stronger focus for play in policy areas such as education, health and physical activity. Its two publications, *Design for Play* and *Managing Risk in Play*, were widely used by stakeholders in 2009 to support work under the Children's Plan (Blades & Gill 2010).

Evaluation of the Play Shaper program, undertaken before its completion, reveals that despite a series of initial challenges some benefits were achieved including an increased knowledge of play, with this translating into strategic plans for individual officers' service areas (Day et al. 2011). This program, embedded within the work of Play England, was possibly the biggest opportunity to change the culture beyond playgrounds and skate parks to more child friendly outdoor environments, but to some extent was a missed opportunity because of the approach taken and delays in starting the program.

From 2010 to 2016: activists to carry the banner forward

As noted earlier, changes in political priorities can influence practice delivery. This is dramatically evident from the situation with child friendly spaces in England. Following 10 years of strong political support from the Labour government, sweeping changes took place after the 2010 general election which brought in a Conservative/Liberal Democrat administration. The new government immediately enacted a range of financial measures to address the country's deficit budget and reduce the bureaucracy.

These measures affected policy, funding and delivery of many organizations and significantly impacted the non-statutory services of the green and open space and play sectors. CABE Space was abolished, and a remnant of their work program was embedded into the Design Council. Play England's funding was not extended and all nine regional offices were abolished, while the London office was reduced to a minimal staff. Play England remains, completely independent of the National Children's Bureau but a member organization. Currently, it has limited staff, and is dependent upon funding for short, time- and site-specific projects, such as promoting 'nature play' and 'street play' with other partners.

The new coalition government sought to reduce the bureaucracy of the planning system and introduce more neighborhood-led initiatives through the instrument of the National Planning Policy Framework. There are pros and cons to this approach, but it has resulted in the abandonment of a range of national policies significant for children's interests, including Every Child Matters, PPG17, the Children's Plan and the Play Strategy.

The current Conservative government, elected with a small majority, is driving their agenda forward without the moderating effects of the Liberal Democrats. So, with no policy, funding programs or delivery organizations where does this leave the agenda for child friendly outdoor environments in the twenty-first century in England? In reality it leaves the country with some improvements in service, although since 2010 many of these have been impacted by the massive funding reductions to local authorities, which in some instances has seen facilities being closed resulting in poorer provision. In other instances, it has initiated exploration for alternative models of funding and delivery. There is, of course, the legacy of high-quality publications from both CABE Space and Play England. Beyond this exists the ongoing fervor of the activists who are still passionate about their sectors. Many of those who were lobbying in the late 1990s are still actively engaged in some way. For the foreseeable future, however, there is no evidence that the Conservative administration will review its approach to the lack of policy, funding and structures for these two sectors.

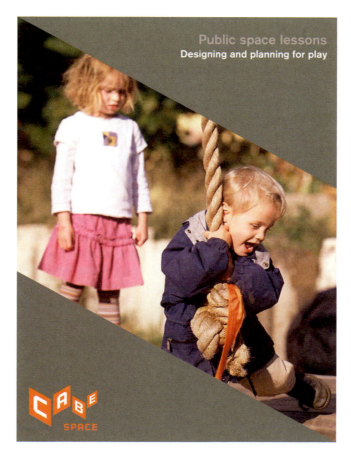

Figure 10.6
Designing and Planning for Play: one example of the legacy of publications (Source: Design Council)

An All Party Parliamentary Group (APPG) on A Fit and Healthy Childhood, which includes Members of Parliament from different political persuasions and many experts, is seeking to influence the new government, and a report from the APPG Play Working Party is currently being finalized. Otherwise, the main way forward will rest with the activists as they work together in networks at the national level but also as they take up the continuing need for children, parents, families, schools, communities, built environment professionals, politicians and funders to more fully understand the many benefits of play and the range of outdoor environments that can support children's activities. Only time will tell the extent to which this will lead to improved and more child friendly outdoor environments in England.

Conclusion

The experience in England in the past 15–20 years demonstrates that passionate activists alone were not able to improve the situation for child friendly outdoor environments in England. To take forward this agenda an evidence base was needed in order to convince national politicians of the importance of both play and green and open spaces and the relationship between the two for child friendly outdoor environments. Following from and accompanying policy development, funding sources were made available to support specific programs for play. Some of these programs were more successful than others; many outdoor play environments were improved but changes to the underlying culture of supporting child friendly outdoor environments was not embedded and sustained.

A lesson from this is that one sector alone cannot change the culture to create and sustain outdoor environments for children. The play and green and open space sectors worked relatively well together, but the relationship could have been improved with closer collaboration. If there is a desire to continue to move towards child friendly outdoor environments, then the partnership needs to reach further afield to engage with other built environment professionals including planners, highway engineers, landscape architects and architects. In addition, there is a need to work with those who are responsible for maintaining and managing urban outdoor environments, such as housing providers, town center managers, police, community organizations, schools and families.

References

Ball, D, Gill, T & Speigel, B 2008, *Managing risk in play provision: implementation guide*, Department for Children, Schools and Families, Nottingham. Available from: www.playengland.org.uk/resources/managing-risk-in-play-provision-implementation-guide.aspx.

Blades, R & Gill, C 2010, *Evaluation of Play England: a summary of years one to four*, National Children's Bureau, London.

Children's Play Council 2000, *Best play: what play provision should do for children*, National Playing Fields Association, London.

Children's Play Council 2002, *More than swings and roundabouts: planning for outdoor play*, National Children's Bureau, London.

Children's Play Council 2006, *Planning for play: guidance on the development and implementation of a local play strategy*, National Children's Bureau/Big Lottery Fund, London. Available from: www.playengland.org.uk/resources/planning-for-play.aspx.

Cole-Hamilton, I & Gill, T 2002, *Making the case for play: building policies and strategies for school-aged children*, National Children's Bureau, London. Available from: http://npi.org.uk/publications/children-and-young-adults/making-case-play-gathering-evidence/.

Cole-Hamilton, I, Harrop, A & Street, C 2002, *Making the case for play: gathering the evidence*, New Policy Institute, London. Available from: http://npi.org.uk/publications/children-and-young-adults/making-case-play-gathering-evidence/.

Day, L, Smith, N & Barham, J 2011, *Play Shaper evaluation: a final report to Play England*, Ecorys, Birmingham. Available from: www.playengland.org.uk/resources/play-shaper-evaluation-report.aspx.

Department for Children, Schools and Families with Department for Culture, Media and Sport 2008, *The play strategy*, Department for Children, Schools and Families, Nottingham. Available from: http://webarchive.nationalarchives.gov.uk/20130401151715/http://www.education.gov.uk/publications/eOrderingDownload/The_Play_Strategy.pdf.

Department for Culture Media and Sport 2004, *Getting serious about play*, Department for Culture Media and Sport, London.

Department for Education 2003, *Every child matters*, Departments for Education and Culture, Media and Sport, London. Available from: www.education.gov.uk/consultations/downloadableDocs/EveryChildMatters.pdf.

Department for the Environment, Transport and the Regions 1998, *A new deal for transport: better for everyone, the government white paper on the future of transport*, The Stationery Office, London.

Department for the Environment, Transport and the Regions 1999, *Towards an urban renaissance: the final report of the Urban Taskforce*, Department of the Environment, Transport and the Regions, London.

Department for the Environment, Transport and the Regions 2010, *An evaluation of the Travelling to School Initiative program final report, October 2010 Executive Summary*. Available from: www.gov.uk/government/uploads/system/uploads/attachment_data/file/4479/travelling-to-school-executive-summary.pdf.

Department for Transport 2005, *Home zones: challenging the future of our streets*, Department for Transport, London.

Department for Transport 2012, An Evaluation of the Travelling to School Initiative Programme Final Report, October 2010. Available from: www.gov.uk/government/uploads/system/uploads/attachment_data/file/4479/travelling-to-school-executive-summary.pdf.

Frearson, M, Johnson, S & Clarke, C 2013, *Findings from the Play Builders 2009 implementation case studies*, SQW, London. Available from: www.sqw.co.uk/files/7413/9059/0629/Play_Pathfinders_and_Play_Builders_Program_Evaluation_RR_231.pdf.

Gill, T 2007, *Can I play out . . .? lessons from London Play's home zones project*, London Play, London.

Greenhalgh, L & Worpole, K 1995, *Park Life*, Comedia and Demos, Bournes Green, Stroud.

Hillman, M & Adams, J 1992, 'Children's freedom and safety', *Children's Environments*, vol. 9, no. 2, pp. 10–22.

National Audit Office 2006, *Enhancing urban green space*, The Stationery Office, London. Available from: www.nao.org.uk/report/enhancing-urban-green-space/.

Neal, P 2014, *State of UK public parks 2014 research report to the Heritage Lottery Fund*, Heritage Lottery Fund, London. Available from: www.hlf.org.uk/state-uk-public-parks#.VXhSZUbqm2k.

Office of the Deputy Prime Minister 2002a, *Green spaces, better places: the final report of the Urban Green Spaces Taskforce*, Office of the Deputy Prime Minister, London.

Office of the Deputy Prime Minister 2002b, *Planning Policy Guidance 17: open space, sport and recreation*, Office of the Deputy Prime Minister, London.

Shackell, A, Butler, N, Doyle, P & Ball, D 2008, *Design for play: a guide to creating successful play spaces*, Department for Children, Schools and Families with Department for Culture, Media and Sport, London.

Smith, N & Day, L 2011, *Children's play program evaluation: final report to the BIG Lottery Fund*, Ecorys, Birmingham.

Urban Parks Forum 2001, *Public park assessment: a survey of local authority owned parks focusing on parks of historic interest*, Department for Transport, Local Government and the Regions, Heritage Lottery Fund, The Countryside Agency and English Heritage, London.

Woolley, H 2003, *Urban open spaces*. Spon Press, London.

Woolley, H 2006, 'Freedom of the city: contemporary issues and policy influences on children and young people's use of public open space in England', *Children's Geographies*, vol. 4, no. 1, pp. 45–59.

Woolley, H 2007, 'Where do the children play? how policies can influence practice', *Municipal Engineer*, vol. 160, pp. 89–95.

Online resources

CABE Space, http://webarchive.nationalarchives.gov.uk/20110118095356/http://www.cabe.org.uk/resources.

Play England, www.playengland.org.uk/news/2010/05/big-lottery-fund-support-for-play-england.aspx.

CHAPTER 11

How are Child Impact Assessments used in planning child friendly environments? The Swedish experience

Maria Nordström

Introduction

Housing developments in urban areas of Sweden have grown rapidly during the last 10 years after a period of slow development since the mid-1970s. Many children will grow up in these new developments. This chapter describes the Swedish situation, where legislation no longer protects children's environmental interests in urban planning but where, in the past, child impact assessments (CIAs) were a way to do so. CIAs are defined here as the process in which children's needs and interests in the physical environment are investigated to determine whether and how they might be affected by proposals for changes brought about by urban development. An example of a successful CIA will be given in this chapter but there will also be a discussion of obstacles and difficulties when doing CIAs. As has been pointed out by Roger Hart and Adrian Voce, work on children's rights stresses formal procedures often at the cost of practical results and accomplishments (Hart 2015; Voce 2015). Also, as this chapter will show, having the procedural mechanism of CIAs is no guarantee that they will be realized, and pressure from powerful institutions like the media is sometimes needed to ensure they are carried out.

The example presented in this chapter will hopefully inspire planners in other countries to start using CIAs, and it invites those already doing so to compare their experiences with those in Sweden. It might also be useful for researchers investigating CIAs theoretically.

Background: The UN Convention on the Rights of the Child and Sweden

The UN Convention on the Rights of the Child (UNCRC, 1989) represents the culmination of several decades of international efforts to gain recognition of children's rights. The UNCRC provides the framework and a basis from which CIAs were developed. Article 3 of the UNCRC states that "the best interests of the child" shall be a guiding principle of the UN Convention and shall be a primary consideration in all actions concerning children. How can children's best interests be known? Children can be asked to express them themselves and their interests can be articulated by adults representing children's interests, who have knowledge of children in general and specific knowledge of those children who will be affected by a specific action. It is particularly important to stress the last provision; that is, that the children who will be affected by a specific development are the ones who should be consulted and asked to participate in a CIA.

Although the UNCRC is a remarkable milestone, as a legal document the UN Convention cannot be enforced directly. For this to happen each signatory nation has to formally incorporate the UNCRC in its domestic legislation and many have not done so, including Sweden. The Committee on the Rights of the Child has noted the lack of Sweden's "formal recognition of the Convention as Swedish law" and of a decision that "the Convention should always prevail when provisions of domestic law conflict with the Convention" (Committee on the Rights of the Child 2015, p. 3). In this light, CIAs can be seen as a means of implementing the UNCRC.

Understanding and implementing children's rights in municipal planning in Sweden

Sweden was eager to ratify the UNCRC in 1990 and nine years later the Parliament passed a bill called *A strategy for the implementation of the CRC in Sweden*. The aim of this strategy was to implement the UNCRC at all levels of society. Municipalities responded positively and some started out with impressive ambitions to apply the UN Convention to all decisions where they found children's issues to be at stake. However, these ambitions turned out to be difficult to implement except in two sectors of Swedish society: urban and traffic planning.

Evidence of a child friendly attitude in urban and traffic planning can be seen in housing areas and road systems built during the twentieth century. Schools and playgrounds were built within walking distance of children's homes in housing areas from the 1950s until the mid-1970s. Pedestrian paths and bike lanes were constructed to separate children's walkways from those of vehicular traffic (see Mårtensson & Nordström in this volume). Research by Swedish psychologist Stina Sandels influenced the development of the traffic-safe planning policy for children in the 1960s. Her experiments showed that, due to the level of their cognitive development, children 12 years and younger are unable to handle complicated traffic situations (Sandels & Hartley 1975). Traffic at that time was transforming Swedish society and Sandels's research was a reaction to the high rates of children's traffic-related injuries and deaths. Her research findings served as a basis for revising Swedish traffic planning policy, which has resulted in a very high level of traffic safety for children (Gummesson 2007; Road Safety Annual Report 2015).

What are child friendly environments?

Child friendly environments are places where children like to be and to play. The physical environment is where children spend their everyday lives and where their physical, social and emotional development takes place, largely through play (Fagen 2011). Children know their immediate surroundings in a detailed way because of their concrete outlook on life. The interaction taking place between the individual child and what surrounds him or her is the result of the activities and interests of the child, as well as of the qualities of the environment and how adults let children use that environment (Nordström 2010).

The concept of 'child friendly environments' is used to draw attention to the fact that environmental qualities are important for children—something that children, especially young children, cannot express very well themselves. The concept is also used to stress the fact that children's perspectives on and experiences of the environment are different from those of adults (Noschis 2008). Adults speaking up for children's environments must not only have good general knowledge of important environmental qualities for children but they must also know which children will be affected by the proposed environmental changes, and how they will be affected. Adults must find out from children how they experience and use their local surroundings at the time of planning a project, and they must also have a detailed understanding of the physical environment where the children who will be affected live, play or go to school.

What are Child Impact Assessments?

A CIA is defined here as the process through which children's interests in the physical environment are investigated to learn whether and how they might be affected by urban planning proposals. The aim of CIAs is to support children's interests in, and need for, supportive environments and environmental experiences. The full process is presented in a document, called the CIA document. The CIA document is intended to be used as basic data in urban planning. In international literature, CIAs are sometimes likened to Social Impact Assessments, SIAs, but in Sweden they have generally been seen as a special process including and addressing the interests and needs of children (Faith-Ell 2015; Svensson 2011).

Swedish child friendly planning in a stage of transition

The Swedish Transport Administration, Trafikverket, has for a long time been the leading actor in Sweden in supporting children's participation in planning, a development related to the previously mentioned traffic safety policy (www.trafikverket.se). Since the early 1990s, the Administration, at that time called the Swedish Road Administration, Vägverket, has cooperated with schools and municipalities in road planning projects, adopting the child friendly perspective of the UNCRC in its activities (Björklid 2007; Strandlund & Saracco 2012).

The national Swedish strategy for the UNCRC states that this Convention should be present at "all levels of society, both in the Government Offices and national authorities and at local and regional levels (municipalities and county councils)"; municipalities and county councils have been advised to set up systems like the CIA to monitor how their child friendly initiatives are delivering outcomes in the best interests of children (Ministry of Health and Social Affairs 2001). The office of the Children's Ombudsman, Barnombudsmannen, has issued a general model for CIAs, addressing any question related to the interests of the child, but it is mainly Trafikverket which has worked with CIAs. Together with the National Board of Housing, Building and Planning, Boverket, and the Public Health Agency of Sweden, Folkhälsomyndigheten, Trafikverket has worked in different municipalities. The power to decide to carry out CIAs lies with the municipalities. Stockholm, the capital and Sweden's biggest city, has decided not to have a general policy for making CIAs compulsory on projects which might affect children. CIAs are only completed in some projects, one example of which will be presented here. This example will illustrate the potential complications associated with completing CIAs.

Completing CIAs in Stockholm

Stockholm, with a population today of approximately 890,000 people, is rapidly growing and the city is estimated to increase to 1 million people by 2022. Approximately 48,000 new apartments will be built between now and then (Sweco Eurofutures 2013). The density of the newest developments in Stockholm surpasses that of any previous building development in the city, which has given rise to much protest by parents, the media and lobby organizations.

The media have held the municipal authority and the planning administration to account for the building policy, stressing the negative consequences for children when their need for outdoor places and for independent movement through the city is ignored. The media have reminded politicians and municipal authorities of the UNCRC and of children's right to have their environmental interests considered in planning projects. With a lot of media attention and pressure, politicians and municipal authorities have had little choice but to agree that CIAs should be carried out. This has sometimes resulted in the production of a CIA document, but not necessarily a full CIA process. CIA documents have been produced only after most, or all, planning has been done, and used by politicians as a symbolic gesture merely to show that they have heard the public. The CIAs implemented in Stockholm have varied in extent and character but most often they have been limited to school grounds and to places already used by children.

Aspects of CIAs that impact child friendly environmental planning

The experiences of political maneuvering in Stockholm reveal an aspect of CIAs which is not generally mentioned but which has consequences for carrying them out and for their success. In the list of the important aspects of the CIA process that follows, the first is the 'power' aspect, on which the outcome of the planning depends. When evaluating CIAs in urban planning, two further aspects are also important for their success.

1   *Who initiates the CIA for the project?* The first question is concerned with who holds the political power in the project. The answer to this question will indicate the likelihood of whether or not the CIA will be carried out or become a CIA document only.
2   *How will the CIA be carried out?* This second question is equally important and is concerned with procedure and methodology. It establishes when the CIA will be started; how it will be incorporated into the planning process; whether children and/or children's representatives will be involved; when children's involvement during the process will take place; what information will be collected about the environmental situation for the children concerned; and how this will be documented. This aspect focuses on both how planners and children will communicate with each other, as well as on how knowledge of children's environments and of places used by the children concerned will be gathered.
3   *What is the outcome of the CIA?* The third question addresses the results of implementing the CIA. The justification and the value of the CIA lies in the results achieved in terms of spaces for children. Therefore the answer to the third question is as important as the answers to the previous questions. The information it seeks

to establish includes the following: what are the tangible, physical results evident in the environment? How do children use the environment after the project has been built and how do they benefit from the new environment? The answers to these questions will show whether the environmental changes have been positive for the children affected and in what ways.

The Aspudden CIA, a case study

The three aspects above will be used here to describe a CIA that solved a critical planning situation where land used by school children during recess was required for building by the municipal authority, who owned the land. On September 7, 2005, one of the major daily newspapers in Stockholm ran an article with a photo of children at the Aspudden school playing outdoors at recess (Engström 2005). The headline read, "Children are deprived of their outdoor space".

The Aspudden school, built during the late 1940s, had recently experienced a growth in the number of pupils and the school playground had become too small for all of them to use. The school children were therefore using the park located next to the school. For several years this became a natural habit for them and there was no objection to this use from the municipality. The children, therefore, thought of the park as part of their school grounds. Until, that is, a building plan developed by the municipal authority incorporated the park as part of a proposed new residential development.

A formal consultation document was sent from the authority to the school informing the school of the change that was to take place. In Swedish urban planning there is a provision that information about a proposed development should be made available to any party that may be influenced by this change, such as neighbors. The arrival of the consultation document at the school marked the start of the school's intense efforts to influence the municipal planners to have the plan changed. This process of challenging the development proposal would never have happened without close cooperation between the school administration, skillful parents (some of whom were landscape architects and knowledgeable about planning) and the media.

A petition describing the negative consequences of the plan for the school children, signed by a large number of parents and school staff, was sent to the municipality. At the same time, this petition was published in the newspaper mentioned earlier with the strident headline in bold text. The headline did not tell the legal truth of the matter (that the school children were to be deprived of something which did not belong to them, as the city owned the land) but readers clearly understood that the school children would no longer be able to use the park during recess.

In Figure 11.1, the proposed residential development is marked by five dark blue squares. Buildings belonging to the school are marked in grey. The light green areas are park space.

After a while the municipal authority reconsidered its decision and changed the plan so that the school children would be able to continue using most of the park, while also permitting some of the planned housing to be built. This change to the plan was made as a result of both the community protest and the findings of the CIA.

Before changing the building plan, children's experts were asked by the municipal authority to conduct what the planners called a 'children's investigation'; an early version of a CIA. This was to verify whether the claims by the parents and the school that the park was important to the school children were true. The investigation showed which parts of the park the school children used and how they used them, as well as which parts of the park they did *not* use. The result of the Aspudden CIA was again published in the same newspaper (Anander 2006). This time the headline declared: "The children defeated the builders".

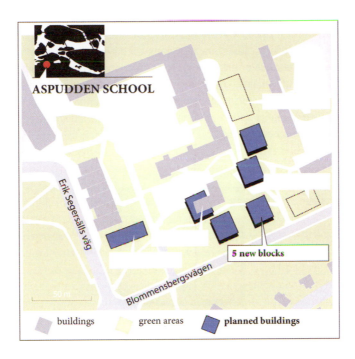

Figure 11.1 Map of the Aspudden school grounds and their surroundings, original building plan, 2005 (Source: Thomas Molén)

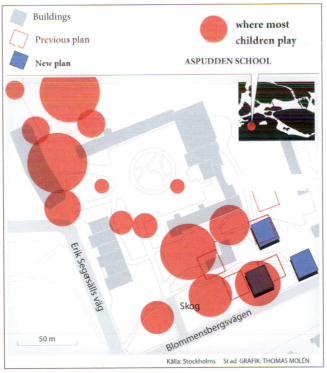

Figure 11.2 Map of the Aspudden school grounds and their surroundings. The revised building plan of 2006 (Source: Thomas Molén)

In Figure 11.2, the final locations of residential development are shown by three dark blue squares. Red dots of different sizes indicate where school children play. The size of the dots indicates the relative number of children playing in the same place.

Applying the three CIA aspects to the Aspudden case

The decision to have the CIA completed for the park area at the Aspudden school was taken by the municipal authority, but only after pressure. The CIA document answered the question about the value of the park for the school children and guided the subsequent action of the municipality. That the municipality respected the result of the CIA for the Aspudden school grounds by issuing a new building plan shows a willingness by the authority to support children's right to a child friendly environment and to fulfill the Swedish commitment to the UNCRC.

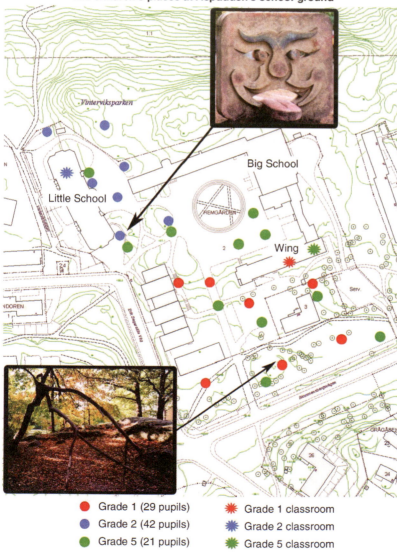

The children's places at Aspudden's school-ground

🔴 Grade 1 (29 pupils)   ✳ Grade 1 classroom
🔵 Grade 2 (42 pupils)   ✳ Grade 2 classroom
🟢 Grade 5 (21 pupils)   ✳ Grade 5 classroom

Figure 11.3 Map made for the Aspudden school children to mark the places they used during recess (Source: Maria Nordström & Ira Lagercrantz, Aspudden CIA document, 2005)

The experts commissioned by the planners to conduct the CIA were free to decide how to collect the information needed for the CIA. On completion, the experts presented their findings to the planners. In the process, an Aspudden CIA document was produced. The planners did not themselves have much contact with the school, the children, their teachers and their parents. The children's experts were the main intermediaries between the planners and the children.

The children's experts first collected all the information they could find about the children's use of the land through observation and detailed photography. Second, they consulted with the school children and teachers to confirm the validity of their observations of the children's outdoor environmental use. The children were interviewed about how they used the outdoors and they were asked to show the places where they spent their recess and to talk about their activities in these places. Easily read maps of the school grounds and the park were provided to the children to mark out these places. Three school classes with children aged 7, 8 and 12 years of age were asked to participate. The analyses of these independent observations, the interviews and the maps were presented in the CIA document. An explanatory text described the value of the grounds to the school children from an environmental psychology perspective.

In Figure 11.3, the neighboring park area is indicated by the photo of some trees. The red star shows the location of the classroom of the first-year school children (aged 7 years old) and the red dots indicate the places they used during recess. The blue star shows the location of the classroom of the second-year school children (aged 8 years old) and the blue dots indicate the places they used during recess. Finally, the green star shows the location of the classroom of the fifth-year school children (aged 12 years old), and the green dots indicate the places they used during recess.

In the revised building plan, the locations of the new buildings were moved to a position where there would be no conflict of use between the schoolchildren and the

Figure 11.4 Part of the 'new' Aspudden school grounds. The trees have been kept and the ground remains uneven. To the left is the school building (Source: Maria Nordström)

Figure 11.5 The new residential buildings (white building in foreground) are close to the Aspudden school (yellow building in background) (Source: Maria Nordström)

future tenants of the new residences. This plan was then realized (Lidbrink 2010). In the end, the school children could keep using 'their' part of the grounds for recess much in the same way as before and the tenants were granted access to the outdoors beside their homes. The revised building plan for the Aspudden school grounds solved the likely conflict between the different user groups of the area before it occurred.

Figure 11.5 shows the close proximity of the new development to the school. Between the three new residential buildings there are lawns and, most importantly for the school children, bushes and trees in an area the children call 'The Jungle'. This area was used regularly by the youngest school children and much loved by them. It was here that two more residential buildings were to be built, something which the planners decided not to do because of the protests by the school, the parents and the media—and because of the Aspudden CIA.

Discussion of the CIA process and the case of the Aspudden CIA

The three aspects of the CIA process identified in this chapter have been used to illustrate important dimensions of CIAs. The first aspect identifies the necessary commitment of the municipality to the UNCRC. As was indicated above, the municipal authority in Stockholm acts differently in different planning situations, thus creating different prerequisites for CIAs. Paying close attention to how a municipality may/may not use the CIA process keeps expectations about the outcomes of a CIA realistic.

The second aspect concerns consultation with children and gaining knowledge about children's environmental experiences. There is a wealth of research on the latter part of this aspect but less on how consultation with children can be done and what the outcomes will be from different methods. There has been considerable focus on how children of different ages express themselves, knowledge which is important to have, but there is less knowledge on how adults (planners, teachers, children's experts and others doing consultation with children in CIA tasks) and children understand each other during consultation. What is still lacking is a focus on how the communicative interaction between children and planners/adults takes place in CIA consultation settings.

The third aspect emphasizes the results and outcomes of the CIA. To learn about the quality of the environmental results obtained by CIAs, children should be observed in the new environment as well as interviewed about its qualities. The views of their teachers and parents are also important. Planners and designers themselves should also be interviewed. An interesting question to ask is, what have planners learned after completing a CIA, and has their understanding developed as to how to create child friendly environments within the usual planning procedures? Or, do they have new notions of how those procedures can be changed for more child friendly outcomes?

Conclusion

Access to physical space is essential for children's possibilities to play, for children's independent movement, and for children's health and well-being. When physical space is contested, as it is today by intense new building in our cities, children are at risk. CIAs are a tool to show how children will be affected by intensified building in places where they live, and therefore are a means to defend children's rights according to the UNCRC. In order for children to be able to play—play being the defining children's activity (Schwartzman 1978; Sutton-Smith 1997)—they need "permission and confidence to use outdoor spaces . . . without the encroachment of adult agendas" (Voce 2015, p. 4). This chapter has shown that the Aspudden CIA helped give children at the Aspudden school that confidence. Creating child friendly environments through urban planning is a way to support and respect children. By making our environments child friendly, we offer children a place in our societies, we enrich our cities, and we improve outdoor urban spaces (Björklid & Nordström 2012).

References

Anander, H 2006, 'Barnen vann över nybygget', *Svenska Dagbladet*, February 8, p. 8.

Björklid, P 2007, *Barnkonsekvensanalyser—Erfarenheter och visioner*, Lärarhögskolan I Stockholm, Stockholm.

Björklid, P & Nordström, M 2012, 'Child-friendly cities—sustainable cities', *Early Childhood Matters*, June, pp. 44–47.

Committee on the Rights of the Child 2015, *Concluding observations on the fifth periodic report of Sweden 2015*, United Nations Convention on the Rights of the Child, CRC/C/SWE/CO/5, March 6.

Engström, A 2005, 'Barnen får ge plats åt nytt bostadsområde', *Svenska Dagbladet*, September 7, p. 15.

Fagen, R 2011, 'Play and development' in *The Oxford handbook of the development of play*, ed. A Pellegrini, Oxford University Press, Oxford, pp. 83–100.

Faith-Ell, C 2015, 'An overview of Swedish research on impact assessment', *Journal of Environmental Assessment Policy and Management*, vol. 17, no. 1. Available from: http://EconPapers.repec.org/RePEc:wsi:jeapmx:v:17:y:2015:i:01:p:1550004-1-1550004-10.

Gummesson, M 2007, *Barns säkra tillgänglighet till skolan*, Chalmers Tekniska Högskola/Chalmers University of Technology, Göteborg.

Hart, R 2015, Foreword in A Voce, *Policy for Play: responding to children's forgotten right*, Policy Press, Bristol.

Lidbrink, J 2010, 'Skolgårdar i stadsmiljö. Utformning, nybyggnationer och utrustning. Studie av fem skolgårdar inom Stockholms stad, pm, Stadsbyggnadskontoret, planavdelningen, juni 2010', Stockholm.

Ministry of Health and Social Affairs 2001, *Child impact assessments: Swedish experience of child impact analyses as a tool for implementing the UN Convention on the Rights of the Child*, Ministry of Health and Social Affairs, Sweden & Ministry of Foreign Affairs, Sweden, Stockholm.

Nordström, M 2010, 'Children's views on child-friendly environments', *Urban Studies*, vol. 47, no. 3, pp. 514–528.

Nordström, M & Lagercrantz, I 2005, 'Lekutredning [Play investigation]. Hur elever på Aspuddens skola i Liljeholmen, Stockholm, använder sin skolgård. Redogörelse utifrån observationer av yngre elevers aktiviteter och deras egna markeringar på en karta över skolans utemiljö i oktober 2005', Kulturgeografiska institutionen, Stockholms Universitet, Stockholm.

Noschis, K 2008, 'Growing up in the city—an opportunity for becoming aware of urban sustainability issues', keynote address presented at the Area Group Meeting for Research in Swedish Environmental Psychology, Stockholm University, 13 October.

Road Safety Annual Report 2015. Available from: www.internationaltransportforum.org/irtadpublic/Sweden.

Sandels, S & Hartley, J 1975, *Children in traffic*, Elke, London.

Schwartzman, HB 1978, *Transformations: the anthropology of children's play*, Plenum Press, New York and London.

Strandlund, L & Saracco, S 2012, *Barnkonsekvensanalyser—hyllvärmare eller faktiska trafiksäkerhetsåtgärder för barn*, Trafikverket, Stockholm.

Sutton-Smith, B 1997, *The ambiguity of play*, Harvard University Press, Cambridge, MA.

Svensson, J 2011, *Social impact assessment in Finland, Norway and Sweden: a descriptive and comparative study*, Degree Project SoM EX 2011-30, Degree Program in Civil Engineering and Urban Management, KTH Architecture and the Built Environment, Stockholm.

Sweco Eurofutures 2013, *Statistik om Stockholm: befolkningsprognos 2013*, Stockholm.

Voce, A 2015, *Policy for play: responding to children's forgotten right*, Policy Press, Bristol.

CHAPTER 12

NSW parliamentary inquiries into children, young people and the built environment

What are they and how did they come about?

Linda Corkery and Kate Bishop

Introduction

When presenting our work on children, youth and environments at conferences, internationally and even in Australia, questions arise regarding the 2005 New South Wales Parliamentary Inquiry that initiated a public discussion focused on children, young people and the built environment. People express surprise that urban planning and design issues were given such a prominent hearing, and are curious about the mechanism that instigated the discussion. Indeed, the parliamentary inquiries, in 2005 and 2009, were significant occasions for individuals, organizations and professionals to air their concerns, present research findings, highlight work already under way and champion the causes of this constituency relative to urban planning, design and development. A number of subsequent initiatives were instigated in response to recommendations issued in the findings of these inquiries, demonstrating the potential of such government mechanisms to influence actions and decision-making that can positively impact children's and young people's lives in a number of ways.

   This chapter provides background information on the two inquiries held in the state of New South Wales (where Sydney is the capital city), which invited submissions and heard presentations that addressed questions and concerns about how the built environment impacts the lives of children and young people. In particular, the discussions focused on the State's major cities which are experiencing rapid and persistent population growth. While governance structures vary from one country to another, and state to state, understanding the mechanics and administration of an inquiry process such as this may be instructive to those seeking a means of generating public discussion about these concerns at their local city or state government levels.

What is a parliamentary inquiry?

In nations governed under the system of parliamentary democracy known as the Westminster system—such as Great Britain, Canada, Australia and New Zealand—at the national level, the government in power has achieved a majority of members of Parliament representing one political party, or a coalition of parties. The leader of the national government is the Prime Minister. At the state level, this is also the case; the party/ies with the majority of elected members forms the government, and in the State Parliament, the leader is the Premier. In both national and state governments, the leader convenes a cabinet of ministers who oversee specific portfolios. Ministerial

Figure 12.1
Learning to read
plans informs the
consultation process
(Source: Advocate
for Children and
Young People)

portfolios deliver a wide range of services and, at the state level, typically include Health, Education, Planning and Infrastructure, Family and Community Services, Environment, the Arts, Transport, etc. Individual state public sector offices support the work of these portfolios. Additionally, there are parliamentary committees, comprising elected members representing all political parties in the Parliament, which consider specific topics and/or oversee specific initiatives or commissions. They are obligated to regularly report back to the Parliament in relation to their specific area of interest.

Parliamentary inquiries are proposed and convened by committees of Parliament, with the approval of the Parliament. They are a means for state government to openly and publicly invite expertise, information and individual perspectives on issues of current concern, to assess how well current issues are being addressed and dealt with by the government, and to recommend actions for improvement or changes of direction.

What prompted the parliamentary inquiries in 2005 and 2009?

The NSW Parliamentary Committee on Children and Young People resolved in May 2005 to conduct an inquiry into children, young people and the built environment. The 2005 Inquiry was the first of its kind in Australia to initiate a discussion about how built environment policies and practices impact the lives of children and young people. With the 'child friendly cities' movement gaining momentum in a number of Australian cities, the Inquiry was regarded as an opportunity to take stock of the success of those projects in NSW locales and open up more public conversation with the wider community (Committee on Children and Young People 2006a, p. ix). It may also have been motivated by the fact that, as a signatory to the UN Convention on the Rights of the Child (UNCRC), Australia was due to report back to the United Nations in 2008 on progress made relative to the UNCRC. Around this time as well, there was also increasing interest and concern for the impacts of increasing urbanization on Australian children and young people, as evidenced in the academic literature and in reports from public agencies, and built environment professionals (Gleeson & Sipe 2006; Woolcock et al. 2010).

As per the Parliament's resolution, the terms of reference to the Committee for the 2005 Inquiry were to consider the following five points:

1 Trends, changes and issues for children and young people in the development, implementation and coordination of policy, design and planning for the built environment
2 The built environment, as it relates to and impacts upon children and young people
3 Strategies to ensure that built environment issues affecting children and young people are readily identified and receive coordinated attention across portfolios and different levels of government
4 The role of the NSW Commission for Children and Young People in giving input to the Government and non-Government sectors on inclusive and integrated planning and policy-making for children and young people in the built environment
5 Any other matter considered relevant to the inquiry by the Committee (Committee on Children and Young People 2006a, p. vii).

The process and the obligation of an inquiry

The inquiry process invites submissions by advertising widely and publicly, for example on the NSW Parliament's website, where advice is offered on how to make a submission and attend hearings as a member of the public:

- **Make a submission:** Committees conducting inquiries welcome submissions from individuals and community groups. Submissions alert committees to factors or information relevant to an inquiry, and show how you, your organization or your community feel about an issue . . . Most submissions received by a committee will be made public
- **Attend a hearing as a member of the public:** Committee hearings are usually held in public and everyone is welcome to attend public hearings, whether they are held at Parliament House or at other sites around New South Wales. Hearing details can be found on each committee's inquiry page (Parliament of New South Wales, 2016).

As described above, the process for making submissions is accessible and unrestricted, with opportunities for anyone to contribute. Specific individuals, agencies and organizations are invited to present at the hearings. Generally, inquiry hearings are open for anyone to attend, but on occasion, if a matter under consideration is particularly controversial, they may be closed to the media (Parliament of New South Wales, 2016). The proceedings of the inquiry are formal processes in which witnesses are sworn and asked whether they give permission for their submissions to be made public. The proceedings are minuted and become part of the official state government record. At the conclusion of the inquiry, a report of the findings prepared by the Committee, including actions and recommendations, is tabled in Parliament.

Figure 12.2 School students engage in collaborative decision-making (Source: Advocate for Children and Young People)

The conduct of the 2005 NSW Parliamentary Inquiry on Children, Young People and the Built Environment

In the case of this specific review, the Inquiry was announced in October 2005 and submissions were sought via major metropolitan newspapers as well as through direct requests to specific organizations, agencies and special interest groups. In May and June of 2006, the Committee held public hearings in relation to the Inquiry, hearing evidence from a range of public sector agencies and departments, local government representatives, academics, professionals and children and youth advocates. In 2005 and 2006, the Committee also participated in two programs of site visits. The first was to Brisbane and included inspections of various suburban and CBD locations and the second was to various locations in the western suburbs of Sydney (Committee on Children and Young People 2006a).

Establishing the first inquiry in 2005: who was involved?

Two central bodies were responsible for the whole process of instigating the inquiries and answering to their recommendations. These were the NSW Parliamentary Committee and the NSW Commission for Children and Young People. A brief summary of the nature of both bodies will be provided here.

The NSW Parliamentary Committee on Children and Young People (hereafter 'the Committee') is a bipartisan committee originally established to oversee the NSW Commission for Children and Young People (hereafter 'the Commission'). (The Commission has now become the Office for the Advocate for Children and Young People which the Committee still oversees.) Other than this, the Committee has no particular responsibilities in relation to children and young people. It reviewed the performance of the Commission and now reviews the performance of the Office for the Advocate. It also responds to changes in issues and trends affecting children and young people in the state of NSW.

The Commission was established in June 1999 as a result of the *Commission for Children and Young People Act 1998*. Its principal functions were:

1   To promote the participation of children in the making of decisions that affect their lives and to encourage government and non-government agencies to seek the participation of children appropriate to their age and maturity
2   To promote and monitor the overall safety, welfare and well-being of children in the community and to monitor the trends in complaints made by or on behalf of children
3   To conduct special inquiries under Part 4 into issues affecting children
4   To make recommendations to government and non-government agencies on legislation, policies, practices and services affecting children
5   To promote the provision of information and advice to assist children
6   To conduct, promote and monitor training on issues affecting children
7   To conduct, promote and monitor public awareness activities on issues affecting children
8   To conduct, promote and monitor research into issues affecting children (*Commission for Children and Young People Act 1998*, p. 5).

Unlike the Committee, the Commission was not a political body and was able to act independently on behalf of the well-being of children and young people in the state. Their projects and activities, representative consultation mechanisms, empowered and engaged children and young people to identify issues and influence decision-making about things that directly affect their lives. It continuously advised both government and the opposition on children's issues. It also played a central role in the processes of the parliamentary inquiries on children, young people and the built environment, and in pursuing the recommendations that came from them.

Ahead of the initial inquiry in 2005, the Commission developed a series of three issue papers to inform the Committee's work. These provided a foundational background for the Committee and were also made available on the Parliament's website to inform the public in the preparation of submissions to the Inquiry. The papers addressed: 1) key concepts associated with the topic of the Inquiry; 2) the evolution of the Child Friendly Cities movement; and, 3) international practice, also commenting on related developments in NSW where children and young people's issues were being given central focus, such as in local government youth advisory councils and the Commission's own Youth Advisory Council (Committee on Children and Young People 2006a, p. 75).

The Commission also made a submission to the Inquiry reflecting their own research with children and young people, alongside 57 other submissions which were received from a range of individuals including academics, planning and design professionals, state and local government agency officers, non-governmental organizations and professional associations. Alongside the written submissions three formal hearings were scheduled and took place between May 9 and June 13, 2006 with 25 witnesses appearing before the panel. This group was also comprised of representatives from community organizations, local government agencies, academics, and design and planning professions.

Themes of the three hearings in brief

Each witness raised particular issues that were salient to their experience and perspectives, and in response to the presentations, the Committee prompted recommendations

Figure 12.3 Young people's input ensures their voices inform planning decisions (Source: Advocate for Children and Young People)

for key policy areas and interventions that they could pursue. Many of the consistent themes that emerged are still relevant today. The topics of discussion included the following: the impact of increased urbanization, resulting in the loss of access to green space and the declining choice of environments for children in city suburbs; safety and restricted mobility due to increased risk aversion; the increase in obesity amongst children; and problems associated with communities' perceptions of young people and the tension they can create in communities.

Consistently recommended areas for policy intervention included building relationships within the development community that ensure more family friendly and child friendly residential developments; accepting that families will be present in high-density, urban consolidation strategies and developments; and the need to protect places for free and formal play/recreation in urban developments (Committee on Children and Young People 2006b, 2006c, 2006d).

The NSW Commission for Children and Young People's Inquiry submission

Although many submissions of a high caliber were received, the only submission that attempted to introduce the voice of young people was the submission from the Commission. No submissions from children or young people were received directly in this process. However, in the absence of direct contributions from children and young people themselves, the Commission's submission reflected the views of children and young people, consulted specifically for the purposes of the Parliamentary Inquiry. The Commission completed consultations with 125 young people aged 4–18 years prior to its submission. The children consulted represented a diversity of cultural and social backgrounds, and included children and young people with physical and intellectual disabilities. In addition to the immediate consultation process, the Commission also drew on relevant feedback from previous consultations with children and young people where issues about the built environment had emerged as a key concern. The Commissioner also introduced the perspectives of these children and young people to the Committee in her presentation to the Inquiry.

Some of the broader socioeconomic realities enumerated in their submission highlighted the following trends over the previous generation:

- **Smaller families**—the number of children under the age of 17 was decreasing and hence the proportion of the population getting smaller. This trend points to the risk of children and young people's issues becoming marginalized, particularly with a focus on the increasing proportion of elderly people in the population.
- **Changing family structure**—increase in two-parent working families, single-parent households and longer working hours per week. This trend has led to more children spending more time in long day care and/or having more unsupervised time at home alone, after school hours.
- **Increasing concerns about child protection**—a combination of concerns about 'stranger danger' in relation to child abduction, although this is a rare event; and a concern about children playing unsupervised in their own yards or streets, and walking to school on their own due to increased volume and speed of vehicle traffic on city streets.

Figure 12.4 Out in the community, young people are active participants in public processes (Source: Advocate for Children and Young People)

- **Increased reliance on private transport**—the impacts on children include loss of a sense of place, decreased independent mobility, less direct contact with local children and local play opportunities, and incidental physical activity associated with getting oneself around by walking or bicycling.
- **Increased urbanization**—more people living in the city and living in increasing density, often with the loss of direct access to yard space and restricted use of shared spaces in the apartment buildings or townhouse developments where they live. In the outer areas of the city, single-family homes are built on shrinking areas of land, leaving precious little space for active play (NSW Commission for Children and Young People 2006).

In combination, the Commission contended, these trends will lead to poor physical health outcomes, a prediction well documented in public health literature, which associates such trends with obesity and diabetes, asthma triggered by poor air quality, and even with mental health issues when children and young people do not have adequate housing, supportive and generally safe neighborhoods (NSW Commission for Children and Young People 2006, p. 6). The Commission's submission also offered the view that there was a link between childhood experiences of the built environment and resulting attitudes carried into adulthood.

> Children develop a strong sense of belonging in a [neighborhood] they are able to engage with. Limiting children's access to their locality is also limiting their opportunity to 'connect' with their community and their understanding of their families' and friends' place within it (NSW Commission for Children and Young People 2006, p. 7).

As reported by the Commission in their submission, the concerns of children and young people included the following:

1 **Community**—being surrounded by good relationships—knowing your neighbors and having friends close by
2 **Facilities**—having access to good facilities like schools, shops, playgrounds which were easily accessible and affordable
3 **Safety**—feeling safe on streets and safe from becoming a victim of violence
4 **Being active**—having access to both informal play areas and formal sporting fields
5 **Public transport**—having access to enable community participation and access to the community's facilities
6 **Participation in planning**—children wanted to be consulted about planning and development decisions (NSW Commission for Children and Young People, 2006).

In concluding their submission, the Commission put forward to the Inquiry three broad areas for targeted action, with associated recommendations:

- **Action Area 1**: Promoting an inclusive environment and an understanding of what that means to those involved in the creation of the built environment
- **Action Area 2**: Promoting children's citizenship and participation through partnerships with key level organizations
- **Action Area 3**: Monitoring the impact of the built environment on children and young people over time.

Figure 12.5
School-based consultations promote leadership and active citizenship (Source: Advocate for Children and Young People)

What were the outcomes—immediate and longer lasting—of the Inquiry?

The 2005 Inquiry resulted in a report released in 2006 which represented both a reflection on and a summary of the submissions and the hearings. The report opens with a list of six recommendations, four of which were for the Commission to consider in response to the Inquiry, including:

1 Convene a steering committee with representation from key peak bodies in state government, the organization representing local government and representatives from the professional institutes of architecture, planning and landscape architecture. (This was established in 2009.)

2 Develop a seminar series aimed at bridging the gaps and building understanding across professional communities involved in the creation of the built environment (This was launched at the end of 2011, and continued throughout 2012.)

3 Launch any or all of the 18 projects based on ideas raised during the inquiry process and related to design, planning and consultation; early childhood and physical environments; housing; education; and monitoring.

4 Partner with a local council to investigate how government can develop and embed participatory practices with children and young people in political processes. (The Commission subsequently partnered with Wollongong City Council on this project in 2007/8.)

In 2007, the Commission also contracted a university research team to develop a set of child friendly community indicators which were subsequently published in 2009 in a publication developed by the Commission called *Built4kids: A Good Practice Guide to Creating Child-Friendly Environments*. From September 2009 to June 2012, this publication was downloaded 155,229 times (Mr. B Williams 2014, pers. comm., 14 March). The Commission also sent out a hard copy of this publication to all 152 local councils in the State at that time. Subsequently in 2010, the Commission contracted the same research team to survey these councils on their use and take-up of this document in their local policies and processes.

One of the projects in Recommendation 3, nested under the heading of 'Education', encouraged investigation of the development of university-level curriculum or course modules for architecture and/or planning degree programs on how to involve children and young people in planning. This has been an initiative of the Landscape Architecture Program at the University of New South Wales and these courses have now become an integral part of the elective offerings within the Faculty of Built Environment. Initially, there was a module on environments for and planning/designing with children and young people in a course called "People, Place and Design" which in 2015 evolved into a separate course called "Children, Youth and Environments".[1] This new course is designed to develop the awareness of young designers and planners of two things principally: the issues surrounding children, youth and environments in cities; and the importance of children and young people's participation in urban planning and design processes.

Another recommendation under the Education category proposed encouraging the establishment of specific professional awards for projects that best reflected the principles of child and youth friendly built environments. In 2012, the NSW Planning Institute of Australia (PIA) recognized the first project in their new award category, 'Planning for Children and Young People', for a project that best demonstrated "how children and young people have participated in a project aimed at encouraging their active and creative use of the built environment" (PIA 2012). This award was sponsored by the Commission.

The follow-up inquiry

A follow-up inquiry was conducted in 2009, specifically to hear from the Commissioner for Children and Young People, "and any other witnesses agreed by the Committee (for Children); and report to both houses of Parliament on the Inquiry" on the progress made on the recommendations as set out in the 2005 Inquiry (Committee on Children and Young People 2010, p. iii). Additional written submissions were not called for in this instance. Rather, two roundtable sessions were convened in March and June 2010, and transcripts from those discussions comprised the final report. The focus of these discussions was on the implementation of the recommendations from the previous Inquiry, and on strategies for ensuring ongoing attention would be paid to the issues raised in the initial Inquiry.

Accountability: how to gauge the impact and effectiveness of the inquiry process?

A major indicator of the effectiveness of a political process such as the inquiries would be evidence of policy changes in relevant policy frameworks. However, these were state government-level inquiries and most of the relevant policy change needs to happen at a local government level. Local governments are able to develop their own planning polices in large part although they are subject to the rules of state government legislation such as the *Environmental Planning Act 1979*. In most cases, the capacity of the state government to affect changes at the local government policy level is limited. However, the Advisory Group established as a result of the inquiries, which was made up of representatives from state government bodies or levels of administration, did look for opportunities to emphasize the recommendations on issues arising from the inquiries to their organizations and constituents in the development of new policies and allocation of public resources. National professional institutes, such as the Planning Institute of Australia, also released position statements during this period, recommending new policies and featuring 'best practice' principles for working with children and young people (PIA 2007).

Many of the strongest outcomes of these inquiries have already been discussed. They took various forms and helped to raise awareness across many social and political levels of the need to pay attention to the environmental opportunities available to children and young people in their communities and the key influences that shape those opportunities in both positive and negative ways. The responses to the recommendations from the original Inquiry gradually unfolded across the next 10 years. The publication of this book will also be an opportunity to revive the interest around the needs of children, young people and the built environment, adding even more people to the network and re-establishing the lines of communication between these groups. This will help keep the issues alive and embed the participatory processes for children and young people – who are now four years older than they were when we convened the original series of workshops! The importance of having further opportunities to assess progress and reflect on the key issues, identifying new challenges, opportunities and barriers, is essential.

Figure 12.6 Communicating their ideas gives young people a platform to express their needs and preferences (Source: Advocate for Children and Young People)

Conclusion

There will always be scope for more training and experience in how to consult with children of different ages, and also how to assist children to prepare for participation in social processes like design and planning. There will also always be a need to remind professional groups and local communities of the need to think about the children and young people who are affected by their decisions. And of course there will always be a need to consult with children and young people about the nature of their experience and the implications for their environmental needs. This work is never done. Processes like the parliamentary inquiries can assist greatly by provoking discussion and debate at the highest political levels and by publicly raising awareness of children's issues and the nature of children's experience. Any cause championed at the state government level can benefit from this focus and level of support. It provides a degree of validation that is tangible, and helps make any issue addressed in this way more accessible and acceptable to the wider community. For children and young people, having the support of people willing to use their significant professional or political positions to champion issues which affect their daily lives is essential.

Note

1   These courses have been developed and taught over the years by both authors, and Kate Bishop now convenes both of them. They are offered to all students in the Faculty, and are taught as interdisciplinary subjects in classes of architecture, landscape architecture, interior architecture, industrial design, planning and building construction management.

References

Commission for Children and Young People Act 1998, NSW Parliament, Sydney.

Committee on Children and Young People 2006a, *Inquiry into children, young people and the built environment, Report No. 8/53*, Parliament of New South Wales, Committee on Children and Young People, Sydney.

Committee on Children and Young People 2006b, *Report of proceedings 9 May 2006*. Available from: www.parliament.nsw.gov.au/Prod/parlment/committee.nsf/0/7E4DA544CFA8382DCA2570260020C057.

Committee on Children and Young People 2006c, *Report of proceedings 16 May 2006*. Available from: www.parliament.nsw.gov.au/Prod/parlment/committee.nsf/0/7E4DA544CFA8382DCA2570260020C057.

Committee on Children and Young People 2006d, *Report of proceedings 13 June 2006*. Available from: www.parliament.nsw.gov.au/Prod/parlment/committee.nsf/0/7E4DA544CFA8382DCA2570260020C057.

Committee on Children and Young People 2010, *Children, young people and the built environment inquiry: follow-up report*, Report No. 8/54, Parliament of New South Wales, Committee on Children and Young People, Sydney.

Gleeson, B & Sipe, N 2006, *Creating child friendly cities*, Routledge, Oxon, UK.

NSW Commission for Children and Young People 2006, *Submission from the Commission for Children and Young People to the NSW Parliamentary Inquiry into Children, Young People and the Built Environment*, NSW Commission for Children and Young People, Sydney. Available from: www.parliament.nsw.gov.au/prod/parlment/committee.nsf/0/A0B77D170AB309A5CA2571920013A25C.

NSW Commission for Children and Young People 2009, *Built4kids: a good practice guide to creating child-friendly environments*, NSW Commission for Children and Young People, Sydney.

Parliament of New South Wales 2016, *Get involved with committees*. Available from: www.parliament.nsw.gov.au/prod/web/common.nsf/key/Getinvolvedwith Committees.

Planning Institute of Australia 2007, *National position statement on child friendly communities*. Available from: www.planning.org.au/documents/item/121.

Planning Institute of Australia 2012, *Planning excellence, 2012 New South Wales awards: nomination book 12*, Planning Institute of Australia, Sydney.

Woolcock, G, Gleeson, B & Randolph, B 2010, 'Urban research and child-friendly cities: a new Australian outline', *Children's Geographies*, vol. 8, no. 2, pp. 177–192.

PART 4

PERSPECTIVES ON PARTICIPATORY PRACTICES WITH CHILDREN AND YOUNG PEOPLE

The final section on participatory practice with children and young people is presented from the perspectives of professional practitioners, recounting projects that have resulted in constructed outcomes. These discussions span education, research and design processes and present tangible examples of how children's participation enhances their experiences, contributes fresh perspectives and facilitates better environmental outcomes. In several cases, the authors reflect on many years of professional practice and their recommendations emanate from long-term commitment and experience with these approaches. They also reveal the challenges and potential points of breakdown that can occur and discuss strategies for avoiding them.

The wide-ranging participatory process described by landscape architect Fiona Robbé highlights the most direct involvement possible for children and young people in the development of a significant, everyday environment. Children's participation in decision-making throughout a real project enhances their personal development, and contributes a unique expression of 'community' in the character and quality of the final constructed environment. Design processes that conscientiously involve children and young people, as described in Robbé's chapter, can readily demonstrate to children and young people what their involvement has influenced.

Research processes that involve children and young people which are linked to immediate design processes, as discussed in environment-behavior researcher Katina Dimoulias's chapter, offer the opportunity for young people to provide continuous input into the creation of the built environment spanning both the general contextual and social considerations, as well as the immediate environmental and design decisions. The project Dimoulias outlines involved young people in setting the brief for a new community youth center—a project type that too often is designed and delivered with little consultation with the end users.

The story of Growing Up Boulder (GUB), in Mara Mintzer and Debra Flanders Cushing's chapter, illustrates a program that allows children and young people to clearly see how their input translates into social and environmental change across time, and to witness what meaningful participation in democratic processes associated with being a community citizen is really all about. As action researchers/facilitators of GUB projects, Mara and Debra have been in an ideal position to monitor and evaluate, shape and encourage young people's participation with the local government of the City of Boulder and this project is widely recognized as an exemplar for implementing child friendly principles.

(Source: Fiona Robbé)

Built environment education, as Angela Million contends, can support children's understanding of their environment and heighten their participation in its creation. This serves both immediate and long-term functions in children's environmental inter-action and their personal growth and development. As an urban planner/designer and academic, Million has undertaken numerous research projects and program evalua-tions in this sphere, and offers a perspective from Germany on how these areas of practice can productively interact.

Ultimately, one of our primary aims for this book is to improve environmental outcomes for children and young people in cities and to influence how, when and with whom they can participate in the process of imagining and realizing the built environment projects that are central to their lives. The power of collaborative and participatory practice is made obvious in the following discussions.

CHAPTER 13

Designing with children

A practitioner's perspective

Fiona Robbé

Introduction

This chapter offers the opportunity to reflect on my 30 years of landscape architectural practice in Australia, much of which has focused on the specialized design of outdoor environments in public places for children and young people. I begin by discussing the context in which public domain playgrounds and design takes place, and why authentic, effective participatory design with children and young people can be elusive to achieve. I will then articulate recommendations for what I consider to be best practice principles for participatory design practice with children and young people, illustrating these with a case study of a school grounds project in a suburban area of Sydney, Australia.

The Australian context

In Australia, much of the design of the public domain which children and young people share with adults has traditionally been undertaken by design professionals. Children's needs and interests in urban spaces are often considered to be neatly and safely covered by providing designated, defined playgrounds which diligently comply with a complex suite of standards and play strategies. Where playgrounds serve children aged 1 to 12 years old, government policy and design processes in Australia are exemplary, with an array of play strategies applied systematically, resulting in the provision of diverse playground venues. However, few of these guidelines include the participation of children in their development.

The concept of children and young people sharing public urban space beyond designated playgrounds receives little consideration in planning and design practice, with the occasional exception. In general, thoughtful, considered design outcomes for young people aged 13 to 18 years old are sadly variable. They are either not given much consideration at all; are partially considered, e.g., including a skate park in an open space; or whole-heartedly considered, e.g., including a dedicated youth space. The latter is rare, however.

At the core of healthy, sustainable, livable cities around the world is the right of citizens to be involved in the ongoing design and redevelopment of the physical environments that shape their urban experience. It is a more recent concept that this thinking extends to children and young people—that they share this right along with adults, to be valued partners in community design and development processes. While the concept of children and young people being actively involved in the planning and design of the public domain has been enthusiastically agreed to in principle in Australia, it remains an elusive process which is rarely embedded into usual practice. When children and young people express what they would like in public environments, their suggestions are not difficult to translate into design, so it remains puzzling as to why the design of public spaces so often fails to meet these age groups' needs.

Research and global policies clearly identify and stipulate the rights, needs and interests of children and young people in relation to the built environment and to participation in design decisions that affect their lives (UNICEF 2002). In practice, there remains a tension between what has been established in regard to children's and young people's rights in the built environment, and the actual daily, practical implementation and recognition of these rights, needs and interests in the design of the public domain. One of the principal outcomes of these tensions is that children and young people are rarely involved in the design of public space. In my experience, children and young people are not involved in participatory design of public space because those in control of the planning perceive that:

1 Young participants will not provide sensible comments and suggestions, but rather fanciful and imaginative ideas which are difficult to implement
2 The process will be too expensive
3 The process will take time to execute authentically
4 There are few known prescribed and agreed processes
5 The group of children and young people may not be representative of a local community. How are they selected and on what criteria?
6 It is not necessary to involve children and young people if there are specialized design professionals who understand their needs already on the project
7 The outcomes of consultation with young participants may not align with the design brief or budget, so "why would we ask children and young people for ideas when we can't implement their ideas, and hence frustrate them?"
8 The logistics required to involve children and young people are considered too difficult to overcome, for example, gaining parental/guardian consent to participate in the consultations
9 Children and young people do not have the capacity to understand complex public domain environments and issues: "What would they know? They are only kids"
10 The time lapse between consultation and the completion of a project negates the usefulness of young participants' involvement as they will have 'grown up' and there will be a new set of perspectives as to what is considered essential in the built environment.

It also seems that children and young people themselves are not yet aware of their rights and the appropriate mechanisms for expressing their views on the urban environments they use, and so are not insisting that they participate in design processes. Design of the public realm is not a readily accessible topic to most school-age children and young people. If they are interested in getting involved in the design of public environments, they do not readily know where or how to engage in the process, or who to approach.

'Coming in from the side' (CIFTS)

When government agencies fail to require engagement with children and young people in planning and design, the process of involving school-age participants falls to other parties. Most commonly it is schools, local governments, occasionally developers, and most frequently planners and designers themselves who initiate the activity. This intervention is not often mandated by government policy, nor by 'bottom-up' community processes, but instead, emerges through professional motivation. It represents what I call 'coming in from the side' (CIFTS); in other words, organizations or designers who understand the value of children's and young people's participation in design, and directly advocate for this in a project at hand. The direct application to a particular design project has an immediacy that is perceived as achievable, which appeals to many organizations and is valued by them. Being a targeted exercise, completed within the scope of a particular project, means that it is also perceived as being free of any other agenda that may be associated with the organizations involved in the project.

The key strategy in approaching the client organizations involved in these projects is to simply suggest the participation of children and young people in the design process; state the reasons it is worthwhile; demonstrate how the process of involvement can take place; and finally, confirm the benefits to the client, children and young people, and the community. Figure 13.1 illustrates the process of coming in from the side.

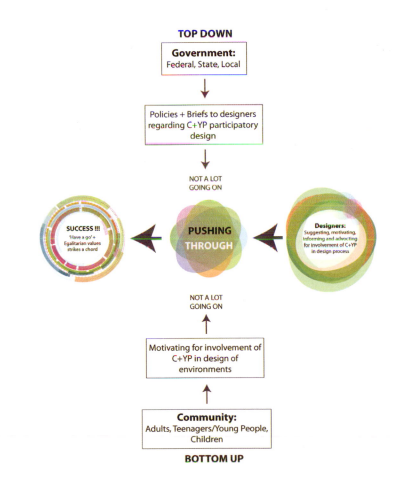

Figure 13.1
The process of coming in from the side (CIFTS) (Source: Fiona Robbé Landscape Architects)

The advantages of a CIFTS approach are that the process of involvement is tailor-made for a specific client and project and very often the direct and delightful results are motivating for everyone. The lack of tightly written and prescribed guidelines for the process often provides a sense of ease to all participants, as participatory engagement in design can be defined by what the group at hand thinks is practical for their project.

However, there are some disadvantages of the CIFTS approach:

1 The process is often incomplete; that is, people lose interest, time or money to realize an authentic process
2 The results can be easily dismissed or disregarded, particularly if politicians or designers overrule the needs and interests of children and young people
3 The process requires all individuals involved in the project to commit to a participatory design process, and if group commitment is not achieved, the process is vulnerable to points of breakdown
4 This form of involvement of children and young people in the design of the public domain is vulnerable, as their interests have to compete with adult agendas and complex design briefs and fixed budgets
5 If children's and young people's input is not a specific component of the project scope, then their interests and ideas are easily disregarded
6 It relies on strong, committed leadership from project team members to insist on including the voice of children and young people at the start of the design process, and giving it attention all the way through to completion of construction.

What can be learned from the CIFTS approach?

We know from successful projects that children, young people and communities benefit hugely from their involvement. Some of these benefits include:

1 The CIFTS approach is tailor-made to a project, and hence is free of set policies and regulations, which can stultify the process
2 Children feel their ideas have been heard, when they usually do not have a voice in the design of urban environments
3 Public space can be designed to better reflect the needs and interests of children and young people, with fewer 'lost in translation', or adult-centric outcomes
4 Children and young people learn about decision-making and design processes, as well as construction realities—invaluable knowledge about the world we all share
5 Children and young people have pride in being part of design outcomes, and feel connected to the environments which they use and share with the community
6 Adults and communities learn to value what children and young people have to contribute to the future design and planning of urban environments.

An additional and valuable benefit of children being involved in design processes is the political advantages that can accrue for a project. Children's consultative outcomes are generally delightful, photogenic and quotable. For example, when a survey finds that '76 percent of children would like real grass in the park', this can be persuasive evidence. Mayors and other officials can justify spending government money on projects by quoting that 'children and young people asked for it'. This often validates the provision of facilities for children and young people, indeed for entire communities, as decision-making has been directly influenced by a group of residents with no political power or agendas. In my professional experience, I have seen this happen numerous times, and I enjoy seeing its effectiveness.

How and when to involve children in the design process: recommendations from practice

A recurring question regarding the involvement of children and young people in the design of the public domain is: should specific policies, models and/or methods be adopted which provide guidelines for the design community to follow? And should these be mandatory? "Looking back at the more than 30-year (now over 40-year) history of children's participation in design and planning, several stages or realms are evident . . . traced to changes in the political and cultural context" (Francis & Lorenzo 2002, p. 160). With each development over time, it has become increasingly clear that there are no agreed universal approaches or methodologies, nor should there be (Department of Economic and Social Affairs 2004).

Consultation techniques used with adults are largely unsuitable and impractical for engaging with children and young people. "It is important that young people are not pushed into replicating traditional adult models . . . but are equipped to create new collaborative approaches" (Department of Economic and Social Affairs 2004, p. 283). Participatory methods should be implemented which are respectful and reflective of children and young people themselves. There are numerous modern methodologies developed by experienced professionals who can guide thinking on this topic. For example, Hart describes a number of relevant approaches—drawings and collages, mapping and modeling, interviewing and surveys, and media and communication (Hart 1997).

Regardless of the method selected, what is vital to a collaborative design process with children and young people is that:

1 The process is flexible in order to adapt to each unique project
2 Children and young people are recognized and valued as partners in the design process, and their perspectives can genuinely inform and underpin the design process
3 Children and young people's needs, interests and requirements are consciously balanced with those of the other project stakeholders, and acknowledged as valuable input
4 The process directly informs design outcomes.

Considering the complexity of designing and delivering contemporary public urban spaces, when should children and young people be involved? I would argue: very early in the design process. Jungk's comment on the importance of "participation at the moment of idea generation" suggests this is the best moment to introduce participatory design (in Sanders & Stappers 2008, p. 9). Ideally, when practical, children and young people should be involved *before* the process of adult idea generation begins. They are quick-thinking, spontaneous contributors to this type of creative activity and, in fact, their ideas can lead the creative design process, if they are enabled to do so.

Sanders and Stappers (2008, p. 7) discuss the idea of "the fuzzy front end". Figure 13.2 illustrates a diagrammatic representation of the design process which represents my interpretation of their concept. The large 'fuzzy front end' is the all-important

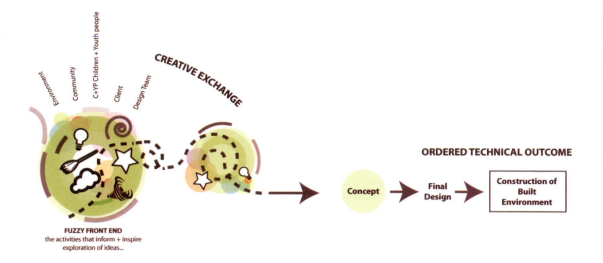

Figure 13.2 From fuzzy front end to final design: charting the creative process (Source: Fiona Robbé Landscape Architects, after Sanders & Stappers 2008)

stage that informs and inspires the development of the design. "The front end is often referred to as 'fuzzy' because of the ambiguity and chaotic nature that characterize it . . . considerations of many natures come together in this increasingly critical phase" (Sanders & Stappers 2008, p. 7).

The 'fuzzy front end' of design is the ideal point in the design process to involve children and young people. They are naturally able to envisage ideas for 'what may be' included on/in the identified site, from a perspective of hope and positive anticipation. Children respond in the moment, uninhibited by self-censoring or hampered by in-depth reflection. This form of spontaneity has been termed 'possibility thinking', or a stance of 'what if' and 'as if', originally coined by Craft (1999). In my experience, this open-minded ability to think through possible scenarios is best encouraged without adult prompts, as their suggestions can pressure children and young people to replicate what adults show them.

So where in the design process is the 'fuzzy front end'?

In a landscape design project, the 'fuzzy front end' stage occurs directly after site analysis and before the first concept sketches are drawn. It is the point at which initial ideas are generated and options are conceived with regard to the site design brief and the community's wishes. Children and young people can get involved at this early stage to generate ideas—from broad concepts to detailed design resolution. For example, they may suggest an overall theme of 'outer space' for a school play area and then provide the details of how to build its component parts, such as a black hole, a rocket ship or a space station.

I find that children and young people can each generate anywhere between 5 and 15 ideas in a relatively short session (which can last from 20 to 40 minutes), inspiring each other through the process. Their ideas can be drawn, written or discussed in a small group setting. A useful technique is to ask the participants to prioritize or rank the design ideas in order of preference, so that there can be a way of identifying their favorite suggestions; pictograms are useful for this step. Gleaning the top three preferences is usually sufficient.

Once children and young people have made this initial contribution, the traditional design process then follows, with the children's ideas being translated into concept development, then final designs, and finally construction drawings. This is the domain of trained professional designers as "they hold highly developed skills that are relevant at larger levels of scope and complexity . . . most designers are good at visual thinking, conducting creative processes, finding missing information, and being able to make decisions in the absence of complete information" (Sanders & Stappers 2008, p. 15). Designers also have expert knowledge, such as safety information and building standards—essential knowledge to translate ideas into three-dimensional built reality.

While we would like children and young people to participate in *all* stages of the design process, it is seldom practical or affordable to do so. Few projects have the extended timelines or budgets for their ongoing and regular input. It is important to acknowledge that children and young people have the ability to contribute to the entire design process; it is simple practicalities that usually preclude this from taking place, particularly time and funding. Ideally, the final design concepts reflect the children's and young people's input, and the resultant design concepts are shared with them for their ongoing input and information. It is good practice to ask their opinion of the developing concepts and get their thoughts on areas for change or improvement.

Another valuable opportunity for involvement of children and young people in the design process is during construction of a project. For example, a small representative group of children can be selected to attend regular site meetings, providing them the required personal protective attire. They can then participate in discussions of construction issues and may be able to contribute to the solutions. Ideally they also take notes to consolidate their input into site issues. A delightful outcome is when these notes are given a voice in weekly or monthly school newsletters.

Once construction has reached 'practical completion' (i.e., completion of construction), it is an important time to involve students in a reflective process, led by a client representative, such as the local mayor or school principal. This is an ideal opportunity to confirm what the young participants have brought to the design and construction process, and thank them for their valued contributions. Media or local magazine coverage also gives their involvement further prominence and positive reinforcement, which has benefits for all those parties involved in the project and for the community's perception of children's capacities to contribute to civic processes.

Benefits for children and young people:

- They feel proud of their involvement, and have a strong sense of ownership of the project outcomes
- They feel empowered and more confident in having input to design projects
- They can see real results for their contributions
- They learn to trust that children and young people can be heard by adults
- They understand some of the democratic processes in our society, and their rights in relation to those processes.

Benefits for the broader community:

- A sense of pride that children and young people have been respected and enabled to contribute to the design of an outdoor environment that they will use in the future

- Provision of an environment which clearly meets children's or young people's needs and interests
- A strong sense of ownership of the environment by children and young people and low levels of vandalism.

Consultation with children and young people, and their ongoing involvement in the design of urban environments, remains susceptible to various points of potential breakdown. During the process of consultation and participation, facilitators need to 'think on their feet', adapt to the situation as required and thoughtfully adjust the process to suit, while focusing on the original intent. This takes skill, commitment and sensitivity. The goal is always to empower children and young people to effect real change in design projects but processes of engagement, completed at the outset of design projects, may not be continued meaningfully through to construction and post-occupancy evaluation. Often this is because clients are unaware of best practice principles fundamental to the process, or may not have the further resources. Many clients rightfully express how proud they are that they consulted with children and young people at the start of a project, but fall short of achieving an exemplary process because they do not continue children's involvement subsequently.

It is important to remember: each design project is specific to its site. Each group of children and young people is unique. Hence, the participatory process needs to be constantly adjusted to suit the situation at hand. Actual processes and methodologies can and should vary from project to project, but it is vital that there is a well-considered, tried and tested approach in every case, and that experienced people are undertaking the work.

Summary list of principles and recommendations for practice

So we are left asking: how can our processes best achieve authentic involvement with children and young people? The list below is a summary only, but gives some guidance to best practice principles.

1 Involve children and young people in the design process for places in the public domain that they will use. Their contributions are valid, contemporary and invaluable. Adults should not guess the needs and interests of children and young people, and should not design according to what they surmise children would like, but rather, what they know they would like. Find out what children would like in their environments, and keep finding out for every project and place.
2 Invite children and young people to be part of the design process *before* sketch designs are commenced to ensure their ideas are embedded in every part of the design (rather than being an add-on to it).
3 Ensure the participants are a representative sample of all children involved, comprising equal numbers of girls and boys, and covering a range of ages.
4 Report clearly and authentically on the outcomes of the involvement of children and young people in the design process. Do not place adult 'spin' on the outcomes as translation often dulls and deflects the directness of the message.
5 Develop a written design brief capturing what children and young people have suggested for a particular project. The design brief powerfully translates children's ideas into traditional design language, e.g., a child may write "real grass" and the

brief may say "provide turfed areas for free play". Use the brief to formulate the first sketch plan and reference it throughout the design process.

6 Involve children and young people in as much of the project design process as is affordable; that is, where 'affordability' is measured in time and money. Each step of children's involvement means that they can adapt and inform the design to better meet their needs. This means involving the original participants in reviewing the design from their perspectives and adjusting it as necessary with the designers. Children's review at concept stage, then final masterplan stage, and again at pre-tender stage would be ideal.

7 Follow-up during construction through several site inspections is invaluable as children and young people can shape decisions as construction takes place. It is often the nuance of constructed detail that supports or fails children.

8 Clearly report back to the children and young people about how their input has shaped the design process and construction outcomes, and thank them for their input so that they realize their ideas have been valued and acted on.

9 Organize media coverage celebrating the involvement of students in a particular project, and involve the group in public project openings.

10 Bring the original participants to the completed design project/s and evaluate the outcomes from their perspectives. This will establish successes and failures for all parties, which is a useful guide for the next project at hand.

The final part of this chapter describes a participatory design process I was involved with that promoted respect for children to be agents of change in their school grounds, and involved them meaningfully all the way through the design process. This is an exemplary project in that their involvement started *before* a designer was engaged!

Kellyville Public School: an exemplary participatory project and process

Background

Kellyville Public School, located in the northwestern suburbs of Sydney and serving children from Kindergarten through to Year 6, has well-developed and -maintained grounds, which offer a varied range of play and learning opportunities. However, until recently, there was little in the school that specifically catered for imaginative, open-ended outdoor play for Kindergarten to Year 2 children. The design brief (a letter to the students) for this project, issued by the school principal and staff, invited the children to research playgrounds generally and design a playground area outside the Kindergarten to Year 2 classes. The Principal was motivated to try a student-led design process, directly reflecting the school's motto 'Play the Game', and upholding the school's tradition of 'excellence and opportunity' for children. She asked my practice, Fiona Robbé Landscape Architects (FRLA), to further develop the participatory design process and continue working with the students, and to translate their ideas into a fully resolved design for construction. This process is outlined below.

Figure 13.3
An example of a student's playground design drawing (Source: Kellyville Public School)

The participatory process for Kellyville

Stage 1: Student research and design project

Twenty-eight children from Years 1 and 2 (aged 6 and 7 years, respectively) undertook a term-long project to research playgrounds and develop playground ideas for their school. This culminated in each child producing a playground booklet titled 'Playgrounds' which summarized their research process, along with a cardboard project sheet outlining each student's diagrammatic design for the playground site (see Figure 13.3). This work had been completed before I arrived to work with the school.

Stage 2: Analysis of student design ideas

The 28 projects and designs were systematically analyzed, qualitatively and then quantitatively, to ascertain common themes and subthemes specific to this project. The children generated 444 separate ideas for the playground—almost 15 ideas per child. Where there was a high proportion of ideas representing a grouping, that identified

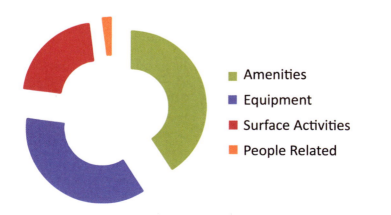

- Amenities
- Equipment
- Surface Activities
- People Related

Figure 13.4
A breakdown of the four main thematic areas from the students' playground projects (Source: Fiona Robbé Landscape Architects)

a 'theme'. An example of a theme is *play equipment*; 161 of the 444 ideas identified specific play equipment elements. Due to its popularity—this represented 38.8 percent of the children's ideas—it became a main theme. Twenty mentions of the 161 ideas (4.8 percent) within that category specifically requested speaking tubes, so that was a subtheme. This information was displayed in graphs, under four main theme categories of amenities, play equipment, surface activities and social outcomes (people related) (see Figure 13.4). Subthemes were represented by color theme coding, in order of popularity, in an additional graph (see Figure 13.5). Similarities and differences in age and gender were also examined. Using simple statistics, we were able to build the case for the children's wishes and preferences.

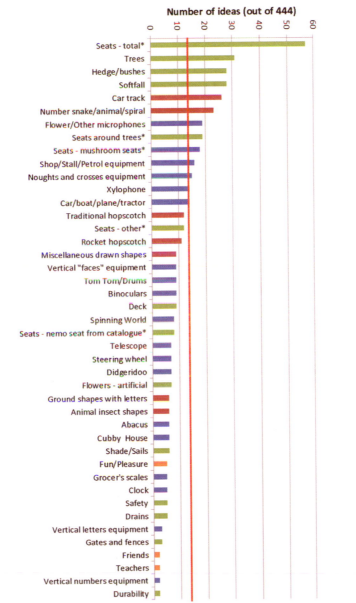

Figure 13.5
Main themes and subthemes from the students' playground projects (Source: Fiona Robbé Landscape Architects)

Stage 3: Formulation of the design brief based on the children's work

Where themes and subthemes were requested by more than half of the students, by age and gender, they were considered essential to include in the playground. (This is represented by the red line in the graph in Figure 13.5.) Naturally, as caring designers we work closely to the stipulated budget, and where possible, try to achieve as many of the subthemes as possible. In the case of Kellyville Public School, we negotiated this carefully with the students who opted to spend more money to achieve their vision, acknowledging that this would take more time and effort. This is a simple, robust and novel way of formulating the playground design brief based on popularity of ideas. The brief was written by the design team, using design language, and supplemented the initial brief written by the principal. The two briefs supported each other, and led the next phase of the design process.

Stage 4: Playground concept plan

The playground design brief was then carefully interpreted into design outcomes by FRLA, and a concept plan was drawn (see Figure 13.6). An accompanying 'opinion of probable costs' (spreadsheet of the cost of each playground item) outlined the anticipated construction expenses.

PATTERNED
RUBBER
SURFACING

DECK

SANDPIT

Figure 13.6
Concept design for new playground, Kellyville Public School (Source: Fiona Robbé Landscape Architects)

Stage 5: Student review of concept plan and costs

The report results, design suggestions and costs were informally presented to a representative group of children from Years 1 and 2, including the Principal, for comment and further design involvement. The informal workshop format allowed for discussions to resolve design questions, confirm the construction budget and agree on when the play area could be built. The children were fully involved in all decisions.

Stage 6: Additional site information gathering

Once the concept was agreed to by all parties (especially by the children), detailed drawings were prepared to tender the playground's construction. The children assisted with gathering additional site information, such as measuring site dimensions and surveying the sloping site to determine levels. Drains were opened and investigated, with considerable interest in what lay under the lids!

Stage 7: Documentation and quotation period

Detailed construction drawings, specifications and schedules were prepared by the design team. Once these were complete and prices had been obtained from experienced landscape contractors, the student group contributed to a discussion about which contractor should be selected to undertake the work and why. The quotations were over budget, and an animated and resourceful conversation was held with the students on the possible options. They debated staging the works, but it was unanimously decided that additional funding should be found so the project could be built all at once, as this was by far the most cost-effective solution.

Stage 8: Interviewing the successful contractor

With the Principal and designers in attendance, the students interviewed the successful contractor. They had thought about their questions ahead of the meeting and were keen to find out how long his team would take to build the scheme, and the order in which the construction would take place.

Stage 9: Construction inspections

Construction work commenced, with weekly inspections undertaken by the Playground Advisory Group of students wearing hard hats and high visibility vests (see Figure 13.7). The students had prepared questions, and took notes to document key construction issues, decisions and progress, which were then relayed back to the school community via the school newsletter. Sometimes a landscape architect was present, but the majority of the inspections were undertaken by the students with their Principal. Formal contractual procedures were undertaken by the Principal.

Stage 10: Playground opening

The playground construction took 16 weeks to complete. The entire school student body attended the official opening, as well as the playground contractor and designers. The playground was named the Sky Walker playground, referencing the space theme as well as the Principal's surname. A red ribbon encircled the playground. Speeches were given by the students, and then the ribbon was cut by the playground advisory group of students and designers (see Figure 13.8). And then everyone played!

LIVERPOOL JOHN MOORES UNIVERSITY
LEARNING SERVICES

Figure 13.7
Overseeing
construction (Source:
Fiona Robbé)

Figure 13.8
The official opening
day (Source: Fiona
Robbé)

Outcomes and reflection

Kellyville Public School's playground represents children's ideas and wishes for their school's outdoor environment. The themes, elements, colors and ideas all came from the children. The professionals involved, including the designers, school administrators and teachers, and the landscape contractor provided the necessary support to enable the children to achieve their ideas. The adults were all united in their enthusiasm to design and build the playground from the student perspective.

Advantages of the process

It was simple, direct, easy to manage and delightful in all phases. Children's ideas and input were authentically obtained through their research processes, class discussions and projects. This initial process was given sufficient time (one school term) to be thorough. The ongoing involvement of students in the concept design phase was genuine, and thoughtful changes were made to the design as it progressed. Continued involvement of the children in the documentation, quotation and construction stages was another strength of the process. Without their ongoing input, compromises would have resulted in the playground having fewer play outcomes than they would have liked. Having the entire student body present at the opening was a highlight, and the playing of the *Star Wars* theme music was not lost on them! The students led the opening ceremony of the playground themselves—another moment of providing the children with respect and opportunities to be empowered in the process of play provision in their school.

Disadvantages of the process

The whole process was time consuming (three years in total from initial contact to opening day). It was expensive to achieve, and only a select group of students could see the whole process through. From the designers' perspective, the authentic child-led design process is expensive, and many aspects of the process were undertaken *pro bono*. From the school's perspective, the process was very long—too long when children are eagerly awaiting outcomes. Funding had to be creatively sourced—typical of many school projects—and this always requires patience and persistence, hence time. Construction was also a slow process due to the highly detailed nature of the work.

Best moments for the designers

Designing the space theme was motivating, the highlight being an 'asteroid belt' around the 'black hole'—achieved with tapered timber decking around a tree with black rubber at its base! Working with the students was enjoyable at all times, and each interaction richly added to the design process. Working with an inspired principal, who shared our vision of child-led decision and design processes, was nothing short of astonishing and was the main reason the entire project was a success.

Best moments for the children

Year 1 and 2 children were highly engaged throughout the design process and enjoyed watching their ideas become a reality. However, the children who were part of the Playground Advisory Group additionally benefited from the experience through their consultations with the teachers, the principal, designers, builders and other students. During construction, these students eagerly participated in weekly site meetings and monitored the progress. They were excited to cut the ribbon at the official opening ceremony, so that everyone could finally enjoy the Sky Walker Playground.

Feedback from teachers

Anecdotally, the teachers describe their new playground as a place where children are very engaged in imaginative play, with few behavioral issues. They highly value this type of play and are proud the school can offer this for their students. There is a high degree of student ownership of the playground, so the students tend to look after it.

Lessons learned

School projects require generous timeframes and budgets, both of which can be challenging to achieve. A shorter project timeline would have rewarded the children at the heart of the process. This requires better funding of participatory design processes, as many of the steps were undertaken for low fees or undertaken *pro bono*, which is a challenge for any landscape architectural practice. A generous construction budget would have saved time pursuing staging and funding options; however, this could not have been anticipated at the outset of the project.

Reflections on the particular success of the participatory design process used

- The students were rewarded by many (at least half) of their ideas having been constructed in the playground; a high percentage compared with consultations on other school projects
- The core student group was involved all the way through the project, which in my experience is unusual in most consultation projects
- The rest of the student and parent body were well informed about the student-led design and construction process and also valued it
- A student-led design process was followed, with students at the center of the process rather than politicians, parents, designers or other competing interests
- The resulting built project is positively viewed by the entire school community and everyone is proud of it.

Conclusion

Involving children and young people in the design of the public domain is a rewarding and valid process for everyone. When children and young people are directly involved, everyone benefits: the client, the project stakeholders, the design community, the broader community and children themselves. Children and young people bring clarity of thought and a positive attitude to design projects, which can often provide direction for fresh design approaches and project outcomes. Even the most perceptive adults cannot fully know what it is to be a child or young person in today's fast-paced, rapidly changing society, and they should not make assumptions and design decisions on behalf of these important groups of people. Children and young people need adults to be strong advocates for their rights to have a voice in the design of public environments that they use, so that their interest in civic participation and the environment is awakened. To invest in the process of children's participation is to invest in a fair, just, egalitarian design process.

References

Craft, A 1999, 'Creative development in the early years: some implications of policy for practice', *The Curriculum Journal*, vol. 10, no. 1, pp. 135–150.

Department of Economic and Social Affairs 2004, *World youth report 2003*, United Nations Publications, New York.

Francis, M & Lorenzo, R 2002, 'Seven realms of children's participation', *Journal of Environmental Psychology*, vol. 22, no. 1–2, pp. 157–169.

Hart, R 1997, *Children's participation: the theory and practice of involving young citizens in community development and environmental care*, Earthscan, New York.

Sanders, E & Stappers, P 2008, 'Co-creation and the new landscapes of design', *CoDesign: International Journal of CoCreation in Design and the Arts*, vol. 4, no. 1, pp. 5–18.

UNICEF 2002, *The state of the world's children*, UNICEF, New York.

CHAPTER 14

At the 'center'

Young people's involvement in youth centers from design to usage

Katina Dimoulias

Introduction

Youth centers are environments that exist specifically for young people to access programs, support or health services, and socio-recreation activities. They can be found in communities across the world. For many adolescents and young adults, these centers serve as a critical point of contact and environment in their lives. Despite their importance to youth development, the majority of youth centers are not purpose-built environments. At best they are renovated or retrofitted buildings, such as converted amenities blocks, church halls or small vacated retail spaces. However, this is starting to change with several purpose-built facilities being commissioned around Australia over the last five years as part of local government initiatives (e.g., Coledale Revitalization Strategy, Shire of Boddington Strategic Community Plan) and several major international initiatives (e.g., Myplace Program, UK, and Youth Café Capital Funding Program, Ireland). Young people's direct involvement in the planning and design of these facilities varies and is not always seen as essential by the governments and professionals involved in the project.

The purpose of this chapter is to encourage authorities and practitioners involved in the development of purpose-built youth centers to prioritize the engagement of young people throughout the planning and design processes. The intent is also to champion the importance of creating an environment that effectively encourages young people's engagement in the delivery of the youth center services after the center's creation. The discussion in this chapter begins with a description of a youth center. The notion of young people's involvement is then discussed as an integral part of creating a youth center setting that is effective in encouraging young people to engage with the center. The chapter concludes with a good practice case study and recommendations to ensure meaningful involvement in research and design projects for the development of a youth center *with* young people.

Youth service and program environments

Public indoor environments for young people range from targeted organized program settings to large, multi-purpose sport or recreational facilities for specific age groups. The focus of this chapter is on center-based youth service and program environments. Within practice, both nationally and internationally, there is little consistency in the way center-based youth services or program environments are distinguished from other types of youth facilities. For the purpose of this discussion, the general term *youth centers* will be used to encompass the range of community or neighborhood site-based services or programs for young people, both within an Australian and the international context.[1] *Youth centers* are defined here as neighborhood or community-based settings for young people and young adults, aged between 12 and 25 years that may deliver a range of targeted support services, organized programs and/or socio-recreational activities in a central and permanent physical structure. Throughout the discussion, the terms *youth* and *young people* will be used interchangeably and inclusively to refer to adolescents or teenagers between the ages of 13 and 18 years. The term *young adults* refers to those aged 19 to 24 years.

Youth centers offer instrumental opportunities for young people and young adults to develop new skills, build relationships with supportive and caring adults, develop proficiencies in a range of interest areas, access educational programs and address personal and/or social challenges (Bond 2010; Dryfoos 1998; Eccles & Gootman 2002; McLaughlin 2000). These are places where a young person can receive relief from and support to deal with family conflict; get an opportunity to complete a high school certificate in an out-of-school program; develop their artistic skills; get help with their homework; and gather legitimately and safely to socialize with friends, play a friendly game of pool or engage in sports or recreational activities.

Despite the developmental and experiential benefits of youth centers, little attention is given to the design of the physical environment to align it with youth needs, organizational objectives and the delivery of services, programs and activities (Dimoulias 2013). It is more common for youth services and programs to be accommodated in non-purpose built structures that are renovated or retrofitted and located in temporary buildings, or co-located with other community services and/or programs. These physical environments are frequently of poor quality, with limited space or unsuitable configurations, restricting the organization's access to the types of spaces needed to provide the full range of services, programs and activities that they want to offer to support young people.

With over 17 years of personal experience, it is disappointing to see many youth centers in metropolitan Sydney continue to present an unwelcoming and ineffective physical environment. This is likely true of youth centers in cities and towns across Australia and in other parts of the world, as funding for purpose-built centers is rare. Youth centers are often situated in geographic catchments that have a large proportion of young people with a high need for support and positive developmental opportunities. A youth center hidden down a narrow side street, surrounded by high wire fencing, with no welcoming entrance, barred windows and no visible youth involvement, is unlikely to attract young people and encourage participation in its range of services and programs. Most importantly, poor physical settings convey to young people that they are not valued by the community.

Purpose-built, youth friendly settings are critical and necessary. Purpose-built centers should include design features that young people perceive as important, such as program and youth spaces, a range of facilities, capacity for personalization, and accessibility (Dimoulias 2013). It is only through young people's authentic participation in the design process (beginning with research about user needs and desires and culminating with evaluation after occupancy) that young people can provide knowledge of the design elements that they prefer.

Figures 14.1 and 14.2 An inner city youth center located in an area with a high proportion of 'at-risk' and disadvantaged young people (Source: Katina Dimoulias)

Youth at the 'center' of their environments

Young people's perspectives are fundamental to our understanding of issues related to their lives. As discussed in previous chapters, within the human and social sciences there is strong evidence supporting advocacy for the invaluable contribution and competency of children and young people to participate in research, either as subjects of research (Christensen & Prout 2002) or as social actors in the research process, including research carried out by children and young people themselves (Christensen & Prout 2002; Prout 2002). Further, Qvortrup (2002) emphasizes that significance must be ascribed to children not only as participants in activities but more so as constructive, value-producing actors.

In addition to their autonomous involvement in the research process, children and young people have demonstrated their capacity to provide critical insight into their own lives and to contribute to a range of areas including policy and decision-making (Morrow 1999; Sinclair 2004; Tisdall & Davis 2004); environmental design processes (Driskell 2002; Sutton & Kemp 2006); and the design of youth programs (Kirshner et al. 2005). In environment-behavior research, while there has been a tradition of younger children's participation (Hart 1978, 1992; Moore 1990), studies involving adolescents' or young people's participation and insights are less numerous. This is changing, however, with a greater number of studies seen in the past decade (e.g., Clark & Uzzell 2006; Derr et al. 2013; Dimoulias 2013; Gerke & Sanyal 2014; Horelli 2006; Sutton & Kemp 2006).

To gain a holistic understanding of the qualities of the settings that are meaningful to and influence the behavioral choices and experiences of young people, it is essential that they are directly involved in the inquiry as active constructors of knowledge (Mayall 2002). As Brodie et al. (2009, p. 6) explain, creating opportunities for meaningful engagement can be a mechanism for improving the "provision of services that are better suited to people's needs and are more efficient".

Youth and adult differences in perceptions of design features

Young people perceive and experience the world around them differently to adults. In planning and designing youth environments, adults' views of needs and preferences tend to be based largely on their personal experiences, their anticipated role in the setting or project, what they know of other similar facilities, and what they believe is best for young people. Frequently their views will be inconsistent with young people's perspectives (Gearin & Kahle 2006; Pretty et al. 2003).

Specifically related to perceptions of the physical environment of youth centers, a recent Australian study compared staff and young people's assessments of physical design features across 10 settings (Dimoulias 2013). Generally, staff put greater importance on physical design features than young people did. On the other hand, staff were less satisfied than young people with almost all of the aspects of the physical environment, such as building size, computer facilities and program spaces. Staff assessments of youth centers are based on how well their design enables service delivery, whereas youth perceptions are based on how well they meet their personal needs and preferences as clients.

Through meaningful engagement in purpose-built youth center projects, young people can participate as research assistants or research partners (Kirshner et al. 2005).

Youth voices can be authentically embedded in the creation of their environments, for example informing the design brief, critiquing designers' concepts and developing their own design ideas. When young people collaborate with adults to develop a youth center, their needs and preferences can be accurately translated into design decisions that result in a setting that is youth friendly, works well for them and fosters greater attendance and program engagement. Involving young people in the design of youth centers also incorporates their contribution to the aesthetics of the building, including its interiors and outdoor spaces. Opportunities to personalize their youth center (e.g., creating murals and artwork, and displays of photographs) are valued by young people, and in turn result in greater involvement in centers and foster a sense of place (Dimoulias 2013).

Involvement in youth centers: from design to access

Youth involvement in the research and designing process and as eventual users of youth centers can range from limited participation to more meaningful and invested engagement. At the lower end, involvement tends to lack an opportunity to gain benefits, occurs at single points in time and results in young people taking part in a more passive manner. In relation to environmental projects, Hart (1999) refers to lower levels of youth involvement as manipulation, decoration and tokenism, which limit genuine engagement in the project. At the higher levels, meaningful engagement involves a more active role, investment in the activity, connectedness and developmental benefits. Chawla (2002) and Hart (1999) describe the higher levels of youth involvement in environmental projects as comprised of characteristics such as self-initiation, collaboration with adults and control by young people.

Youth programs and support services aim to achieve a range of outcomes, in the short and/or long term, to assist young people to positively navigate adolescence, the transition to adulthood, and/or deal with difficult circumstances. Short-term, in-program outcomes can range from point-of-service behavioral outcomes to psychosocial improvements, including instances of direct contact with a program, intensive engagement and increases in a sense of belonging. Longer-term outcomes include the development of competencies, academic achievements and skill development, which are achieved over many months of meaningful and consistent engagement in program activities. Walker et al. (2005) suggest that if the length of time or intensity of engagement in the center and programs is intermittent or short term then it is not sufficient to achieve beneficial outcomes for young people. To achieve beneficial outcomes, youth center designs created with young people should encourage them to attend centers regularly and engage sufficiently in programs and activities so that they can experience the full benefit of their involvement.

Creating a youth center with young people: barriers and challenges

In practice, involving young people in the creation of a youth center continues to be challenged by several common barriers, as discussed below.

1. Lack of valuing young people's voice and contribution in the design of youth environments

In practice, many adults continue to approach youth center design from a position of 'knowing what is best' for young people or 'the professional is the expert'. In doing so, they act as gatekeepers to opportunities for young people's participation. Hence, young people's involvement in the creation of youth centers, their delivery and evaluation continues to be uncommon. To address this, strategies must be put in place to ensure that young people are acknowledged as the experts and genuine partners in the creation of their environments. This is achieved by embedding consultation and engagement methods in design project processes from the outset; ensuring advocates for young people are part of the project team; engaging a youth reference group as assistants or partners; prioritizing young people's voices; and placing their knowledge at the center of design decisions.

Figure 14.3 In 2012 a purpose-built inner city youth, family and community center in Sydney replaced a youth service that had formerly operated from a converted amenity block with no involvement from young people and community members (Source: Katina Dimoulias)

2. Lack of funding to support staff engagement of young people

Limited funding is a significant issue across the youth service sector. Youth center staff often have little funding and staff capacity to support consultation activities beyond their regular program delivery when a new facility is proposed to replace an existing center. Furthermore, funding for new facilities often does not have the scope to incorporate youth engagement as a critical component of the design process. Funding restrictions prevent youth workers and the design team from spending time engaging young people throughout the design process.

*3. Lack of practitioners with skills and experience to engage young
   people authentically*

Another major barrier to young people's involvement in the development of youth
centers is attributed to the limited skills, experience and knowledge of practitioners to engage young people in research and design processes. Strategies to ensure
practitioners are skilled in youth participation include:

- training youth workers and/or a youth reference group in skills to consult and
  engage young people throughout the design process
- employing a consultant experienced in youth participation to collaborate with
  young people in research and design activities
- commissioning an architect/design team who is experienced with youth engagement, values the contribution of young people and is willing to work with young
  people.

Good practice in involving young people in the process of creating a youth environment

There is no universal solution or template for developing an effective youth center
environment that encourages engagement in programs and facilitates the achievement of developmental outcomes. Young people are not a homogenous group; their
needs and user group characteristics vary and are complex. Therefore, local young
people must be given an opportunity to voice their specific needs and preferences in
the planning and design of purpose-built youth center projects.

Over the past decade several purpose-built youth center projects have been commissioned across Australia. Some of these projects were completed with little or no
youth involvement; others incorporated a greater extent of meaningful participation.
Even with the latter, young people's perspectives and involvement were not always
integrated into the design process. A recently completed, purpose-built youth center
in a rural community in regional New South Wales is a noteworthy example of comprehensive youth engagement in practice. The community's unique demographic
characteristics, needs and issues were the driving force behind ensuring that consultation with community members—specifically, with young people—was at the center
of the facility's development. This project will be used to illustrate principal aspects of
good practice in youth participation and engagement, and point out where gaps can
occur in young people's meaningful involvement.

Case study: a rural youth center

The case study youth center is located in a low socioeconomic community in regional
New South Wales. It is an area with high unemployment and low income. Compared
to other districts in the region, this community houses the majority of the Torres Strait
Islander and Aboriginal population, has the highest concentration of social housing
and has a considerably high incidence of crime. In addition, 25 percent of the population in this area is aged between 10 and 24 years (Regional Council Tamworth 2015a).
The youth center targets 12- to 18-year-olds and services the broader region, which
in 2011 had 7,861 young people aged 10 to 19 years (Regional Council Tamworth
2015b).

The need for a purpose-built youth facility emerged as a recurring priority through extensive research and analysis conducted in the community over a four-year period. The research also suggested that the co-location of services and an integrated service delivery approach would be an effective solution for the community. The youth facility project is part of a broader local government revitalization strategy for the area. It is a key initiative that endeavors to address the significant youth challenges and issues inherent in this area, and provide positive opportunities and activities and to support young people in developing positive futures. It was proposed that the youth center would offer a range of cultural/creative, health, education and training, social and recreation service programs and activities.

Planning for the new youth center had two phases. Phase one was a research inquiry, conducted by a consultant, which involved young people and the wider community and resulted in a long-term youth development strategy for the area (Dhinawan 2010). A variety of methods—formal and informal—were employed to consult community members, young people, and government and non-government representatives, including:

- Asset-based Community Development survey with 129 residents (including young people)
- Kids in Action survey with 158 young people
- Focus groups with 50 young people
- A community-wide workshop with 20 local residents and Aboriginal Elders
- Eight 'kitchen table' consultations with 50 community residents, including young people in their homes and at the community center
- Two 'World Café'-style consultations with 60 local government and non-government agencies and potential stakeholders
- A community petition of support with over 500 signatures (Dhinawan 2010).

Phase two consisted of research activities to identify the most suitable site for the youth center and a skate park, and understand gaps in local service provision. The methods employed included:

- A two-day forum with 20 young people
- Door knock of 40–50 residents situated in close proximity to the two proposed sites
- Local resident survey (Dhinawan 2010).

Participatory activities with young people and community members were also planned for the consultations that focused on the youth center design concept. It is understood by the author that the skate park designers conducted a pre-design workshop with young people and community members in which participants generated concept designs and identified preferred design elements. The workshop outcomes were used to produce a vision and a design brief for a new skate park. Further to this, young people were invited to be part of creating a personalized physical environment for the center. An indigenous artist was employed to work with the community to create a unique setting that respected local young people and their contributions, and that reflected the local indigenous culture.

In addition to the formal research activities, a key member of the project working group—the existing center's Youth Services Coordinator—regularly engaged young

Figure 14.4
A youth friendly
method of engaging
young people in
the planning of
their youth center
(Source: Stephen
Blanch)

Figure 14.5
Local young
people involved
in consultations to
decide on a site for
their youth center
and skate park
(Source: Stephen
Blanch)

people in informal conversations about their views for a new facility. Through these
conversations, the coordinator sought to understand what concepts were of importance to young people, such as creating a safe and welcoming place, or a place
they could be proud of. These qualities were embedded in the project's design principles and informed the design brief. This knowledge was invaluable, providing a

strong foundation for the youth representatives to advocate for design decisions that represented young people's voice and expressed their desires. For example, during the design process when the notion of safety was raised, some stakeholders recommended a heavy-duty security mesh covering all center windows as a preferred design option. However, this solution was not consistent with young people's views of creating an appealing, youth friendly and welcoming safe haven. The youth representative argued that a less obtrusive option would be better suited to creating a setting that was not only safe, but also respected young people's preference for a friendly and welcoming place.

On reflection

This project involved processes with a number of critical elements that generated a more supportive and congruent youth center for local young people and the community. These included: 1) proponents of youth involvement being key members of the project team; 2) a bottom-up approach allowing young people and community members to be essential actors in identifying the main issues, youth and community needs and solutions for the local area; and, 3) indirect community and youth involvement in the design of the center which enabled them to have some part in creating an outcome that met their needs.

Several areas for improvement were also highlighted in this project. The role of young people in these research processes positioned them as key informants in the planning and design of their center. Greater direct, more active and ongoing involvement in the design process would have provided young people and the community further opportunities to more closely align the design outcome with their needs. Finally, a post-occupancy evaluation of the youth center once it was completed and in operation—which was not planned for the project—would generate valuable information about the performance of the new facility.

Recommendations for practice

Five principal recommendations that have emerged from analysis of this case study, along with research and practical experience with purpose-built youth facilities, are discussed below.

1. Research community and young people's needs and desires

The development of a youth center environment should begin with a research inquiry to identify both the broader community needs and, more specifically, young people's needs and preferences. A combination of youth friendly research methods and approaches that allow all young people, including those experiencing social exclusion, to be involved in the research process at different levels is recommended as this yields a broader range and depth of views.

2. Engage with young people to uncover the meaning of key descriptions
of the physical setting, e.g., 'youth friendly', 'safe place', 'place of pride',
so as to ensure their accurate translation into design decisions

This principle is one that is often neglected in the development of youth centers and as a result contributes to design decisions being made that do not accurately represent young people's needs and views. Engaging young people in conversations that draw on their perceptions and experience to uncover the meaning of environmental qualities is paramount. Young people's experience in public settings, youth centers and their community make them experts on the environmental qualities that support positive development. Using formal techniques to uncover the meaning of concepts is important, but the value of informal discussions with young people in their everyday settings should not be underestimated.

3. Value young people's participation throughout the design process
and be willing to respect young people's insights in the design

Working with design teams that respect young people's participation and are committed to working closely with them is fundamental to a successful project outcome. As emphasized throughout the chapter, this engagement should involve young people at critical stages throughout the center's design process.

4. Give young people opportunities to 'put their stamp' on the setting

When young people have the opportunity to make design choices that personalize the center's program spaces—with artwork, murals, soft furnishings, carpeting, etc.—the aesthetic qualities of the place reflect a more youth-oriented, appealing and welcoming environment. Often purpose-built center designs do not allow scope for this kind of personalization. However, these things can foster a sense of ownership and give young people a feeling of belonging within their community, which in turn encourages regular visits and program participation. Importantly, personalized spaces also visibly communicate the value of young people and their contributions to the center and to the community.

5. Conduct post-occupancy evaluation with young people with the
support of staff and other design professionals

Post-occupancy evaluations (POEs) generate valuable knowledge of the performance of environments. POEs are rarely undertaken on purpose-built youth centers; however, this kind of evaluation would be invaluable for learning about what works and does not work in youth centers' design. With an understanding of salient design features, youth preferences and how the physical environment supports developmental outcomes and positive experiences, we can improve the new facility and inform the design of future similar projects. Engaging young people in the evaluative process has the potential to increase their sense of ownership and control in the delivery of their youth center and its programs.

Conclusion

In the past 10 years, several major government initiatives, within Australia and internationally, have invested in the development of purpose-built youth centers. In addition to these initiatives, there has also been an increase in the number of individual projects of new youth centers. Many of these projects have recognized the significance of involving young people in youth center development processes. However, youth engagement in projects is not guaranteed and may be limited to the initial planning process only, or simply ignored. The success of youth centers to support young people, motivate them to visit centers and engage in beneficial programs and activities is partly reliant on young people's involvement in creating an environment that effectively meets their needs. Researchers, practitioners, funders, policymakers and governments are strongly encouraged to prioritize young people's engagement in the creation of youth centers and to ensure that meaningful and authentic involvement occurs throughout all stages of the project. Giving young people opportunities to collaborate with adults on these projects, conduct research, translate their perspectives into the design principles and project briefs, and make design decisions, can lead to better environmental and social outcomes for youth and their communities.

Note

1   The term *Centre-Based Youth Service* was developed by the author (Dimoulias 2013) for the Australian context; it refers to community-based settings for young people aged between 12 and 25 years that deliver support services, referrals, programs and activities in a central and permanent physical structure. The term *youth center* is based on this term and is used here to have broader international relevance.

References

Bond, S 2010, *Integrated service delivery for young people: a literature review*. Brotherhood of St. Laurence. Available from: www.bsl.org.au/pdfs/Bond_Integrated_service_delivery_for_young_people_lit_review_2010.pdf.

Brodie, E, Cowling, E, Nissen, N, Ellis Paine, A, Jochum, V & Warburton, D 2009, *Understanding participation: a literature review*, National Council for Voluntary Organizations, London.

Chawla, L (ed.) 2002, *Growing up in an urbanising world*, UNESCO/Earthscan Publications, Paris.

Christensen, P & Prout, A 2002, 'Working with ethical symmetry in social research with children', *Childhood*, vol. 9, no. 4, pp. 477–497.

Clark, C & Uzzell, DL 2006, 'The socio-environmental affordances of adolescents' environments' in *Children and their environments: learning, using and designing spaces*, eds C Spencer & M Blades, Cambridge University Press, Cambridge, pp. 176–195.

Derr, V, Chawla, L, Mintzer, M, Cushing, DF & Van Vliet, W 2013, 'A city for all citizens: integrating children and youth from marginalized populations into city planning', *Buildings*, vol. 3, no. 3, pp. 482–505.

Dhinawan, N 2010, *Coledale youth space: a report of first phase consultation*, The Youthie.Org. Available from: www.theyouthie.org/Get-Involved/Services/research-reports.

Dimoulias, K 2013, *Valuing youth settings: the environmental context of center-based youth services and its influence on young people*, PhD thesis, University of Sydney.

Driskell, D 2002, *Creating better cities with children and youth: a manual for participation*, UNESCO/Earthscan Publications, Paris.

Dryfoos, J 1998, *Safe passage: making it through adolescence in a risky society*, Oxford University Press, New York.

Eccles, J & Gootman, JA 2002, *Community programs to promote youth development*, National Academy Press, Washington, DC.

Gearin, E & Kahle, C 2006, 'Teen and adult perceptions of urban green space Los Angeles', *Children Youth and Environments*, vol. 16, no. 1, pp. 25–48.

Gerke, G & Sanyal, N 2014, 'Engaging youth in the planning process: walking reflections', *Children Youth and Environments*, vol. 24, no. 3, pp. 201–212.

Hart, R 1978, *Children's experience of place*, Irvington, New York.

Hart, R 1992, *Children's participation: from tokenism to citizenship*, UNICEF International Child Development Center, Florence, Italy.

Hart, R 1999, *Children's participation: the theory and practice of involving young citizens in community development and environmental care*, Earthscan Publications, London.

Horelli, L 2006, 'A learning-based network approach to urban planning with young people' in *Children and their environments: learning, using and designing spaces*, eds C Spencer & M Blades, Cambridge University Press, Cambridge, pp. 238–255.

Kirshner, B, O'Donoghue, J & McLaughlin, MW 2005, 'Youth-adult research collaborations: bringing youth voice to the research process' in *Organized activities as contexts of development*, eds JL Mahoney, RW Larson & JS Eccles, Psychology Press, New York, pp. 131–156.

Mayall, B 2002, *Towards a sociology for childhood*, Open University Press, Buckingham.

McLaughlin, MW 2000, *Community counts: how youth organizations matter for youth development*, Public Education Network, Washington, DC.

Moore, RC 1990, *Children's domain: play and place in child development*, MIG Communications, Berkeley, California.

Morrow, V 1999, '"We are people too": children's and young people's perspectives on children's rights and decision-making in England', *The International Journal of Children's Rights*, vol. 7, pp. 149–170.

Pretty, GH, Chipuer, HM & Bramston, P 2003, 'Sense of place amongst adolescents and adults in two rural Australian towns: the discriminating features of place attachment, sense of community and place dependence in relation to place identity', *Journal of Environmental Psychology*, vol. 23, no. 3, pp. 273–287.

Prout, A 2002, 'Researching children as social actors: an introduction to the children 5–16 programme', *Children & Society*, vol. 16, no. 2, pp. 67–76.

Qvortrup, J 2002, 'Sociology of childhood: conceptual liberation of children' in *Childhood and children's culture*, eds F Mouritsen & J Qvortrup, University Press of Southern Denmark, Odense, Denmark, pp. 43–78.

Regional Council Tamworth 2015a, *Community profile*. Available from: http://profile.id.com.au/tamworth/five-year-age-groups?WebID=10.

Regional Council Tamworth 2015b, *Community Profile*. Available from: http://profile.id.com.au/tamworth/five-year-age-groups?WebID=230.

Sinclair, R 2004, 'Participation in practice: making it meaningful, effective and sustainable', *Children & Society*, vol. 18, no. 2, pp. 106–118.

Sutton, SE & Kemp, SP 2006, 'Young people's participation in constructing a socially just public sphere' in *Children and their environments: learning, using and designing spaces*, eds C Spencer & M Blades, Cambridge University Press, Cambridge, pp. 256–276.

Tisdall, EK & Davis, J 2004, 'Making a difference? bringing children's and young people's views into policy-making', *Children & Society*, vol. 18, no. 2, pp. 131–142.

Walker, J, Marczak, M, Blyth, D & Borden, L 2005, 'Designing youth development programs: toward a theory of developmental intentionality' in *Organized activities as contexts of development*, eds L Mahoney, RW Larson & JS Eccles, Psychology Press, New York, pp. 399–418.

CHAPTER 15

Engaging children and adolescents in local decision-making

Growing Up Boulder as a practical model

Mara Mintzer and Debra Flanders Cushing

Introduction

For three years, children and adolescents in Boulder, Colorado, USA, had been studying, modeling and discussing their ideas for the Boulder Civic Area, a public space in the heart of downtown Boulder. Primary school children designed tree houses for the space so they could see birds, touch trees, read books and simply hang out, and their secondary school peers readily endorsed these ideas. In May 2015, the city's planning board unanimously passed an amendment to incorporate the "ideas from Growing Up Boulder, including . . . a tree house for children" into the Boulder Civic Area Master Plan (https://bouldercolorado.gov/pages/previous-planning-board-decisions). This outcome was a result of activities facilitated through Growing Up Boulder, an ongoing child and youth friendly city initiative that has enabled community leaders to embrace young people's design and planning ideas and codified them into city policy (Derr et al. 2013).

This chapter will discuss the establishment, organizational structure, funding sources and engagement techniques for a child and youth engagement program

Figure 15.1 Tree house with pillows, slide, books and a ladder, envisioned by a Boulder primary school child (drawing by 8-year-old child from Whittier International Elementary School) (Source: Mara Mintzer)

called Growing Up Boulder (GUB), focusing on the strong partnerships at its core. This discussion will present GUB as a practical model from which other communities can learn in order to support and engage children and adolescents in community decision-making. As a long-running initiative, GUB continues to evolve and reflect on successes and challenges, seeking to incorporate best practices from research and practice. The chapter concludes with a reflection on GUB's impact and offers recommendations for other communities looking to establish their own child friendly city initiative.

The context and establishment of the Growing Up Boulder initiative

Founded in 2009, GUB empowers Boulder's children and adolescents by providing opportunities for inclusion, influence and deliberation on local issues that affect their lives. GUB emphasizes the inclusion of young people from a diversity of income levels and ethnicities, while concurrently recognizing that all children and adolescents deserve a voice in community decision-making. As a child and youth friendly organization, GUB combines the rights-based focus of the United Nations Convention on the Rights of the Child (UNICEF 2014) with the participatory approach of Growing Up In Cities (Chawla 2002). GUB is also aligned with the global Child Friendly Cities (CFC) movement that developed from a long history of social justice efforts.

GUB operates in Boulder, Colorado, an American city of approximately 100,000 people nestled at the foothills of the Rocky Mountains. Boulder is an unusually dynamic city for its size; it hosts the state's flagship public university, the University of Colorado Boulder, numerous start-up companies and large, established corporations. More than 72 percent of its citizens aged 25 years and older hold a four-year bachelor's degree or higher, compared with 29 percent of citizens nationally (US Census Data 2009–2013). In addition, its civically engaged citizens have contributed significantly to the character of the city. For example, in 1969 a group of residents started a movement for open space conservation, which led citizens to approve a government tax to purchase land for a green belt around the city. This has grown to a network of 45,000 acres that surrounds the city today.

In spite of its progressive politics and largely affluent and well-educated citizenry, not all of Boulder's residents share equally in the good fortunes of the city. Fourteen percent of Boulder's children live in poverty. During the 2012/13 school year, only 61 percent of low-income children read at or above grade level by third grade, versus 91 percent of their more affluent peers. Similarly, 63 percent of Latino children read at grade level or above versus 90 percent of Anglo children. Mirroring these examples of inequity, Boulder's most actively engaged citizens are primarily financially advantaged, educated, white adults. People of color, of limited means, parents with young or school-aged children, immigrants and young people themselves tend to be left out of the civic engagement process (Community Foundation 2013).

Working to rectify this situation, GUB not only empowers and supports individual children and adolescents through select projects, but also takes a broader, more systematic approach to involve multiple organizations and stakeholders. Three primary organizations founded GUB: the University of Colorado, the City of Boulder and the Boulder Valley School District (the area public schools for K-12 children). GUB operates out of the Environmental Design Program at the University of Colorado Boulder. This academic setting enables a focus on place-based approaches and projects that have a

Figure 15.2
University and high school students work together to offer design solutions for dense, affordable housing in the city (Source: Lynn M. Lickteig)

strong connection to the physical environment, an important aspect that has not been fully explored in the child friendly city literature (Woolcock et al. 2010).

As the first founding partner, the University provides in-kind resources to coordinate the initiative, ensures the initiative is grounded in best practices and current research, and broadly disseminates outcomes of the work. The University benefits from the initiative by enabling researchers to study theoretical and practical elements, while university students gain valuable skills.

The second collaborator and founding partner is the City of Boulder. The city's Executive Director of Community Planning and Sustainability for Boulder, David Driskell, was instrumental in establishing the initiative. Driskell has extensive experience involving children and adolescents in community development and served as the UNESCO Chair for Growing Up In Cities. Having a champion for young people's voice in a government leadership position was key to GUB's beginnings, but the strong partnerships with other city departments developed because of GUB's track record of worthwhile processes and products. As a result of being able to offer projects at low or no cost in the beginning, GUB now has ongoing relationships with the city's Parks and Recreation, Transportation, Library, and Open Space and Mountain Parks departments.

The third founding partner is the Boulder Valley School District (BVSD), which provides the initiative with legitimacy in the schools and helps negotiate bureaucratic hurdles. GUB, in turn, facilitates projects that support the District's mission to ensure students are "prepared for successful, civically engaged lives", and develop into "lifelong learners who confidently confront the great challenges of their time" (www.bvsd. org/goals/Pages/default.aspx).

Soon after GUB was established, the three key partner organizations created and signed an auto-renewing memorandum of understanding (MOU). This important agreement has helped maintain continuity and generate institutional memory as staff and organizational structures change. The MOU focuses on relationships between the partners and deliberately does not involve funding to avoid being constrained by economic fluctuations.

The next section provides an overview of the organizational structure of GUB and describes the roles played by various stakeholder groups.

A multi-tiered organizational structure

Over its six years, GUB's organizational structure has evolved to support high-quality work that requires consistent but manageable time commitments from partner agencies. The initiative focuses on developing both top-down and bottom-up partnerships, since both are key to GUB's model.

Committees

The GUB executive committee, comprised of department heads and leaders from the three founding partner organizations, meets bi-annually; its role is to set the direction and support the GUB vision. The steering committee, in contrast, meets bi-monthly and is comprised of on-the-ground partners, including representatives from city departments, child and adolescent serving organizations, and non-profit organizations. On average, eight organizations are active in the steering committee at any given time; however, this group is dynamic, with participation shifting as organizational priorities and staff availability changes. This fluctuating composition of the steering committee is effective, as only those with current GUB interests attend the meetings. Because the GUB coordinators network continuously throughout the university, city government and the community-at-large, there is a steady flow of new and continuing partner organizations involved in GUB. As Chawla et al. (2005) note, it is this building of multilevel alliances that helps sustain effective participatory processes with children and adolescents.

GUB coordinators

From the outset, two part-time coordinators have shared the responsibility for day-to-day tasks and project development, keeping GUB running smoothly. One coordinator focuses on connections within the University and academic writing, while the other focuses on relationships with the outside community and day-to-day administration.

Participating children and adolescents

Children and adolescents, aged 3 to 18 years, are at the heart of all GUB projects and activities. GUB primarily works in established school classrooms or after-school programs.

University students

Undergraduate students at the University of Colorado also represent an important part of the GUB team. As students studying environmental design, including architecture, landscape architecture and planning, they contribute technical and graphic communication skills, and an understanding of the physical environment. Students gain experience in the areas of community organizing, consensus building and facilitating participatory processes, which are particularly relevant to community-oriented design and planning professions (Angotti et al. 2012).

Visiting scholars from around the world, including PhD students, master's students and postdoctoral researchers, are also interested in learning from GUB. They conduct research, assist with activities, contribute expertise and share GUB outcomes with international audiences.

Teachers

Teachers in the public school system serve as gatekeepers to their classrooms and are essential partners to meaningful engagement with children and adolescents. They ensure that GUB's projects are sensitive to their students' age, culture, socioeconomic status and personalities, as well as to the teachers' curricular goals. The GUB team and teachers develop a GUB curriculum together and revise it throughout the process. The most successful projects include teachers who commit extra time outside of the classroom and whose classes are relatively flexible, without rigid curriculum requirements or state testing expectations.

Partner community organizations

When not working in school classrooms, GUB relies upon partners to lead their own GUB projects, often within established out-of-school programs. For example, two long-time GUB partners include the city's Youth Services Initiative (YSI), an after-school and summer program, and the Boulder Journey School, a private local preschool.

Figure 15.3
YSI students pose behind picture frames that they used in photographs of positive and negative elements for a new city park (Source: Victoria Derr)

City staff and leaders

City staff and city council members visit each GUB classroom at some point during the project. This serves as an opportunity for the city to hear directly from young people, and proves to the children that their work and ideas have importance and real-world impact.

Parents and families

GUB offers opportunities for parental and caregiver engagement in multiple ways. Parents volunteer as field trip chaperones, serve as experts on given topics and assist behind the scenes. When children are involved with civic projects in their classrooms, parents are also more likely to take interest and become engaged. For example, when Boulder Journey School's preschool children shared their recommendations for the Boulder Civic Area redesign at a city council meeting, more than 20 parents joined them in the council chambers.

Foundations of the GUB model

GUB builds upon the foundations of the 2006 Denver Child/Youth Friendly City Initiative, a project based out of the University of Colorado's Children, Youth and Environments (CYE) Center. The CYE Center, now the Center for Engaged Research and Design (CEDAR), gave birth to GUB and imparted several important lessons based on experiences with other cities. First, it is crucial to establish relationships with non-profits, funders and government entities before requesting resources. Second, community engagement takes significant time to be successful. Third, it is important to learn which government agencies wish to engage with a child friendly city initiative, build upon those relationships and let go of relationships which feel forced or are met with hostility (Kingston et al. 2007; Wridt 2008).

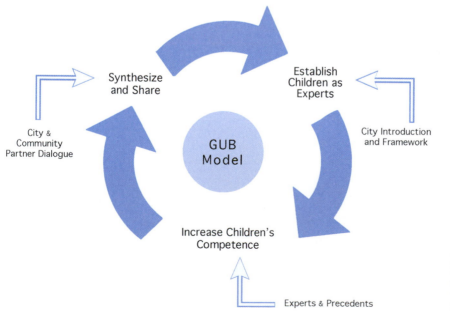

Figure 15.4 GUB model diagram (Source: Adapted from Derr & Yilmaz 2015)

Growing Up Boulder operates by using these lessons learned and builds upon new principles as well. GUB's iterative process, developed into a model, helps the team design consistent interventions or curricula across projects. The GUB model is composed of three key phases, which together form a continuous feedback loop (see Figure 15.4).

Phase 1: Establish children as experts

A project begins by framing a problem for a group of young people: how should the city redesign the heart of downtown Boulder? What should a new city park look like? Why do these issues matter to young people and to the city? To answer questions like these, GUB begins with the assumption that young people are experts in their particular community. They know best what it is like to be a child or adolescent today living and experiencing the city. GUB establishes children as experts by bringing the question to the individual level, whereby each child has something meaningful to contribute and is always correct in her assertions. When children, especially those least likely to have a voice in society, are valued for their contributions from the inception of a project, they are more likely to engage and continue to contribute throughout. The other goal of the 'children as experts' component of the process is to capture young people's ideas before they are influenced by adult and expert solutions, as children are often more flexible and creative in their thinking (Derr 2015; Levitt & Dubner 2014).

Phase 2: Increase children's competence

Next, GUB increases children's competence by expanding their knowledge in the topic area of study. For example, if the city wants to design a nature play area, what are the best examples of nature play in the world and why? How do students feel about these precedents? Through slideshows, videos, field trips, independent research and conversations with experts, young people learn about similar problems and solutions around the world.

Phase 3: Synthesize and share

The last step of the GUB model is for students to synthesize what they have learned from others with their own ideas then share their recommendations with key decision-makers. Students debate their ideas with peers, refine their thinking then present their projects to a wider audience. 'Share-out' events might take the form of group digital presentations to a panel of experts or might involve experts visiting table displays where students discuss their 3-D models, persuasive writing or photo exhibits. In culminating GUB events, the city and community partners engage in an authentic, two-way dialogue with the children and adolescents. Adults are invited to enter the students' space, where students are most comfortable and are supported by familiar teachers and adult mentors. Visiting young people in their space shifts the power dynamic and empowers students to speak more freely. As the young people have spent weeks dissecting the given topic, they are well prepared to hold informed discussions with their adult visitors (see Figure 15.5).

As GUB's cyclical model illustrates, GUB projects are works in progress. A project may end after a large share-out event, or it may repeat the cycle as interest and time allow. In order for the model to thrive, the conditions below are essential.

Creative, multimodal methods of engagement

At the center of GUB's model is the use of creative, multimodal methods for learning. By using a variety of engagement methods, at both the individual and group level, GUB curricula provide opportunities for every child to experience success. Methods of engagement include photovoice, 3-D model making, mapping, persuasive writing, drawing and digital presentations (Derr & Yilmaz 2015). The GUB team itself is continually learning about new methods of engagement through conferences and papers and incorporates them into lesson plans. GUB selects student groups to work with that have flexible curricular needs, allowing for optimal creativity in the curriculum development.

While a GUB coordinator spearheads the curriculum development, it is developed collaboratively with teachers, after-school program mentors, city staff and GUB interns or scholars.

Build upon established networks

Based on GUB's six years of experience, the majority of GUB projects now take place in school classrooms and in after-school programs (Derr et al. 2013). The initiative does this for two reasons. First, the organized group setting offers a diverse group of students with whom to work and an ongoing structure for productive meetings. Second, building upon established relationships is an important technique for enlisting youth engagement (Blanchet-Cohen & Torres 2015). An adult leader who already has a trusting relationship with young people allows GUB to build upon that connection and bring students into the learning process more quickly.

Figure 15.5 A city leader listens to third graders explain their ideas for the Civic Area site plan (Source: Catherine Hill)

Figure 15.6 GUB employs the 'City as Play' method, developed by urban planner James Rojas, to help intermediate school students envision a new Civic Area (Source: James Rojas)

Value and reflect students' culture in projects

While Boulder's population as a whole is not particularly diverse, the young people with whom Growing Up Boulder works come from a variety of backgrounds. Many GUB children or their parents are born in other countries, come from low-income backgrounds and speak languages other than English. For this reason, when possible GUB engages team members who reflect the children's cultural, linguistic and/or socioeconomic background. GUB also builds opportunities for the appreciation of students' cultures into the curriculum by asking young people to include elements of their own and their peers' heritage into their projects. For example, Boulder high school students proposed adding a walkway with quotes from Boulder's varied languages into the Civic Area in order to make a more inclusive public space.

Customized deliverables

GUB coordinators also work with city staff to develop customized outputs that meet their department's needs. Often GUB delivers a report that summarizes children's recommendations and uses words, tables and images to support their ideas. Less traditional deliverables can also be successful, as demonstrated by an adapted graphic illustration. When a professional artist for the city's bike-walk visioning summit included input from GUB's children, youth and parents into the overall graphic, the GUB team took the illustration a step further and adapted it to highlight the young people's recommendations. Since its creation, the Director of Transportation

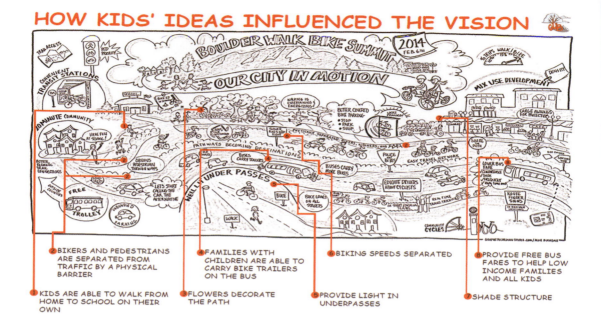

HOW KIDS' IDEAS INFLUENCED THE VISION

② BIKERS AND PEDESTRIANS ARE SEPARATED FROM TRAFFIC BY A PHYSICAL BARRIER

④ FAMILIES WITH CHILDREN ARE ABLE TO CARRY BIKE TRAILERS ON THE BUS

⑥ BIKING SPEEDS SEPARATED

⑧ PROVIDE FREE BUS FARES TO HELP LOW INCOME FAMILIES AND ALL KIDS

① KIDS ARE ABLE TO WALK FROM HOME TO SCHOOL ON THEIR OWN

③ FLOWERS DECORATE THE PATH

⑤ PROVIDE LIGHT IN UNDERPASSES

⑦ SHADE STRUCTURE

has repeatedly shared this graphic with others to represent the concerns of those who are so often absent from the public discussion (see Figure 15.7).

Figure 15.7 GUB applied an overlay highlighting child, youth and parent contributions to a graphic designed for Boulder's Transportation Master Plan (Drawing by Alece Birnbach at Graphic Recording Studio with overlay by Anna Reynoso)

Challenges

Operating with limited funding

It has taken time for GUB to become established and grow into a valued community initiative. In the beginning stages, the initiative was supported through small contributions from private individuals, the city and school district, small university grants, volunteer time, and service and research requirements for university staff. More recently, GUB has combined funding from several city departments and university grants to stretch resources, while also relying on in-kind contributions from the founding partner organizations. In spite of the growing financial support, the initiative is still underfunded. As an initiative and not a service-providing entity or non-profit, GUB is often ineligible or overlooked for community grants. Likewise, it is less likely to receive significant research funding because it does not focus on traditional research outputs.

Absence of champions, relevancy or organizational alignment

GUB projects are less successful when there is no city leader to serve as a champion; children and adolescents cannot see the relevance of the project to their own lives; or there is limited organizational alignment between GUB and the potential partner.

One example of this stems from a child and youth bill of rights project. At the request of a city council member and several GUB executive team members, GUB staff facilitated projects with intermediate and secondary school students to create a child and youth bill of rights for the city. Although elements of the project were successful, it also ran into two problems. First, when the city councillor left office, few other city leaders considered a bill of rights a priority. Without a champion from the city, the project felt less important and meaningful to the students. Second, students in an elective after-school program for low-income and immigrant youth proved unenthusiastic about the topic, as demonstrated through their project evaluations and through diminishing attendance at meetings. Whether the topic of a bill of rights was too vague, too academic or just not relevant to some of the youth in this program, the GUB team agreed that future projects were likely to be more successful if they focused on more personally meaningful and tangible outcomes.

Organizational alignment is equally important, as GUB's experience with a local non-profit illustrated. GUB requested to work with a well-known out-of-school program that provides lifelong learning skills to children and families of limited income. After several meetings, however, it became apparent that the organization was not a good fit. The non-profit was overextended with other partnerships in the community, and the goals for their program (performing math and reading at grade level) were quite different than the goals for GUB's projects (giving children a voice in decisions that affect them). Although GUB facilitated several activities with this group, the partnership has since faded.

GUB's challenges, while frustrating at times, have helped the initiative choose more successful projects, partners and ways of working. The challenges and successes have led GUB to refine its operations and make a positive impact at multiple levels.

Positive impact at multiple levels

GUB has had a positive impact on the young people, community partners and undergraduates with whom it works. GUB evaluates its work in a variety of ways, ranging from the use of questions from the *Child-Friendly Cities and Communities (CFC) Assessment Toolkit* (IRC/CERG 2011), to an analysis of the process, which asked children and adults what they liked and what they would change about a project. Emails and interviews from partners have also helped GUB complete the story of how its work affects participants.

In response to the question of how GUB has been most effective, David Driskell, the city's Executive Director of Community Planning and Sustainability, responded:

> The thing that stands out for me . . . is that . . . [young people] engage in a co-educational process so that it's a dialogue rather than just coming and voicing [their] perspective. They're actually listening to the perspectives of others and in the process, maybe changing their perspective and coming to a . . . more complex understanding of all the things that go into creating a community (Driskell 2014, interview by Derr, August 25).

Parents are also appreciative of the valuable opportunities their children have in the community through GUB. One preschool parent expressed her excitement in a public online forum:

> My five-year-old's preschool class recently partnered with Growing Up Boulder on submitting ideas to revamp the Boulder Civic Area. Not only did the City Council and designers listen to the kids and take their ideas seriously, the winning bid for the design consists mostly of ideas that came FROM THE KIDS! How cool is that?!

Figure 15.8
A preschool child interacts with a presentation about her class's work (Source: Lauren Weatherly)

> When Boulder has an amazing, functional, family-friendly Civic Area to enjoy, you'll have a bunch of five-year-olds (among others) to thank (Anna, preschool parent, 2013, *Boulder Rock'n Moms Yahoo group post*, December).

While other GUB papers describe the impacts of individual GUB interventions (Derr 2015, Derr & Kovács 2015, Derr et al. 2013), Table 15.1 summarizes the impacts of the work overall.

The majority of GUB projects show statistically significant increases in the pre- to post-test CFC assessment statement, 'The government asks me my opinions about my life or my community'. Perhaps the most significant indicator of the initiative's success is the increasing number of requests from city departments, teachers and schools, developers, non-profits and outside municipalities that GUB now receives for its services and guidance. A city department head recently told GUB staff, "We need GUB more than GUB needs us".

Table 15.1 The impacts of the GUB project.

	Primary and Secondary Teachers & Students	Undergraduate Students & Faculty	City partners
Most effective?	Authentic connection with partners Respectful attitude, genuine listening Opportunities for peer-to-peer dialogue Showing how ideas can be translated into plans All students are engaged in learning by use of creative & multiple methods	Participation with young people and a broad range of community partners broadens perspectives Sequential process of engagement, from in-depth outreach to integrated seminar and studio Project of professional interest	Engaging people of all ages in a co-learning process Longer time frame allowed for dialogue, seeing different points of view Leverage city funding significantly
Most significant results or changes?	Kids having a voice and feeling that their work mattered A sense of agency and empowerment Development of relationships over time Feeling heard by city government and leaders	Holistic problem solving Idea of duty and stewardship Students start to find themselves Relevance of issue Learning values and effective methods for participation	Instilling a value, a mindset within young people and city leaders

(Source: Adapted from Derr 2015 and Derr & Kovács 2015)

GUB as a transferable model of practice

Based on GUB's research and the reports of others, GUB is the only project of its kind worldwide that has had such longevity and continued success. It can be a valuable model for other communities wishing to develop child friendly initiatives that successfully intersect with civic projects and processes for the benefits of children, young people and the community as a whole. The essential elements of the GUB model, which could be effectively transferred to other locales, include:

- Bringing together founding partners that include a municipality, a research institution and a public school system or similarly established group that works with young people
- Establishing strong relationships with partners first before requesting significant funding
- Finding leaders within each institution who will champion the child friendly city concept

Figure 15.9
Primary school
students dialogue
with GUB partners
about dense,
affordable housing
(Source: Lynn M.
Lickteig)

- Ensuring that each community partner's organizational mission has elements which align with those of the CFC; if there are none, then find a different organization which is a better fit
- Working within existing programs of young people, such as school classrooms or structured after-school programs
- Choosing student groups that have flexible curricula in order to optimize collaborative and innovative program design
- Using creative, interactive and varied methods of engagement to support multiple types of learners
- Providing opportunities for authentic, two-way dialogue between city leaders or decision-makers and students
- Offering the first project(s) free of charge or at a low cost, then requesting remuneration for future projects after partners have seen how a CFC project can add value
- Employing a continuous feedback cycle to gather feedback from young people, their teachers and community partners to learn and refine what works best for their community.

Conclusion and moving forward with GUB

Persistence, commitment and a willingness to learn from past experiences are key to achieving deeper change within child friendly efforts (Bartlett 2005). This is true for GUB. The development of effective partnerships is a dynamic, ongoing process and after six years, partners understand how rich the work can be when each stakeholder contributes.

Looking towards the future, GUB will continue running high-quality projects with Boulder's children and adolescents, while also seeking opportunities to transfer GUB's knowledge to others in the community. The GUB team is developing new evaluation tools to better measure the initiative's efficacy; training colleagues in partner organizations how to implement the model themselves; and finding additional ways to integrate the GUB philosophy into university classes. As the requests continue to grow, Growing Up Boulder uses its mission as guidance in its evolution: to empower Boulder's young people with opportunities for inclusion, influence and deliberation on local issues that affect their lives.

Bibliography

Angotti, C, Doble T & Horrigan, P (eds) 2012, *Service learning in design and planning: educating at the boundaries*, New Village Press, Oakland, California.

Bartlett, S 2005, 'Integrating children's rights into municipal action: a review of progress and lessons learned', *Children, Youth and Environments*, vol. 15, no. 2, pp. 18–40.

Blanchet-Cohen, N & Torres, J 2015, 'Enhancing citizen engagement at the municipal level: youth's perspectives' in *Handbook of children and youth studies*, eds J Wyn & H Cahill, Springer Science+Business Media, Singapore, pp. 392–402.

Breitbart, M 1995, 'Banners for the street: reclaiming space and designing change with urban youth', *Journal of Planning Education and Research*, vol.15, pp. 35–49.

Chawla, L 2002, 'Insight, creativity and thoughts on the environment: integrating children and youth into human settlement development', *Environment and Urbanization*, vol. 142, no. 2, pp. 11–21.

Chawla, L, Blanchet-Cohen, N, Cosco, N, Driskell, D, Kruger, J, Malone, K & Percy-Smith, B 2005, 'Don't just listen—do something! Lessons learned about governance from the Growing Up in Cities project', *Children, Youth and Environments*, vol. 15, no. 3, pp. 53–88.

Community Foundation Serving Boulder County 2013, *Boulder trends report*. Available from: www.commfound.org.

Crafton Walker, A 2013, 'Re: Improve North Boulder!', *Boulder Rock'n Moms Yahoo Group*, November 12.

Derr, V 2015, 'Integrating community engagement and children's voices into design education and community planning', *Co-Design: The International Journal of CoCreation in Design and the Arts*. DOI:10.1080/15710882.2015.1054842.

Derr, V & Kovács, I 2015, 'What does child-friendly, dense, affordable housing look like? A case study of participatory neighbourhood design from Boulder, Colorado, USA', *Journal of Urbanism: International Research on Placemaking and Urban Sustainability*. DOI:10.1080/17549175.2015.1111925.

Derr, V & Yilmaz, S 2015, 'Effective means of communication for children and youth to have a voice in environmental decisions in their city', paper presented at 'Bridging Divides: Spaces of Scholarship and Practice in Environmental Communication', The Conference on Communication and Environment, Boulder, Colorado, June 11–14.

Derr, V, Chawla, L, Mintzer, M, Cushing, DF & Van Vliet, W 2013, 'A city for all citizens: Growing Up Boulder's approach to engaging children and youth from marginalized populations', *Buildings*, vol. 3, pp. 482–505.

Gurstein, P 2003, 'Youth participation in planning: strategies for social action', *Canadian Journal of Urban Research*, vol. 12, no. 2, pp. 249–274.

Horrigan, P 2006, 'Design as civic action and community building' in *From the studio to the streets: service-learning in planning and architecture*, eds MC Hardin, R Eribes & C Poster, Stylus Publishing, LLC, Sterling, Virginia, pp. 127–138.

IRC/CERG 2011, 'Child-friendly cities and communities assessment toolkit'. Available from: www.childwatch.uio.no/projects/activities/child-friendly-cities-and-communities-research-project/finaltoolkit2011.html.

Kingston, B, Wridt, P, Chawla, L, van Vliet, W & Brink, L 2007, 'Creating child friendly cities: the case of Denver, USA', *Municipal Engineer* 160, Issue ME2, pp. 97–102.

Levitt, S & Dubner, S 2014, *Think like a freak: the authors of Freakonomics offer to retrain your brain*, Harper Collins, New York.

UNICEF 2014, *Convention on the Rights of the Child*. Available from: www.unicef. org/crc/index_30160.html.

US Census State and County QuickFacts 2015, *State and county QuickFacts*. Available from: http://quickfacts.census.gov/.

Woolcock, G, Gleeson, B & Randolph, B 2010, 'Urban research and child-friendly cities: a new Australian outline', *Children's Geographies*, vol. 8, no. 2, pp. 177–192.

Wridt, P 2008, 'Visioning and implementing a child- and youth-friendly city: organization, strategy and findings from Denver', paper presented at the 'Child Friendly Cities Conference', Rotterdam, The Netherlands, November 3–5.

CHAPTER 16

Preparing children and young people for participation in planning and design

The practice of built environment education in Germany

Angela Million

Introduction

In Germany, there is a rising interest in creating better public participation today, fuelled by previous unsuccessful participation processes, for example 'Stuttgart 21', a plan to refurbish the main train station in that city, and the development plans for Tempelhofer Feld in Berlin, which resulted in a successful public poll against any future development. Due to demographic change there is a focus in German city planning on families—parents, children and youth—to make inner cities more attractive for them (Bundesstiftung Baukultur 2015, p. 44). Practices in built environment education (BEE) with children and young people offer an excellent opportunity to prepare them for participation in the current design and planning processes. The rationale for, and benefits of, BEE for children and young people, built environment professionals and projects will be outlined in this chapter.

Children and young people are enthusiastic, intensive users and navigators of city spaces (Christensen & O'Brien 2003). Their awareness of their environment, with 'feel-good' places and 'no-go' areas, is one of their most basic experiences and makes them experts in their own everyday lives. However, the participation of children and young people often fails to be influential (BBSR 2013). Participation is influential when "actions aim to intervene in existing conditions", "involvement is part of the public dialogue and decision making" and "engagement is influential and changes are significant" (Mullahey et al. 1999, pp. 3–4). To date, participation by children and young people has not become part of German planning culture (Moser 2010, p. 19). In fact, planners and architects are still often unsure how to involve young people, especially in formal planning processes.[1] This is especially true for young people under the age of 18 and is the case not only in Germany, but also in other countries such as the US and Australia (Frank 2006, p. 351).

There are several reasons for this, including the demanding and complex nature of planning and designing, the failure to reach children and young people and to keep them interested, or a failure to implement their ideas. The *German National Baukultur-Report* for 2014/15 therefore asks for a new culture of participation, which includes enabling strategies and the strengthening of building and planning skills "in formal and extracurricular education and linking Baukultur education and participation more intensively than before" (Bundesstiftung Baukultur 2015, p. 94).[2]

This chapter presents methods of BEE which teach children and young people about the built environment. In the first part, the obstacles to children's participation in urban planning and design will be discussed. Then BEE, with its aims and values, will be defined. The chapter ends with a discussion which links built environment education with young people's effective participation and finally it looks at the implications for planners' and architects' education. The reflections presented here are based on several research and participatory projects conducted by the author with different partners over the last 10 years. The work of JAS Jugend Architektur Stadt e.V. (a non-profit organization which promotes built environment education and the participation of children and young people in urban planning and design) will be introduced to provide a window into BEE practice and how it can help prepare children and young people for more effective participation.

Defining children's participation and its value for urban planning and design

Current challenges for German cities in the field of urban planning and design include the demographic change towards an older and more diverse population; increased cultural pluralism and social fragmentation; new trends in living, working and shopping; the Smart City movement; climate change, and the transition to renewable energies; differences in the urban development of growing and shrinking cities and regions; the lack of public sector funds; and renovation of public infrastructure, such as roads, bridges and schools (Bundesstiftung Baukultur 2015, p. 58). In recent years there has been growing acknowledgment of children and young people as stakeholders who should be involved in urban planning and design processes. Children and young people are increasingly seen as experts in their own lives and are also recognized as "producers of cities" (BBSR 2013).

Planning practitioners, politicians and researchers identify a long list of convincing justifications for and benefits of children and youth participation, especially in the areas of civil law, democratic and political theory, educational, ethical and moral theory, and service orientation (Betz et al. 2010, p. 3). Specifically:

1   Intergenerational exchange through participatory processes can improve communication and understanding between younger and older people in society
2   Being involved in planning and decision-making gives young people an opportunity to bring forward their own ideas and present themselves as equal discussants. This helps decrease the negative prejudices which adolescents frequently face in society
3   By actively involving different groups, environments can be created which suit the needs of all groups in a society. Involving young people and their interests becomes even more important
4   Participatory processes foster integration in a neighborhood and identification with a community by being involved in shaping the environment and by being taken seriously in the process and appreciated
5   Participatory processes foster social and democratic learning (Frank 2006; Hart 2009; Million & Heinrich 2014).

Table 16.1 contains scales, topics and subjects useful for indicating how and when children's and young people's participation should take place in German city planning

Table 16.1 Scales and themes of participation by children and young people in city planning and design in Germany.

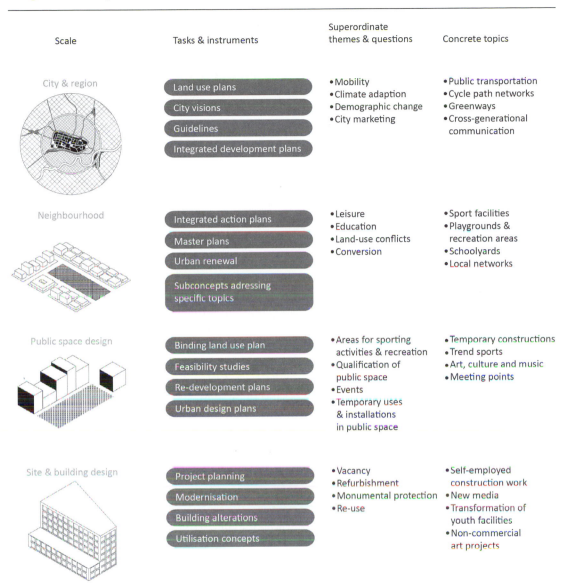

Scale	Tasks & instruments	Superordinate themes & questions	Concrete topics
City & region	Land use plans City visions Guidelines Integrated development plans	• Mobility • Climate adaption • Demographic change • City marketing	• Public transportation • Cycle path networks • Greenways • Cross-generational communication
Neighbourhood	Integrated action plans Master plans Urban renewal Subconcepts adressing specific topics	• Leisure • Education • Land-use conflicts • Conversion	• Sport facilities • Playgrounds & recreation areas • Schoolyards • Local networks
Public space design	Binding land use plan Feasibility studies Re-development plans Urban design plans	• Areas for sporting activities & recreation • Qualification of public space • Events • Temporary uses & installations in public space	• Temporary constructions • Trend sports • Art, culture and music • Meeting points
Site & building design	Project planning Modernisation Building alterations Utilisation concepts	• Vacancy • Refurbishment • Monumental protection • Re-use	• Self-employed construction work • New media • Transformation of youth facilities • Non-commercial art projects

(Source: Adapted from Uttke et al. 2013)

and design. It is derived from a research project titled *A Practical Test of Youth Participation*, which evaluated 55 pilot participatory projects involving young people (Niemann et al. 2013; Uttke et al. 2013). The pilot projects and their evaluation were funded by the German Federal Ministry of Transport, Building and Urban Affairs. They aimed to provide an exploratory setting for testing methods, instruments and strategies for involving youth in urban planning and decision-making processes by funding real-life youth participation projects (BBSR 2013).

The table identifies themes and topics that have a strong relation to the needs and interests of youth, as indicated in the participatory pilot projects by children and young people themselves. It explicitly shows where children and youth need to be involved in the processes of planning at several scales, including the region, city or neighborhood; public space design; or at the micro-level of a building or site.

The list in the table is not complete, as trends and developments continue to highlight new ideas about how and where participation is needed. For example, in Germany recently, the influx of refugees is creating new demands on planning for housing and neighborhood development. As planning tasks differ, participation concepts also have to be strongly rooted in the local and regional context of each project. The appropriate level of participation is closely related to this also. The table thus does not specify what level of participation or "agency or participatory engagement of children and young people" (Hart 2008, p. 23) is necessary for different scales of planning and design.

Our study (Heinrich & Million 2016 based on Uttke et al. 2013) showed that the larger the spatial setting of planning, the more likely there were to be strategies for child and youth participation. However, as city and regional planning often deals with the long-term development of a whole region, city or city district, this presents challenges to a successful participation process as there is a high degree of abstraction, long planning horizons of sometimes more than a decade, and a huge gap between planning and implementation with a lack of personal contact between decision-makers and adolescents. In these instances, planning practitioners named eliciting any interest at all from the children and young people in the participation process as the biggest challenge.

The most successful level of involvement for children and young people, in particular, occurred when they were part of the design process for public spaces and buildings for which they were the main user groups (such as schools, youth centers and daycare centers). This also included the design of outdoor spaces, meeting places, shelters, street furniture, performances and events, and installations that (re-)designed public squares and green spaces. At this scale of planning there was more child-initiated, directed and shared decision-making with adults. The young people realized a number of youth-led pilot projects at the scale of sites and buildings demanding a high level of professionalism, self-organization and project coordination from them. The major obstacle for such youth-led projects is the availability of and/or access to suitable spaces. Availability in this context refers to whether neighbors and property owners accepted dedicated spaces for children or youth.

These few examples show that participation in urban planning and design is a challenge, not only for the professionals directing participatory planning projects, but also for the children and young people involved. At times, there is little fun for them, given the high expectations of their involvement. This is where children's and young people's education on architecture, urban design and planning can help. BEE offers children the opportunity to:

- develop awareness and an understanding of the local environment and an appreciation for architecture and design
- learn about stakeholders, rights and responsibilities in the design of the environment and possible careers in the built environment
- understand the roles, rights and responsibilities of professionals in the creation of the built environment as a contribution to society and sustainable development

- broaden personal, learning and thinking skills such as creativity, confidence, self-management, teamwork, critical reflection and judgment, participatory and communicative skills
- experience analytical and conceptual working methods (Engaging Places network 2012; International Union of Architects 2008, p. 5).

Built environment education for children and young people

Built environment education is as multifaceted as its subject: the built, designed environment. It incorporates a broad field of activities, focuses and approaches to education such as environmental, architectural, design and (visual) arts education, mostly for children and young people. All of these types of learning activities for children and young people use buildings, places and spaces as topics and contexts for learning (Uttke 2012).

The number of initiatives dedicated to teaching children and young people about architecture and the culture of building has risen in the past 10 years beyond existing activities (such as architects-in-schools) to include the national chamber of architects in Germany (and also in the US and in other countries). It has also become a more interdisciplinary movement, bringing together professionals from different fields, including architects, urban planners, landscape architects, environmental planners, educators and artists. Educational projects are run by education officers in museums or dedicated architecture centers; people working in the wider sector of culture and the arts; design and planning practitioners, and architects working either independently or through their professional bodies; and, of course, teachers in schools and kinder-gartens. What they share is a link to the built environment as a focus and a setting for formal and informal learning. In addition, over recent years there has been a shift from activities with purely educational aims to those offering participation in real planning and design projects (Uttke 2012).

Table 16.2 lists the aims related to built environment education. It was published in 2006 by an international group of BEE educators who formed the international association of built environment education (PLAYCE = play + space). As there are countries in Europe which do not have urban planning as a separate profession from architectural design, PLAYCE uses the term 'architecture' synonymously with the term 'built environment'. In international built environment education practice, the designa-tion 'architecture education for children and youth' is used equally often and does not refer only to education about buildings (Laaksonen & Räsänen 2006).

When it comes to participation processes, built environment education can directly assist by providing concrete knowledge and skills before, just in time for or within the planning and design process or 'hands-on' building process. Built environment education can also give young people knowledge and an understanding of long-term visioning and planning processes and foster their skills in dealing with abstraction. As such, built environment education can be beneficial in several ways: it can improve the quality of results; promote young people's ability to analyze, reflect, criticize and formulate their own ideas while bearing in mind the demands and aims of other stake-holders and interest groups; and it allows them to present their results professionally in public forums.

To give an insight into BEE teaching practice, the work of the non-profit organiza-tion Jugend Architektur Stadt e.V. (JAS) will be discussed. This organization promotes

Table 16.2 Aims of built environment education focused on architecture and the built environment, children and education as defined by PLAYCE.

Architecture-focused aims

- To promote reflection on and constructive criticism of the built environment and related practices
- To support built environment professionals in working with children in the design process
- To support multi-disciplinary collaboration between professionals and children
- To improve the built environment

Child-focused aims

- To broaden children's experience of the built environment
- To promote enjoyment and exploration of the built environment
- To promote the development and use of creative skills and processes
- To support children's identification with the environment and society
- To support children in experiencing the richness of cultural diversity

Education-focused aims

- To support the use of a range of approaches to learning
- To support the use of architectural education in the school curriculum, as a vehicle for multidisciplinary learning
- To encourage creative and critical thinking
- To support architectural education in informal education
- To promote the role of built environment professionals in education

(Source: Adapted from Laaksonen & Räsänen 2006)

built environment education and the participation of children and young people in urban planning and design. JAS conducts educational workshops and participatory planning projects for and with children and young people in cooperation with different partners, such as private initiatives, schools, municipalities, universities and other institutions.

A specific approach to learning about the built environment: the work of JAS

Multiple methods are available to enable children and young people to learn about the city and processes of space production and to express their ideas about the city and architecture based on their own strengths, via speech, text, images, film or models. Looking back at a decade of educational projects and participatory planning, three areas of learning have been identified by the JAS educators, each of which also have a strong capacity to improve children's and young people's experience of participation:

1 Space investigation: See & Explore
2 Developing ideas and designs: Design
3 Communication to the public: Present & Implement.

The aim of the methods is to foster competencies and skills in a communicative, interactive process of participation. (The JAS projects mentioned are presented online with their methods and outcomes and will therefore not be discussed in detail here.)

Space investigation

When JAS conducts participatory planning and design, it never starts with a wish list of ideas, nor jumps into a design process without knowing the space and the inhabitants' needs. Just as professionals do an investigation before they start the design

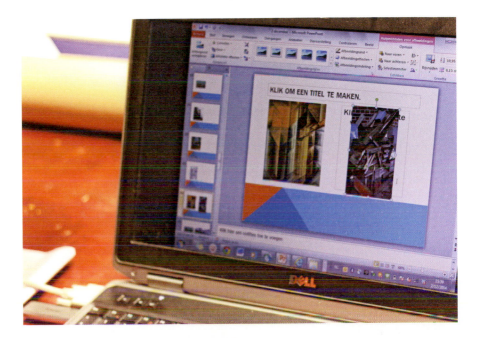

Figures 16.1 and 16.2 Challenging young people's views about their neighborhood by using historic paintings (Source: JAS Jugend-Architektur-Stadt e.V., Essen)

and planning process, it is crucial not only to find out about the children's and young people's perceptions of good and bad spaces but also to look for hidden qualities to plan and build upon. In BEE there are a number of exercises that are useful to encourage children and young people to explore the built environment with all their senses, to understand connections and to form their own opinion. For example: traversing buildings and districts; mapping out and recording sensory impressions; marking out movements; listing the positive or negative aspects within a space; holding interviews; or taking photos and videos. Depending on the planning and design focus, they can also carry out a conventional site analysis including working with maps, aerial photos and existing master plans. This was done, for example, in the Greven youth-built projects, which consisted of planning and designing youth meeting points providing shelters in public spaces. At the same time the young people were taught through discussions with planners and architects about the background of planning, such as ownership, building codes and land use regulation.

JAS often works very visually, preferably with media that are familiar to children and young people. Through searches for scenes from films or paintings in their neighborhoods, participants are challenged to change their views on their everyday surrounding and identify the hidden potential of a site. Built environment education is also connected with actively entering the city and exploring it on foot, by public transport or by bicycle. It includes site visits, sometimes also to learn about other spaces in the city that may not be within the everyday sphere of children—an approach not often found in traditional planning processes as they generally only focus on the spaces to be designed or planned. Engaging intensively with the city and its inhabitants promotes children's ability to read, assess and understand space and the forces that shape it. This fosters an understanding of the complexity of planning. It can also produce criticism which children may respond to with suggestions for change. This usually leads to the next step: the development of ideas and designs.

Developing ideas and designs

The investigation and experience of spaces and people are the basis on which young people develop their own spatial vision. The JAS projects showed that short exercises to study colors, forms and materials enhance the quality of the final, built product. The aim is to encourage young people to gain the means of creative expression and to develop various, meaningful ideas for spaces, buildings or whole urban districts. Ultimately, it is to prevent them from jumping on the first ideas which come up. For example, young people in Greven wanted to simply buy a garden house from the home improvement store to use as their new shelter, but it did not meet demands such as resistance to vandalism, nor flexibility for reuse and redesign.

The design process relies on the visualization of ideas, and techniques for communicating ideas are taught using collage making, drawing or storytelling. Sometimes films are also produced to convey the main ideas. Here the aim is usually to foster peer learning as the young people often are highly competent in this area.

One very successful method in participatory planning and design has proved to be testing children's and young people's ideas as temporary, 1:1 scale installations in buildings, on streets or in plazas (see Figure 16.2). In Hannover, a school hallway was transformed into a parkour course and pupils monitored the reaction of their fellow students. In the city of Aachen, a street was temporarily closed to study its potential as an extended schoolyard (see Figure 16.3). In a national workshop to develop a manifesto for youth participation in planning and design, one idea was to test the main messages as slogans using a megaphone (see Figure 16.4). Sometimes these temporary prototypes or events proved to be the start of a design and planning discussion with politicians, residents and other stakeholders.

Figure 16.3 Testing ideas for public space in a temporary event such as the closing of a neighborhood street in Aachen (Source: Patricia Eichert)

Figure 16.4 Testing the main messages of a manifesto for youth participation in planning and design using a self-built megaphone (Source: Andreas Meichsner)

Presenting and discussing ideas

Good presentation skills proved to be crucial for children and young people to make positive impressions on officials at public hearings and committee meetings, and to win advocates and supporters for their ideas and projects. In planning processes especially, young people (and occasionally children) got involved in heated discussions with city officials, politicians and residents. Role play and escalation training can help to prevent young participants' motivation from dwindling after hard discussions, negative press articles or protests by residents.

Figure 16.5 Young people presenting their ideas for public spaces to be part of a neighborhood development plan via a billboard campaign in Aachen (Source: JAS Jugend-Architektur-Stadt e.V., Essen)

Figure 16.6 High school and university students producing a game to be played in public to define the elements involved in redesigning Karl-Marx-Platz in Berlin (Source: JAS Jugend-Architektur-Stadt e.V., Essen)

As children and young people do not just want to announce their views, JAS tries to combine participatory processes with visible results, which can be temporary in nature. Depending on the planning target, street signs, postcard series and performances, for example, are created to let children and young people present their ideas in public. A billboard campaign was a result of a brainstorming process for the development of a city district where children and young people conveyed their ideas for rethinking public streets and plazas in the Aachen city center (see Figure 16.5). Participating in the redesign of a plaza resulted in the development of a board game by children, assisted by university students. The children played it with the wider public on a farmers' market day to collect further ideas for redesigning the plaza (see Figure 16.6).

The links between built environment education and young people's participation

As presented in the educational work by JAS, there are a number of ways to enhance participatory planning processes as a means of learning about planning and design and to foster the quality of the outcome and the communication of young people's ideas. Hart's (1997) ladder of children's participation defined different means and degrees of participation alongside different levels of expression of children's agency. Hart (2008) states that there can be many interpretations of the ladder and that the degree of participation needs to suit the individual project. The more children and young people take the lead in participation processes, the greater the expression of agency but the more demanding it is likely to be for them.

Different competencies, skills and knowledge help in children's mastery of participatory planning processes. As in some of the JAS projects mentioned, when children and young people participate in urban analysis and design tasks, knowledge about planning processes as well as presentation and communication skills are helpful. Built environment education is a way to help children and young people better master different levels of participation in various planning processes and can be a stepping stone to more successful participation for children and young people. Therefore, built environment education can be regarded as a necessary component of successful participation processes in planning and design (Bertelsmann Stiftung 2009; Knauer & Sturzenhecker 2005).

There is also an academic discussion on what pedagogical participation should be like. It can be clearly stated that there is a distinction between participation and education, as their primary goals differ (Parnell 2006, p. 74). In particular, Mullahey, Susskind and Checkoway (1999, p. 4) contend: "young people's work that focuses on individual learning and development, rather than on changing their surroundings, is not real participation". Knauer and Sturzenhecker (2005) also conclude that, by definition, youth participation is not pedagogical because it allows young people to be political actors and policy-makers.

Nevertheless, there is also a general agreement that participation automatically implies educational processes. Studies show that participation itself leads to key areas of personal growth, such as self-reliance, communication skills and developing one's own point of view (Million & Heinrich 2014, referring to Knauer & Sturzenhecker 2005, p. 3; Winklhofer & Zinser 2008). Hence, even if participation is not intended to be educational, educational processes do, in fact, take place.

This makes planners—and anybody else organizing a participatory planning and design process—educators, whether they like it or not. Planners have long been portrayed as facilitators and mediators, who need to be able to work and communicate across professional and non-professional boundaries and with diverse groups (Selle 1996; Udy 1991). Forester (1999) too, stresses that planners need to be teachers because "they can promote effective processes of public learning" (p. 61).

Since the 1990s there has also been a discussion on the role of BEE in participation processes. Critical reflection on this approach ascertains that it works as a learning experience for children, young people, planners and designers but does not always result in an improved or changed built environment (Francis & Lorenzo 2002, p. 164). Planners need special training to carry out participatory planning and design (Francis & Lorenzo 2002; Gaus-Hegner et al. 2009). This is not something that is usually explicitly pursued in higher education, except in courses for future professional teachers. However, if one frames the task of planning and designing in these terms, then one option that arises is to offer students the opportunity to become 'teachers' themselves through their education.

Conclusion

This chapter began by clarifying current issues in German city development at various scales and discussing the themes of child and youth participation in Germany today. Participatory obstacles for children and young people were discussed, as well as failures by planners to organize influential participation. With a focus on enabling children and young people to master the participation processes, built environment education was introduced to link the demanding and complex nature of planning and design with child and youth participation. Built environment education methods have enhanced the recent practice of participation, transforming it into a more communicative learning process, which helps solve some of the current issues in planning participation. Planners also need to develop the skills and capacities of educators, helping children and young people master different levels of participation. Lastly, we can only imagine how children and young people who have engaged with urban planning and design at a young age will take action as adults. It may be that increasing children's and young people's knowledge of cities and spaces and their participation skills could lead to a better culture of building and planning in the future.

Acknowledgments

This paper is based on research and practice carried out together with a number of dear colleagues. Special thanks go to Juliane Heinrich and Felix Bentlin for joining me in researching youth participation and cities as settings for learning. Special thanks also go to Päivi Kataikko, Silke Edelhoff, Carla Multhaup, Sebastian Schlecht, Thorsten Schauz and Ralf Fleckenstein of JAS Jugend Architektur Stadt e.V. for their joint efforts in built environment education in the past 10 years.

Notes

1   Formal planning processes are urban planning processes defined by building law; in Germany, they are defined for example in the Baugesetzbuch.
2   "Baukultur is understood as the joint and interdisciplinary effort to implement processes which help improve the (physical) quality of urban places" (Wesener 2011, p. 426). The term *Baukultur* includes striving for better planning and design processes as well as for an improved physical quality of urban places.

Bibliography

BBSR—Bundesinstitut für Bau-, Stadt- und Raumforschung [Federal Institute for Research on Building, Urban Affairs and Spatial Development] 2013, *Adolescents in urban neighborhoods*. Available from: www.bbsr.bund.de/BBSR/EN/RP/ExWoSt/FieldsOfResearch/TeenagersUrbanQuarter/01_Start_dossier.html?nn=386162.

Bertelsmann Stiftung (ed.) 2009, *Mitwirkung (er)leben. Handbuch zur Durchführung von Beteiligungsprojekten mit Kindern und Jugendlichen* [Effective action: a handbook on the implementation of participation projects for children and adolescents] (2nd ed.), Verlag Bertelsmann Stiftung, Gütersloh, Germany.

Betz, T, Gaiser, W & Pluto, L 2010, 'Partizipation von Kindern und Jugendlichen. Diskussionsstränge, Argumentationslinien, Perspektiven' in *Partizipation von Kindern und Jugendlichen. Forschungsergebnisse, Bewertungen, Handlungsmöglichkeiten* [Participation of children and adolescents: research results and societal challenges], eds T Betz, W Gaiser & L Pluto, Wochenschau-Verlag, Schwalbach/Ts., Germany, pp. 11–31.

Bundesstiftung Baukultur (ed.) 2015, *Baukultur report 2014/2015: built living spaces of the future—focus city*, Federal Foundation of Baukultur, Potsdam, Germany.

Christensen, PM & O'Brien, M 2003, *Children in the city: home, neighborhood, and community*, Routledge, London.

Engaging Places network (ed.) 2012, *Built environment education*. Available from: www.engagingplaces.org.uk/about%20us/art63734.

Francis, M & Lorenzo, R 2002, 'Seven realms of children's participation', *Journal of Environmental Psychology*, vol. 22, pp. 157–169.

Frank, KI 2006, 'The potential of youth participation in planning', *Journal of Planning Literature*, vol. 20, no. 4, pp. 351–371.

Forester, J 1999, *The deliberative practitioner: encouraging participatory planning processes*, MIT Press, Cambridge.

Gaus-Hegner, E, Hellmüller, A, Wagner, E, Weber-Ebnet, J (eds.) 2009, *Raum erfahren—*

Raum gestalten [Experience space—design space], Athena Verlag, Oberhausen, Germany.

Hart, RA 1997, *Children's participation: the theory and practice of involving young citizens in community development and environmental care*, UNICEF, New York.

Hart, RA 2008, 'Stepping back from "the ladder": reflections on a model of participatory work with children' in *Participation and learning: perspectives on education and the environment, health and sustainability*, eds A Reid, BB Jensen, J Nikel & V Simovska, Springer, New York, pp. 19–31.

Hart, S 2009, 'The "problem" with youth: young people, citizenship and the community', *Citizenship Studies*, vol. 13, no. 6, pp. 641–657.

Heinrich, AJ & Million, A 2016, Young people as city builders: putting youth participation in German municipalities to the test. *Dis-P The Planning Reivew*, vol, 52, no. 1, pp. 56–71.

International Union of Architects UIA (ed.) 2008, *Built environment education guidelines* (2nd ed.). Available from: http://uiabee.riai.ie/downloads/uia_bee_en.pdf.

JAS Jugend Architektur Stadt e.V. n.d. Available from: www.jugend-architektur-stadt.de.

Knauer, R & Sturzenhecker, B 2005, 'Partizipation im Jugendalter' [Participation in adolescence] in *Kinder- und Jugendpartizipation. Im Spannungsfeld von Interessen und Akteuren* [Participation of children and adolescents: between interests and stakeholders], eds B Hafeneger, MM Jansen & T Niebling, Barbara Budrich, Opladen, Germany, pp. 63–94.

Laaksonen, E & Räsänen, J (eds) 2006, *Play+space=playce: architecture education for children and young people*, Alvar Aalto Academy, Helsinki, Finland.

Million, A & Heinrich, AJ 2014, 'Linking participation and built environment education in urban planning processes', *Current Urban Studies*, vol. 2, pp. 335–349.

Moser, S 2010, *Beteiligt sein. Partizipation aus der Sicht von Jugendlichen* [Participation from adolescents' viewpoint], VS Verlag für Sozialwissenschaften, Wiesbaden, Germany.

Mullahey, R, Susskind, Y & Checkoway, B 1999, *Youth participation in community planning*, American Planning Association, Chicago.

Niemann, L, Schauz, T, Andreas, V, Uttke, A, Heinrich, AJ & Edelhoff, S 2013, *Kompass Jugendliche und Stadtentwicklung* [Youth and urban development compass], Bundesministerium für Verkehrs, Bau und Stadtentwicklung, Berlin, Germany.

Parnell, R 2006, 'Serious play in design: students and children exploring architecture' in *Play+space=playce: architecture education for children and young people*, eds E Laaksonen & J Räsänen, Alvar Aalto Academy, Helsinki, Finland, pp. 67–75.

Selle, K 1996, *Planung und Kommunikation: Gestaltung von Planungsprozessen in Quartier, Stadt und Landschaft. Grundlagen, Methoden, Praxiserfahrungen*, Bauverlag, Wiesbaden, Germany.

Udy, JM 1991, *A typology of urban and regional planners: who plans?*, E. Mellen Press, Lewiston, New York.

Uttke, A 2012, 'Towards the future design and development of cities with built environment education: experiences of scale, methods, and outcomes', *Procedia—Social and Behavioral Sciences*, vol. 45, pp. 3–13.

Uttke, A, Heinrich, AJ, Bentlin, F, Bombach, S, Niemann, L, Schauz, T, Andreas, V & Edelhoff, S 2013, 'Jugendbeteiligung im Praxistest' [A practical test of youth participation], Berlin, Dortmund, unpublished final report.

Wesener, A 2011, 'Improving quality of place: strategic approaches in Germany and the UK' in *Proceedings of REAL CORP 2011*, eds M Schrenk, VV Popovich & P Zeile, pp. 425–435. Available from: http://programm.corp.at/cdrom2011/files/CORP2011_proceedings.pdf.

Winklhofer, U & Zinser, C 2008, 'Jugend und gesellschaftliche Partizipation' [Youth and societal participation] in *Die Gesellschaft und ihre Jugend. Strukturbedingungen jugendlicher Lebenslagen* [The society and its youth: structural conditions of adolescents' situation], eds G Bingel, A Nordmann & R Münchmeier, Barbara Budrich, Opladen, Germany, pp. 71–93.

Conclusion

Kate Bishop and Linda Corkery

Throughout this book, we have presented numerous initiatives, strategies, projects and processes from around the world that have had an impact on built environment outcomes for children and young people and, in the best situations, have engaged them in decision-making. Ideologically, there is a lot of overlap in the chapter content as all the authors fundamentally support the ambition for children and young people to have greater opportunity for active civic participation. What we can draw out from the projects summarized here is that the rights of children and young people, enshrined in the UN Convention on the Rights of the Child are—25 years later—still to be fully and consistently implemented. Nevertheless, the CRC resonates as a guiding force for realizing children's rights in the governance processes of our communities.

Despite expressing good will towards the UN Convention and its ambitions, most signatory nations have not translated its principles into their domestic legislation, nor used it as a basis for changing policy or practice in any domain of children's lives. So the CRC continues to be an inspiring, aspirational stand-alone document with tremendous potential to influence social directions, but remains poorly implemented at this point in time. Certainly, the greatest losers in this are children and young people themselves, but society as a whole also misses out when we do not create processes and places that enable all citizens to contribute to the world we share.

In both the seminar series convened in 2012 and this book, we have covered the major processes involved in the creation of the built environment, highlighting main points of breakdown in those processes and recommending ways to amend our approaches and procedures for children's and young people's benefit, in particular. At the culmination of the seminar series we asked participants for their feedback on three questions:

1 What are some points of immediate change for you to make in your professional practice, or for your organization?
2 What were your 'aha!' moments in the series?
3 Where will you go from here? What are your recommendations for extensions to this series? Where would you like further attention/training to focus?

The overwhelming response to the first question was that participants wanted to undertake more consultation with more children and give them the opportunity to voice their opinions throughout projects, programs and policy development. They also wanted to review how they could use participatory methods to evaluate the outcomes that explicitly incorporated children's perspectives.

These responses reflect a willingness among built environment professions to 'do the right thing' by children and young people, and it is fair to say that people are generally willing to include children and young people in civic processes. But in practice, it is difficult to activate. On reflection, we might also have asked: 'What do you perceive are the barriers to doing this in your organization?' Although the barriers are well known, they remain issues that need more consideration.

Involving children and young people in civic processes is often perceived as difficult, too time consuming, resource intensive, risky and of limited value to a project in many instances. It is easy to dismiss doing it. These are standard reasons given by local government organizations, clients and/or practitioners, particularly for routine design or planning projects. It is still an exception for a local government to regularly include a program of children's consultation or participation as part of capital works projects—even those that have specific outcomes for children and young people. This fight for children's right still needs champions. As stated by Chawla, "children's participation depends on committed adult support" (2002, p. 237). It always has and it always will.

The second question, although somewhat less relevant for the book, still generated some interesting responses that flag directions or considerations for the future. The speakers that made the largest impact on their audiences were the social researchers who pointed out the extent of social change that has taken place in our society between the last two generations. What struck the participants was just how profound these changes were and how quietly they had become the norm. The indicators included the drop in birth rate; the increase in emphasis on an aging population and the implications of this for children's issues on political agendas; the loss of natural spaces in urban environments and children's access to the few remaining areas; the increase in privatization of public space; changes in family composition and in the definition of 'family'. Many of the authors raised these issues in their chapters.

Australia, like many other developed economies, is experiencing the lowest birth rate in our nation's history. There is an increase in one-person households and single-parent families, and our population is unquestionably getting older. All these social changes serve to reduce children's social presence and social voice and, therefore, increase the need for more vocal defenders to advocate on children's behalf.

Along with demographic change, we are also experiencing an increase in urbanization, a loss of natural settings and a loss of public space in our cities. These changes affect the whole community. As is well documented, contact with nature is fundamental to community well-being, as is access to quality public space—for all citizens (Ward-Thompson et al. 2008). Both types of place provide settings for recreation, social activities and experiences that can counter the impact of lives that are increasingly lived in private spaces, with fewer and fewer people. We know that childhood is also being affected in this way and that modern childhoods are increasingly urban, socially isolated and lived mainly in private spaces (De Visscher & Bouverne-De Bie 2008; Freeman & Tranter 2011).

The third question to the seminar participants produced more concrete, operational recommendations. In answering this question, participants recommended needing more training in involving children and young people; wanting to see more evidence of best practice, how it is done and what it looks like; having greater access to relevant information and relevant case studies; hearing more from children to get their unique perspectives. None of these recommendations were surprising, and there is nothing inherently wrong with any of them, but they were a little disappointing for those of us who have been working in this area for many years, as they show how difficult it is to transfer knowledge and experience across sectors, across disciplines and across time.

Nevertheless, a lot of ground has been gained in all these areas in the last 25 years. There is a lot of 'how to' information easily available now and there are many 'best practice' case studies from around the world of projects and programs that have involved children and young people and are extremely successful—we have included a few current ones in this book. What the responses from our seminar participants really tell us is that the process of advocating for children and young people is never finished. We will never reach a stage where it is possible to say that our attention can now be turned away from these issues. Children's rights, children's participation, children's well-being, children's environmental opportunity will always need active, vocal campaigners keeping these issues in the social consciousness and on political agendas.

This book has aimed to do just that. The authors have contributed many salient discussions of participatory research and practice; recommendations for professional practice; and rich reflections from years of experience working as advocates for children and young people in research, policy or practice. For the sympathetic reader it provides a window into four major regions of the world and where they are at in relation to promoting children's and young people's rights and participation in the development of the built environment and the benefits of doing so. For the uninitiated reader, we have provided a resource which might assist in understanding the key components of successful approaches, programs and projects that could be implemented in new circumstances.

The built environment represents a universally relevant platform that has a profound impact on all our lives. It also provides the stage on which we demonstrate social values, beliefs and characteristics. For the most part, people are unaware of its impact on everyday behaviors, moods, opportunities and quality of life, and they do not give it a second thought. However, the built environment influences and impacts all aspects of our lives—physically, intellectually and emotionally—regardless of age, gender, ability or culture. Because of this, all community members stand to benefit from having a say in its creation. Children and young people represent two of the most impressionable groups for whom decisions about the built environment can have the greatest impact. Harnessing their participation in envisioning future scenarios introduces this constituency to an opportunity to experience relevant civic processes at work for their own and others' benefit. What we must do at all times is adopt approaches that we know to be beneficial to the outcome of a built environment project and involving children and young people is one of them.

Accommodating the majority of the world's population in cities will be an ongoing challenge to human ingenuity, creativity and intelligence. Like all experiments, it will not always result in positive outcomes. Urban development is driven by continually shifting economic and political partnerships, agendas and capacities. Cities must also respond to the constantly changing needs of its social populations. The outcomes for *all* people must always count.

We hope that in reading this book, the reader gains respect for the commitment, tenacity and passion that many people have brought to these issues for many decades now; and for the benefits to the wider community that have come about through choosing to promote the interests, voices and capacities of children and young people in civic processes such as urban planning and design. We hope we are supporting their efforts by promoting the need to focus on the importance of the processes that are involved in the creation of the built environment, as it is these that consume most of the energy and effort of these passionate individuals, and it is the integrity of these processes that underpin the ultimate environmental opportunities that remain for children.

The clear message from all the chapters is that we need to remain attentive to the issues of children's participation and inclusion in civic processes, particularly urban planning and design. The ground gained is not stable and new generations of professionals need to be continually recruited to the cause if achievements are to be maintained and children and young people are to continue to have a voice in our communities. The optimal outcome is to see children's inclusion in social processes become fully embedded in organizational and/or institutional cultures—truly 'business as usual'—asking to hear their views and valuing their perspectives. When that change occurs, it will really represent a coming of age.

References

Chawla, L (ed.) 2002, *Growing up in an urbanising world*, UNESCO and Earthscan, London.

De Visscher, S & Bouverne-De Bie, M 2008, 'Children's presence in the neighbourhood: a social-pedagogical perspective', *Children & Society*, vol. 22, pp. 470–481.

Freeman, C & Tranter, P 2011, *Children and their urban environments: changing worlds*, Earthscan, London.

Ward-Thompson, C, Aspinall, P & Montarzino, A 2008, 'The childhood factor: adult visits to green places and the significance of childhood experience', *Environment & Behavior*, vol. 40, no. 1, pp. 111–143.

CASE STUDIES

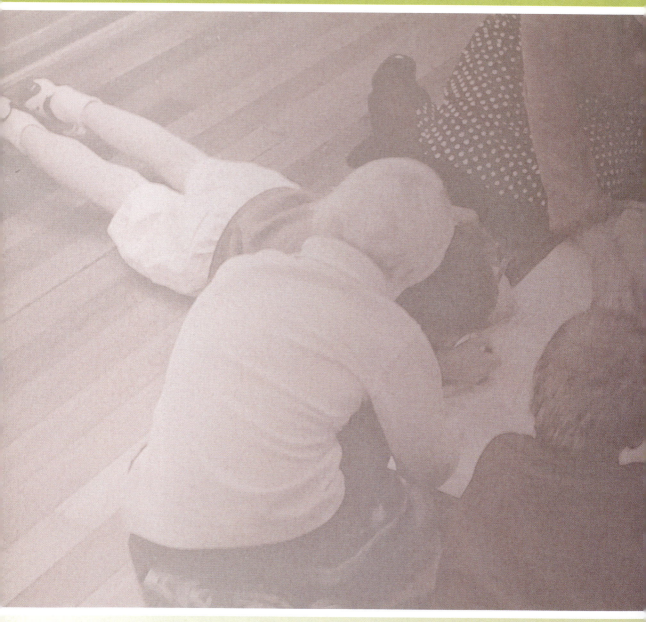

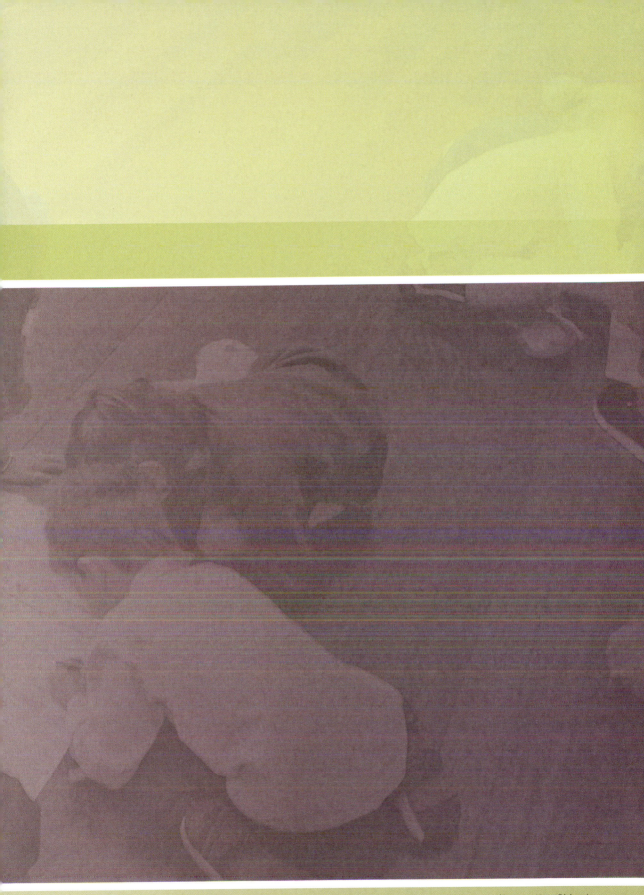

(Source: Kate Bishop)

ACTIVE & SAFE ROUTES TO SCHOOL

Type of case study example: Program
Country: Canada
Website: www.saferoutestoschool.ca/
Contact: Green Communities, Active & Safe Routes to School, 416 Chambers Street, 2nd Floor, Peterborough, Ontario

Case Study Synopsis

VISION: Ensuring that children have independent mobility.

BACKGROUND

The Active & Safe Routes to School (ASRTS) program is a community-based national movement dedicated to children's active transportation for the daily journey to school. It also addresses "health, physical activity, and traffic safety issues while taking action on air pollution and climate change" (www.saferoutestoschool.ca/).

The concept of Safe Routes to School (SRTS) began in Odense, Denmark in the 1970s (Macridis & Bengoechea 2015) and soon after spread internationally. In 1996, pilot projects were initiated in three schools in Toronto. The positive reception of the program led to it spreading nationwide.

WHAT THEY DO

The Active and Safe Routes to School program champions school travel planning (STP) through many initiatives to increase children's active transportation (www.saferoutestoschool.ca/programs).

The Canadian school travel planning model involves the collaboration between key stakeholders such as governments, school staff, parents and children. It involves five stages: "program setup, data collection and problem identification, action planning, implementation, and ongoing monitoring" (Macridis & Bengoechea 2015, p. 562). The Active and Safe Routes to School website is a comprehensive resource that provides various tools and implementation strategies; for instance, the 'School Travel Planning Toolkit' to assist schools and communities to create their own, tailored program. The program utilizes a flexible, multidisciplinary approach that can be modified for the needs of specific communities.

SUCCESS / IMPACT

By 2013 the Active and Safe Routes to School program had spread to over 120 schools nationwide with some schools achieving a modal shift of over 20 percent towards walking and cycling (http://toolsofchange.com/en/case-studies/detail/635). Numerous schools have appointed school transportation committees and local governments have incorporated the model into policy.

REFERENCES

Macridis, S & Bengoechea, EB 2015, 'Adoption of safe routes to school in Canadian and the United States contexts: best practices and recommendations', *Journal of School Health*, vol. 85, no. 8, pp. 558–566.

ARCHIKIDZ!

Type of case study example: Program
Country: Netherlands/Australia
Website: www.archikidz.com.au/
Contact: Suite 65/61 Marlborough Street, Surry Hills NSW 2010

Case Study Synopsis

VISION: Inspiring tomorrow's thinkers and city-makers: inviting children to participate and to contribute to creating their own (living) environment.

Archikidz aims to help children in an accessible and fun way to become acquainted with architecture and the (urban) environment. Furthermore, the free program offers children the opportunity to meet other children from diverse socioeconomic backgrounds, and to collaborate and learn from one another (Archikidz Rotterdam Project Plan 2015). In hands-on workshops, children are under the supervision of architects, volunteers and other arts and built environment professionals who share their knowledge and expertise with the next generation of city-shapers. Each event is based on a built environment theme (e.g., shelter, floating homes, sustainability, green walls, soundscapes, reimagining the city, playgrounds, building bridges, etc). Ultimately, the workshops aim to bring a younger audience into the world of architecture in an educational, fun and creative way.

HISTORY OF ARCHIKIDZ

The concept for Archikidz had its inception in 1998 in Amsterdam, the Netherlands, as the brainchild of Robert Mulder. Mulder had the idea of organizing an architecture festival for children. The initial event was called 'Bouwen in the Beurs' (Build in the Beurs). The workshop aimed to offer children the opportunity to put themselves in the shoes of an architect, question architectural concepts and get acquainted with their built environment. The concept was soon established as a non-profit foundation. The innovative child-focused program has since been replicated in many cities around the world including Rotterdam, Bergen, Barcelona, Buenos Aries, Lisbon, Santiago and Sydney.

AUSTRALIAN CHAPTER

In 2012 the inaugural Archikidz event was held in Sydney, Australia. Since then more than 6,000 kids and over 400 built environment professionals have participated in an Archikidz event in Australia (www.archikidz.com.au).

In 2015, the most ambitious Archikidz was held in Sydney as part of the VIVID Festival. PLAY[ground] was held over a three-day weekend and engaged more than 6,000 attendees and 96 volunteers, with the support of 24 partners and event collaborators, including Sydney Living Museums, the City of Sydney Council and international architectural firm HASSELL. The program included more than 33 workshops about city-making and the built environment.

"HASSELL and Archikidz explored what happens when a child's vision of play is inserted into the adult world. Ideas were tested with kids throughout the design process and their responses to the final outcome were recorded" (www.hassellstudio.com/en/cms-projects/detail/playground/).

CITY BLOSSOMS

Type of case study example: Program
Country: USA
Website: http://cityblossoms.org/
Contact: 516 Kennedy St NW, Washington, DC 20011

Case Study Synopsis

VISION: City Blossoms envisions a nation of neighborhoods and schools with green spaces that inspire healthy living, creativity and innovative learning.

HISTORY / BACKGROUND

City Blossoms began in the late 1990s as a volunteer gardening project in Columbia Heights, by two high school students, Lola Bloom and Rebecca Lemos-Otero (current co-founders and co-executive directors). The project evolved into City Blossoms and became a non-profit organization in 2009. The core philosophy of City Blossoms is "collaboration with community stakeholders to create holistic, accessible green spaces for people of all ages to engage with the environment and each other" (www.cityblossoms.org). City Blossoms is a child-centered organization dedicated to engaging community and empowering children, youth and local organizations to develop dynamic and productive green projects. To date, City Blossoms has worked on 42 projects in Washington, DC, Baltimore and Philadelphia, and has developed 34 green spaces which have directly engaged over 9,500 children and youth through in-school, after-school and summer projects (www.cityblossoms.org).

WHAT THEY DO

The program is free and provides after-school, in-school and summer programming for predominantly Latino and African-American youth, ranging from age two through to teenagers. The main demographic targeted by City Blossoms is low-income neighborhoods where children and youth may not otherwise have access to green space (www.cityblossoms.org).

City Blossoms facilitates the transformation of unused or underused land, to educate children and young people about caring for themselves and for the environment. Participants acquire skills and knowledge across areas including nutrition, math, science, environmental awareness and community building. Business skills are also acquired by students through the 'Mighty Greens' Youth Entrepreneurship Program, where they sell produce from their garden projects at local farmers' markets.

COLLABORATION

City Blossoms develops partnerships with schools and community-based organizations both in Washington, DC, and nationwide. In 2012, through a partnership formed between CSX (a leading rail-based freight transportation organization) and The Nature Conservancy, City Blossoms implemented a garden-based curriculum (building 'pollinator' gardens) with local schools to actively engage children and communities through education. The success of the City Blossoms model has led to ongoing partnerships with over 21 gardens (schools and community-based organizations).

EVALUATION AND TRAINING

To ensure the relevance of City Blossoms' programming, they incorporate a cycle of evaluation, practice, testing and recording (www.cityblossoms.org). Beyond the design and implementation of urban gardens, City Blossoms' consultants train educators and community-based organizations (over 300 to date), through partnerships with The Nature Conservancy, local schools and the Food Corps in addition to distributing their bilingual teaching tools, which include an early childhood curriculum development (with consideration to learning standards) and the CGS (Community Green Spaces) cookbook. Furthermore, they provide supplemental programming to other youth-serving programs that intend to include a gardening component in their own programs (www.cityblossoms.org).

MELBOURNE FOR ALL PEOPLE STRATEGY 2014–2017

Type of case study example: Policy
Country: Australia (City of Melbourne)
Website: www.melbourne.vic.gov.au
Contact: 120 Swanston Street, Melbourne, Victoria, Australia

Case Study Synopsis

VISION: The *Melbourne for All People Strategy 2014–2017* aims to create a more holistic approach to planning and service delivery, with the aim of developing "more resilient, healthier and better connected individuals and communities" (City of Melbourne 2013, p. 3).

BACKGROUND

The 2014–17 strategy consolidates a number of previous plans. Extensive consultation was undertaken with children and young people who live, study and visit the City of Melbourne. It is the integrity and depth of this process that is in focus here.

Since 1996, the City of Melbourne has demonstrated its commitment to young people through the implementation of a range of strategic plans and policies. In 2006, the City of Melbourne commissioned the Australian Youth Research Centre (YRC) to conduct research examining national and international literature on the civic engagement of young people and best practices in other Victorian local government areas, and to provide recommendations for Council's strategic direction and priorities for the City's young people.

One of the recommendations from the final report, *Civic Engagement and Young People*, released in 2007, was to consult young people in order to improve the City's decision-making and practices. In the development of *Empowering Young People—Young People's Policy 2010–2013*, the City of Melbourne consulted with more than 140 young people, including international students, to further understand the needs and interests of young people. Young people were also invited to provide feedback on the draft version of the policy.

While the City of Melbourne has a long-standing commitment to young people's civic engagement, the inclusion of children in early and middle childhood received less attention until 2009, when the City funded a project to consult children from birth to 12 years of age about their views on and ideas for the City of Melbourne to inform the development of the City's first children's plan. Similar to the research carried out for young people, the project involved a literature review in addition to analyzing relevant national, international and state policies.

The consultation process was designed to ensure that a "diverse sample of children most affected by City of Melbourne policy could be best consulted and contribute" (Kotsanas et al. 2014, p. 12). One hundred and thirty children aged 3–12 years old participated in the research, with the addition of 43 parents or carers of children under two years old, who spoke on their behalf.

The consultations culminated in the publication of two children's plan documents: one pictorial document for children titled *Children's Voices,* and one adult document.

REFERENCES

City of Melbourne 2013, *Melbourne for All People Strategy 2014–2017*, City of Melbourne, Melbourne.
Kotsanas, C, Smith, K & MacNaughton, G 2014, *Creating a children's plan with children, Research Report 43*, Youth Research Centre, University of Melbourne, Melbourne.

CHILD AND YOUTH FRIENDLY STRATEGY

Type of case study example: Policy
Country: Canada
Website: www.surrey.ca/community/3191.aspx
Contact: City of Surrey, BC, Canada

Case Study Synopsis

BACKGROUND

Surrey in British Columbia, Canada, has a long-standing commitment to being a family friendly city. This commitment is reflected in the City's plans, policies, programs and initiatives. Released in 2006, the City's 'Plan for the Social Well-Being of Surrey Residents' identified children and youth as a top priority. One of the key recommendations from the Social Plan was for the City to develop policies to ensure that child and youth friendliness become one of the key objectives pursued in the decisions made by the City.

DEVELOPMENT OF THE 'CHILD AND YOUTH FRIENDLY CITY STRATEGY'

The 'Child and Youth Friendly Strategy' covers three main areas: 'child and youth engagement', the 'physical environment' and 'civic services'. The City has divided 'young children' into three age categories, in recognition that each grouping has differing needs and interests. These are: early years children (0–5 years); middle years children (6–12 years); and youth (13+ years).The process involved in the development of the strategy is as follows.

Phase 1: Research

In order to ensure that the 'Child and Youth Friendly Strategy' incorporated 'best thinking and promising practices', research was conducted that examined child friendly policies and practices from other cities around the world, along with reviewing academic literature on child friendly cities. The research provided the foundation for the development of the Strategy. The results of this review were assembled into the supporting report: *Creating a Child and Youth Friendly City: What does it Mean? A Review of Child and Youth Friendly Policies and Practices from other Cities*.

Phase 2: Child and Youth Consultations

During the spring and summer of 2009, over 811 children (511 aged 0–12 years), youth (300 aged 13–18) and parents (250) participated in the consultation process. Acknowledging that needs and interests vary with age, different consultation methods and techniques were used with each age group.

Phase 3: Staff and Community Stakeholders Consultations

The ideas and suggestions that arose from the community consultation with young people shaped the agenda for this stage in the consultation process. Consultation workshops were conducted with staff from multiple City departments; representatives from community and government agencies concerned with children; the Social Planning Advisory Committee; Parks and Community Services Committee.

ACTION AND EVALUATION

A major component of the 'Child and Youth Friendly Strategy' are the 'action points' which address existing initiatives or new projects or approaches for the City to implement. Each action point identifies a 'target age', the time frame and the department responsible for the item. Since the Strategy was adopted, ongoing evaluation occurs through corporate reports to council and updates in initiatives.

FREMANTLE ESPLANADE YOUTH PLAZA

Type of case study example: Project
Country: Australia
Website: www.fremantle.wa.gov.au/youthplaza
Contact: City of Fremantle, Town Hall Centre, 8 William Street, Fremantle

Case Study Synopsis

VISION: "To create a community space activated via community events, programs and action sports. Enhancing an iconic park setting and creating a focal hub for the community of Fremantle. Capturing the rich historic essence of site within a contemporary youth focused design" (City of Fremantle 2013, Part 2, p. 5).

BACKGROUND

The Fremantle Esplanade Youth Plaza (EYP) is an internationally awarded activity hub for young people and families located in the heart of Fremantle, Western Australia. Officially opened in 2014, the EYP is a "multipurpose skate-able play space that complements existing uses and facilities at the Esplanade Park Reserve" (www.parksleisure.com.au/regions/wa/2014-pla-wa-awards-of-excellence).

The Youth Plaza, while including a world-class skate park with facilities to cater to all ages, is much more than simply a skate park. The plaza includes a BMX course, a parkour park, table tennis and ping pong facilities, slack lining and rock climbing equipment, a stage for youth festivals and performances, along with ample shelter, lighting, Wi-Fi areas and a community space for events, activities and art.

"The plaza is not just an iconic facility due to its functionality and dynamic uses, but also due to its striking aesthetics and contemporary design, positioning the plaza as one of the flagship public space developments in Australia" (worldlandscapearchitect.com/the-esplanade-youth-plaza-fremantle-australia-convic/).

The City of Fremantle actively engaged children and young people in the development of the EYP. The City of Fremantle placed a high priority on engaging with children and youth within the community, as reflected in the 2010–2015 Strategic Plan and the Youth Plan 2012–2015. In the process of developing the Youth Plan, the City of Fremantle consulted with 190 young people.

ESPLANADE YOUTH PLAZA CONSULTATION PROCESS

The children and youth component of the consultation process involved two youth plaza design consultation workshops, with more than 80 children and youth participating. An additional 220 children and youth provided feedback via an online survey. Furthermore, 74 face-to-face surveys were conducted with young people who attended skate workshops that were held during the school holidays. Additional community-wide consultation included 214 surveys completed online, 72 participants at two pre-design workshops, 96 participants who provided feedback on the two concept designs.

BIBLIOGRAPHY

City of Fremantle 2013, *Fremantle Esplanade Youth Plaza concept design report*, Part 1 of 2, City of Fremantle, Western Australia. Available from: www.fremantle.wa.gov.au/sites/default/files/Convic%20Report%20-%20Part%201.pdf.

City of Fremantle 2013, *Fremantle Esplanade Youth Plaza concept design report*, Part 2 of 2, City of Fremantle, Western Australia. Available from: www.fremantle.wa.gov.au/sites/default/files/Convic%20Report%20-%20Part%202.pdf.

THE GREENWAY PRIMARY SCHOOL SUSTAINABILITY PROGRAM

Type of case study example: Program
Country: Australia
Website: www.greenway.org.au/arts-and-community/schools

Case Study Synopsis

PROGRAM OBJECTIVES

To promote quality, authentic, experiential learning in the students' local neighborhood, involving a combination of in-class and outdoor activities for primary school students (5–12 years).

To integrate the state of New South Wales' (NSW) cross-curriculum priority of sustainability into the new syllabus subjects of English, Science and History (www.greenway.org.au/arts-and-community/schools).

BACKGROUND

The GreenWay Primary Schools Sustainability Program is an award-winning, accredited, place-based primary school sustainability educational program that promotes experiential learning in the students' local neighborhood (http://observatoryhilleec.nsw.edu.au/special-projects/). The program was developed within the larger GreenWay Sustainability Project, 2009–2012. The Project, located in Sydney's Inner West, focused on the development of a sustainable governance model for the GreenWay, which included improving urban biodiversity, community and volunteer engagement, and promoting active transport.

DEVELOPMENT OF THE PROGRAM

The foundation for the program was developed over a 10-year period by staff and parents at Kegworth Public School in Leichhardt, a primary school in Sydney. The GreenWay Primary Schools Sustainability Program began formally as a pilot project in 2011 and involved four local councils, the NSW Department of Education and Communities and three local primary schools. The free program uses the GreenWay corridor as an outdoor classroom to introduce kids to sustainability issues, local history and the urban environment. Through a series of local history and environment walks and accompanying activities (outlined in the comprehensive GreenWay Primary Schools Sustainability Program teacher's manual—developed as part of the project), students learn about key themes:

- Built environment/natural environment (in an urban context)
- Infrastructure/wildlife corridors
- Urban water cycle
- Local history (i.e., place names, Aboriginal heritage)
- Past and present use of buildings
- Transport
- Caring for the local environment
- Community connections
- Multiple use of open space

The success of the program has resulted in it being accredited by the NSW Teachers Federation in addition to being adopted by the Observatory Hill Environmental Education Centre as a 'best practice' case study and a local model for urban sustainability education. While the larger project that the program sits within was completed in 2012, ongoing grants and funding have enabled the educational program to continue.

ONGOING RECOGNITION

The program receives funding from the four local councils positioned along the GreenWay as well as from the NSW Environmental Education Trust. In 2015 the NSW Environmental Education Trust funded 10 Inner West primary schools to participate in the program.

The program is closely aligned with the NSW primary schools curriculum, where all activities are linked to 'Key Learning Areas' (KLAs) including the Creative Arts, Human Society and Environment, Mathematics, Personal Development, Health and Physical Education and Science and Technology.

HAMPTON YOUTH COMMISSION, VIRGINIA, USA

Type of case study example: Policy
Country: USA
Website: http://hampton.gov/
Contact: 22 Lincoln Street, Hampton, Virginia 23669

Case Study Synopsis

VISION: Young people with the power and voice to shape the future of Hampton.

BACKGROUND

"Widely recognized as one of the most successful and long-running initiatives in the field, the Hampton, Virginia Youth Civic Engagement (YCE) model has empowered local youth for nearly 20 years. This initiative has led to a fundamental shift in City leaders' perceptions of young people" (National League of Cities 2009, p. 96).

The City of Hampton has placed a high priority on empowering local youth in planning and decision-making for the city. The focus on youth began in 1990 when the Mayor and City Council created a master plan for children, youth, and families. In support of this, the newly formed Coalition for Youth was responsible for surveying over 5,000 of Hampton's young people and adults to understand the issues the City's young people faced. The City's commitment to engaging youth in the workings of local government was reinforced in 1995 when the Coalition for Youth was made a formal city department. The Coalition was assigned the responsibility for youth-focused issues. The goal of the Coalition was to ensure that youth would grow into productive members of the workforce and the community. Furthermore, the Coalition "serves as a clearinghouse for youth development and capacity building practices for agencies and other organizations" (Sirianni 2005, p. 13).

In recognition of the importance of having the youth voice heard, in 1997 the City Planning Department hired two young people to serve as 'youth planners' to uncover what the young people believed would improve Hampton. The Youth Planners (an ongoing initiative) determined two fundamental methods for youth to become involved in Hampton's planning, policy and decision-making. First was the development of a Youth Component to the City's Comprehensive Plan, and secondly, the creation of a Youth Commission. Both of these initiatives were sanctioned by the City Council in 1997.

HAMPTON YOUTH COMMISSION

The Youth Commission, a city-appointed board, was designed by the Youth Planners to be an effective voice for the youth of Hampton. They are responsible for the Youth Component of the Comprehensive Plan. The Commission consists of 20–25 high-school teens from across the City of Hampton. Commissioners are appointed on two-year terms. Each year, Youth Commissioners determine the issue(s) they will tackle. In partnership with the Youth Planners, they conduct research to support the Commissioners to make informed decisions or create appropriate strategies to address specific issues.

The Youth Commission is leading the effort to engage young people in the Hampton community. Each year the City Council provides the Youth Commission with USD40,000. These funds are a source for grants which the Commissioners can then use to fund community-based, youth-led initiatives that are dedicated to serving and involving young people.

REFERENCES

National League of Cities 2009, *The state of city leadership for children and families*, National League of Cities, Washington, DC.
Sirianni, B 2005, 'Youth and civic engagement: systems change and culture change in Hampton, Virginia', CIRCLE, Washington, DC. Available from: www.civicyouth.org/PopUps/WorkingPapers/WP31Sirianni.pdf.

STEPS INITIATIVE—EMERGING ARTIVISM PROGRAM

Type of case study example: Program
Country: Canada
Website: www.stepsinitiative.com
Contact: c/o Art Hub 27, 39 Queens Quay East, Suite 100, Toronto, M5E 0A4

Case Study Synopsis

STEPS: Sustainable Thinking and Expression on Public Space

OVERVIEW

The STEPS Initiative is a community-based public art organization that began in 2010 at the Centre for Social Innovation in Toronto, Canada. Built on the premise that public art can bridge the gap between the cultural, social and environmental sectors, the STEPS initiative fosters community capacity building through the creative transformation of public spaces—what they refer to as public space 'ARTivism'.

The STEPS Initiative's programming is not exclusively limited to youth; however, their most successful programming has been youth-driven. The youth program has resulted in positive changes to neighborhoods and public spaces, as well as an increase in young people's confidence and interest in civic issues (Solanki et al. 2014).

EMERGING ARTIVIST PROGRAM

The Emerging ARTivist program and workshops have been facilitated in both community and school settings, resulting in several large-scale youth-led projects. This program challenges young people to approach the city through a critical lens, and question their role in making public places more vibrant. The Emerging ARTivist program "provides a platform for young people from some of Canada's most diverse and low-income communities to animate public spaces in their communities" (Solanki et al. 2014, p. 39). Program outcomes have improved the urban experience of local residents in addition to building capacity for participating youth as civic leaders engaged in urban design issues, empowering them to transform their urban environment (Solanki et al. 2014). Projects range from the world's tallest mural, which transformed Toronto's skyline, to a 200-linear-foot Fence Reclamation Project along a pedestrian corridor. In these projects, the youth participants led the process from conception through to design and installation (www.stepsinitiative.com).

TORONTO EMERGING ARTIVISTS (TEA)—YOUTH-LED ARTIVIST PROGRAM

The Toronto Emerging ARTivists (TEA) program is a collective of young people (14–22 years) from some of Toronto's most underserved communities, who are committed to improving their communities through their engagement with public art (www.stepsinitiative.com). The TEA program collaborates with a group of artists from a range of disciplines, who work in conjunction with local youth to co-facilitate public art workshops with young children. "The artists bring the technical skills, while the youth bring the local knowledge to make the workshops relevant for their younger peers" (Solanki et al. 2014, p. 42). The program has allowed participants to build an extensive network of young people across the city, who are recognized as an important voice in local planning initiatives (www. stepsinitiative.com).

REFERENCES

Solanki, A, Kane Speer, A & Huang, H 2014, 'Youth ARTivism: fostering civic engagement through public art', *Journal of Urban Culture Research*, vol. 9, pp. 38–51. Available from: www.cujucr.com/downloads/JUCR%20Vol9%202014-F.pdf.

Y-PLAN—UNIVERSITY OF CALIFORNIA BERKELEY

Type of case study example: Program
Country: USA
Website: http://y-plan.berkeley.edu/
Contact: Institute of Urban and Regional Development, 318 Wurster Hall, #1870, University of California, Berkeley, CA 94720{hy}1870

Case Study Synopsis

GOAL: "The goal of the Y-PLAN is not only to engage schools and students/youth in community development projects, but also to foster learning experiences for all participants" (McKoy & Vincent 2007, p. 389).

BACKGROUND

The original Y-PLAN initiative is a form of Social Enterprise for Learning (SEfL) project methodology developed by the University of California Berkeley Graduate School of Education. Established in 2000, Y-PLAN (Youth—Plan, Learn, Act, Now) is based in Berkeley's Center for Cities & Schools. Y-PLAN is a pedagogical and professional development tool, in addition to being a planning studio that addresses specific issues in local communities. Y-PLAN facilitates positive community outcomes by partnering university graduate and undergraduate urban planning students (the mentors), local high school students, and teachers, with government agencies, private industry and other community parties to work on real-world planning issues, in addition to providing meaningful opportunities for young people to serve as key stakeholders in their community (McKoy et al. 2015).

Over the past decade, Y-PLAN has engaged over 12,000 young people and 250 civic partners in over 75 community development projects across 16 cities in the United States, Japan, China and Sub-Saharan Africa (McKoy et al. 2015, p. 230).

The 5-step Methodology:

Phase 1: Start Up + Project Identification
Phase 2: Making Sense of the City
Phase 3: Into Action
Phase 4: Going Public
Phase 5: Looking Forward—Looking Back

Through a rigorous project-learning curriculum, students engage in research, conducting interviews and surveys, mapping, observation and analysis; and generate visions for change, presenting their evidence-based solutions to clients and stakeholders (McKoy et al. 2014, p. 28). The Y-PLAN model engages students in a critical analysis of the places where they live. Through the main focus areas of housing, transport, public space and schools, services and amenities, students examine and realize solutions to critical community issues (McKoy et al. 2014, pp. 27–28).

REFERENCES
McKoy, D, Buss, S & Stewart, J 2014, 'Blueprints for hope: engaging children as critical actors in urban place making', *Early Childhood Matters*, November, pp. 27–30.
McKoy, D, Stewart, J & Buss, S 2015, 'Engaging students in transforming their built environment via Y-PLAN: lessons from Richmond, California', *Children, Youth and Environments*, vol. 25, no. 2, pp. 229–244.
McKoy, D & Vincent, JM 2007, 'Engaging schools in urban revitalization—the Y-PLAN (Youth—Plan, Learn, Act, Now!)', *Journal of Planning Education and Research*, vol. 26, no. 4, pp. 389–403.

Index